THE LITTLE AFRICAN HISTORY BOOK

*Black Africa from the Origins of Humanity to the Assassination of
Lumumba and the turn of the 20th Century*

CHUKWUNYERE   KAMALU

Dedicated to Emmanuel Amadi

It is most appropriate, given his African-centred and human–centred political views, to dedicate this book to the loving memory and life of my late father-in-law, Emmanuel Amadi, who was as inspiring in his personal kindness as he was in his erudition. He will always be greatly missed.

First published in 2007 by Orisa Press, London, England.

© 2007 Chukwunyere Kamalu

Cover design: C. Kamalu

Printed by Lulu: www.lulu.com

ISBN: 978-0-9557131-0-1

CONTENTS

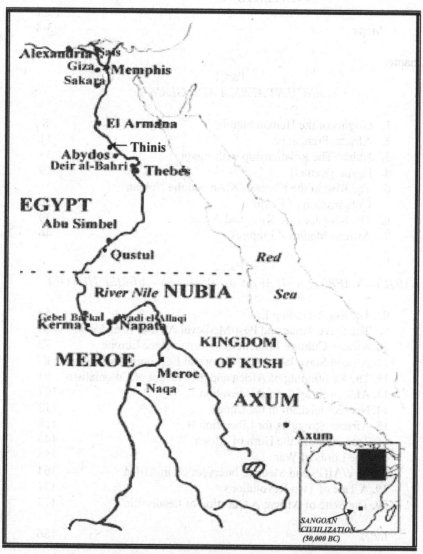

ANCIENT AFRICAN CIVILIZATIONS (50,000 BC – 600 AD)

The achievements of the Nile Valley Civilizations (Nubia, Egypt, Kush, Meroe and Axum) are relatively well known, but all were preceded by a Sangoan civilization (approx. 50,000BC) in central Africa, in the region of the modern Democratic Republic of Congo. The people of this region would later make the first known lunar calendar and table of prime numbers carved on the ISHANGO BONE (between 11,000 and 30,000 BC) and further south in modern Swaziland, become the first miners of iron (43000 BC). Hence the sciences of astronomy, mathematics and metallurgy all began in the southern region of Africa.

Africa 2007

In contrast to the past achievements and great wealth of the Nile Valley civilizations, the past zenith of African civilization, Africa in 2007 was besieged by war, hunger, ethnic and religious strife and the HIV/AIDS epidemic. In the time of the empire of Ghana in the 11ᵗʰ century AD (or even Mali in the 13ᵗʰ century AD), Africa remained in the forefront of world civilizations, as it had been since the birth of Nubia, prior to 3200 BC.

PART ONE

ANCIENT AFRICA AT A GLANCE

Chapter One

The Origin of the Human Family

According to a monogenetic theory* of human evolution, only in the last few millions of years did our ancestors emerge on the continent of Africa. Some of our earliest ancestors came from Ethiopia. One of the earliest was our mega-great Granddad, Ramidus (full name Australopithecus Ramidus) who lived as long as 4.4 million years ago. Ramidus got his name from the Afar people of Ethiopia. In their language the word "ramid" means "root"[1] , which is very appropriate. Then there is Lucy (who is also nicknamed "Eve" because she was one of the earliest women on the Earth). Lucy lived 3-4 million years ago. She was very little, only about 4 feet tall. We know this because scientists discovered her bones in Tanzania in east Africa[2]. In fact they found almost all of her complete skeleton, so they were able to measure her height. By one of the Great Lakes at Olduvai Gorge also in Tanzania the scientists also discovered the bones of Zinjanthropus (full name: Zinjanthropus Bosei) who lived about 2 million years ago[3].

In the Ice Age, our ancestors, the ancient Africans trekked across North Africa into what later became Europe. Diop says that ancient Africans went out to populate the rest of the world by walking out of Africa by one of three possible routes: through the Strait of Gibraltar, the Isthmus of the Suez, and maybe through Sicily and southern Italy"[4].

It was very cold in Europe. It was the Ice Age. This was about 20,000-40,000 years ago. The first of our ancient African ancestors to settle in Europe was Grimaldi. He would have had a difficult time trying to survive in the unwelcoming European Würm Glaciation (Ice Age). Grimaldi's predecessors[5] had trekked all the way across North Africa into the Pyrenees Mountains which separate modern France and Spain. Grimaldi may well have died of the cold, covered in the snow of the mountain steppes. Grimaldi, it so happened, is one of the closest African ancestors of European people. But although Grimaldi was African and had dark skin as today's Africans do, future generations of his clan would lighten in skin colour to survive in a climate with very few hours of sunlight.

One of the problems of survival for Grimaldi's people was that this absence of sunlight made less vitamin D available in their skin. In his native Africa the sunlight was abundant and allowed Grimaldi's ancestors (Homo Erectus and clan) to absorb enough vitamin D to have strong healthy bones. The sun in Africa would pour out abundant light and heat

---

* In 2007, monogenetic theory took a great step closer to becoming indisputable fact. See reference 4.

all day long and every day. But in the dark sun starved European Ice Age, they could not absorb sufficient amounts to prevent the diseases caused by lack of vitamin D such as rickets, a bone disease. In the African sun the ancient Africans had developed a chemical in their skin called melanin, which darkened their skin, as darker skin blocked out more of the harmful ultra violet rays given out by the sun.

The absence of sunlight in Europe killed many of Grimaldi's clan as a result of health problems caused by the lack of vitamin D. These problems may have included deep depression or unhappiness caused by the lack of sunlight which could have caused some family members to take their own lives, and rickets. But nature had found a way to save some of Grimaldi's clan and allow the family line of Grimaldi to survive. It turned out that lighter skin can absorb more vitamin D than darker skin. So those of Grimaldi's family with lighter complexion fared better. Grimaldi's family would have included some albino members. By accident these members of Grimaldi's family had been born without the usual amount of melanin chemical to make their skin dark. These albino family members would have fared best of all in the European climate as their light skin was able to absorb enough vitamin D from the weak sunlight to ward off bone diseases. Over the generations to follow nature adapted Grimaldi's family to the European climate by gradually making the clan lighter and lighter in skin colour by a process scientists call "natural selection"[6]. This just means the traits of the family that made it more able to survive became more and more common in the children that were born out of Grimaldi's clan, until eventually the clan became predominantly more like white skinned modern Europeans than the black skinned ancient Africans who were their ancestors, and who had trekked across the Pyrenees mountains from north Africa.

The great ancestor of the modern European people was Cro (full name: Cro magnon) who was born about 20,000 years ago at the end of the last Ice Age[7]. Cro was born on the threshold of a new era in human history. For about 20,000 years or so our adventurous ancestors, including Grimaldi and his clan only had time to be pre-occupied with surviving in very harsh conditions. Cro magnon was a hominid (that is, a user of tools). He was more advanced than Neanderthal who earlier had mysteriously disappeared. That was 35,000 years ago. Possibly, the offspring of migrations from Africa before Grimaldi, had failed to survive through the ice age.

Cro magnon's family developed to the level of becoming artists, hunters and sailors. At about Cro's time the ice in Europe had started to melt. This still took thousands of years, so that as late as 8000 years ago much of Europe was still under ice.

References

Chapter One - Origins of the Human Family

1. White, T., G. Suwa and B. Asfaw, *Australopithecus Ramidus, a new species of early hominid from Aramis, Ethiopia,* Nature, Vol. 371, 22 September 1994, p.306-312.
2. Johanson, Donald C. & Maitland Edey. *Lucy: The Beginnings of Humankind* Touchstone Books (1990)
3. Leakey, L.S.B., *The Evolution of Man on the African Continent;* Tarikh Vol. 1, No.3; Man in Africa, Longman, 1966, p.7-11.
4. Diop, Cheikh Anta, *Civilization or Barbarism: An authentic anthropology,* Lawrence Hill Books, New York, 1991, p.11. <u>Also note</u>: In 2007, the African monogenetic theory (the theory that humans came from a single source in Africa) was virtually confirmed by the study of Cambridge University scientists, using a large data set of people from around the world combining skull measurements with genetic evidence, showing that the further away human populations are from an African source of dispersal, the less diverse they are. This implied a singular African source of humanity's origin with African populations being the most diverse. See Mania, A., W. Amos, F. Balloux, & T. Hanihara, *The effect of ancient population bottlenecks on human phenotypic variations,* Nature, Vol. 448, 19 July 2007, p.346-348.
5. Grimaldi's ancestral family: the clan of Homo erectus and Homo sapiens that walked out of Africa 150,000 years ago.
6. Murray, F.G., *Pigmentation and Sunlight,* American Anthropologist, 1934, Vol. 36, p.438-445.
7. Diop, Cheikh Anta, *Civilization or Barbarism: An authentic anthropology,* Lawrence Hill Books, New York, 1991, p.26.

Chapter Two

African Prehistory

8,000 years ago when much of Europe was still under ice, the Sahara desert in Africa was green, fertile and teeming with life. We know that the area was inhabited by our ancient relatives, who left us their cave paintings to look at and try to understand[1].

Who were these ancient Saharans? Perhaps the cave paintings leave us a clue. These people were nomadic hunter-gatherers – they moved from place to place and the men hunted while the women gathered berries and other wild fruits for food. They must be the oldest known Africans after the hominids, our ancient forefathers and foremothers described in the last chapter.

Again, the paintings in the caves of the Sahara give us an idea of what life was like for these Saharan nomads. The scenes painted show them herding cattle - cows, sheep and goats - and their dwellings are shown as circle shaped huts. There are scenes of men drawing water from the well using a bucket attached to a long rope. One 6000 year old painting on the rocks of Tassili, in the region of modern Algeria, shows a group of men in a form of dance or initiation ceremony. Another rock painting shows women gathering grain which may have been wild grain. There were also scenes of music and dance. Another picture appears to show two musicians playing together on what look like a harp and another stringed instrument, possibly having only one string. Some paintings also display costumery which reminds us of the later head dress of the Ancient Egyptians and others show dancers wearing masks, loin cloths and flared leggings that remind us of the attire of Zulu warriors[2].

The paintings show that the Sahara was not only green and fertile in those times but that it was also a peaceful environment. In later painted scenes, however, we do increasingly see scenes of battle with men armed with bows and arrows. These may have been battles with rival clans to settle disputes over herd or territory. In some cases the enemies may have been invaders into their desert home. Painted scenes also show that the ancient Saharan peoples had processes of justice. One scene shows what looks like a court in session dispensing justice and the guilty party being led off towards his punishment[3].

About 3,500 years ago, the Sahara began to dry out forcing some of the desert peoples to move towards the Nile for survival. Others may have migrated further southwards and continued their nomadic lifestyle. The settlement of Saharan peoples led to the establishment of one of the earliest agricultural civilizations in the world. Becoming a settled society allowed the Nile Valley natives to pursue high culture and develop ancient Nubia and then ancient Egypt, with its arts and sciences, philosophy, astronomy and mathematics[4].

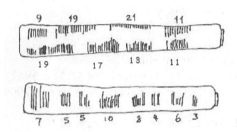

Figure 1. Sketch of the Ishango Bone. Found at Lake Edward, DRC.

It may well be that the ancient Saharans were wanderers and their offspring today, many generations later may be the Khoisan bushmen of the Kalahari Desert deep south of the foot of the Nile. If so, these prolific cave painters who were hunter gatherers continued their art in caves in the Kalahari in Southern Africa. They had created a peaceful society conducive to the flourishing of art. Their art was not simplistic, but had already developed to a stylised level which might be described as "abstract art" (that is, not created with the purpose of painting a faithful copy of reality, but in a style designed to emphasize certain things like, for instance, dance movements). These hunters were keen marksmen and hunted with bows and arrows.

It is plainly a grave mistake to suppose that there was no established human civilization in Africa before the Egyptians in ancient Egypt and the Nubians in ancient Nubia. In the region of Lake Edward in former Zaire (now Democratic of Congo – DRC) the discovery of an 11,000 year old bone [5], later to be known as the "Ishango Bone" marked with prime numbers and even numbers is the earliest evidence of mathematical activity anywhere on the earth. Indeed, the bone is the first table of the small prime numbers, as well as being the earliest lunar calendar. Further south in Swaziland researchers discovered a 43,000 year old iron mine[6] evincing the development of the science of metallurgy in Africa at an early stage. As Renton et al have noted, archaeological evidence points to the presence of a civilization described by writers as Sangoan in the central African region as much as 50,000 years ago[7].

References

Chapter Two - African Prehistory

1. Davidson, B., (and editors of Time-life books) *African Kingdoms,* Time-Life Books, Amsterdam, 1966, p.43-57.
2. Ibid., p.46-47.
3. Ibid., p.56-57.
4. Watterson, B., *Ancient Egypt*, Sutton Publishing, 1998, p.1-4.
5. De Heinzelin, J., *Ishango*, Scientific American, 206:6 (June 1962), pp105-114. Later studies put the age of the bone at closer to 30,000 years old.
6. New York Times (South African edition), 8 February, 1979.
7. Renton, D., Seddon, D. and L. Zeilig, *The Congo: Plunder & Resistance*, Zed Books, London & NY, 2007, p. 7.

Chapter Three

Nubia: The Relationship with Egypt

Although our main barrier to understanding Nubia still remains the undeciphered Meroitic script we do know that Nubia, probably the earliest known state of any size in Africa, and in the world[1], covered part of the modern Sudan. At Qustul in the south, an incense burner and tombs belonging to Nubian kings predating the start of the Ancient Egyptian first dynasty in 3200 BC were discovered[2]. This civilization, Nubia, was the source of the traditions and culture of ancient Egypt. Unfortunately, because we cannot read the Nubian script (Meroitic) which came into being in 200 BC, the ancient Nubians are not the voices telling their own history. We must be content with seeing them through the accounts of the Egyptians. So characters like Kamose who came into much contact with the Nubians are in the foreground, because we have texts such as that found on the Carnarvon Tablet which tell us of his expeditions and trade relations in Nubia.

There were earlier figures of the Old Kingdom, like Sneferu, who came into close contact with the Nubians. According to the writings of the Palermo Stone, King Sneferu (or Snofru) (2613-2589 BC) the first king of the 4th dynasty conducted a military campaign against the Nubians to secure Egyptian borders[3]. The fourth dynasty is famous for its pyramid builders, but Sneferu is often regarded as the greatest of these pyramid builders simply because he built so many structures. Some say Sneferu made the prototype for the great pyramids, but that honour surely belongs to Imhotep, prime minister to King Djoser of the 3rd dynasty[4].

In the time of the Egyptian Old Kingdom a certain pattern had emerged in Egyptian relations with Nubia. Whenever Egypt was united under one pharaoh and strong as a nation, it was in the position to exploit Nubia for its riches in natural resources. When Egypt was weak and politically unstable, Nubia was left to develop free of interference. Thus Nubia, which encompasses part of the Sudan and modern Ethiopia and Eritrea was periodically exploited by its ancient Egyptian neighbour. The Egyptians obtained raw materials from Nubia such as the rock with which they built their grand monuments. How they transported such vast quantities of this rock is still an unsolved mystery. The rock used for instance in the building of the second great pyramid of Khafre came from Nubia. As well as stone, Nubia had gold, copper, and many semi-precious stones like jasper, cornelian and amethyst. It was important as a corridor to trade with tropical Africa to the south as well as being quite a cosmopolitan trade centre with traders from the near east such as the

Hyksos of ancient Persia. It was also a route for trade in ivory, ebony, incense, exotic animals and slaves as well as other luxuries[5].

During the first intermediate period (2181-1991 BC) political instability in Egypt prevented its continued trade and interference in Nubia. At this time there was relatively easy travel between the two countries and many Nubians had settled peacefully in Upper Egypt, possibly in search of a better quality of life. The Nubians travelling north sold their skills as labourers, artisans and mercenaries, playing an important role in the civil conflicts in Egypt. It is well known that Nubian military men, particularly archers were highly regarded as is demonstrated by the discovery of Nubian archers found in a tomb of this period[6]. Nubia was also known as the land of the bow in reference to its revered archers[7]. At about this time, Egypt managed to re-unite and entered another period of strength and political stability under the Mentuhoteps who founded the 12th dynasty. This era is also known as the middle kingdom.

As well as trade, Nubia and Egypt engaged in occasional conflict, probably brought about by competition for trade and trade routes, since Nubia was an important trade corridor for Egypt. In the middle kingdom period, when Egypt was once again strong and in a position to exploit its southern neighbour, military campaigns were again made to subdue the Nubians to the will of the Egyptian state. The Egyptian kings tried to conquer and annex all of lower Nubia and did this mainly through the power of the 12th dynasty rulers such as Senusret I and Senusret II. At about this time the Egyptians began to refer to Nubia as the land "Kush". To protect the new gains made the Egyptians built military buildings or forts at important points along the River Nile to prevent the Nubians travelling into Egypt using boats on the river[8]. Thus the Egyptians tried to defend their southern border with Nubia by pushing their forces into Nubia and forcing the Nubians away from the border with Egypt to create a buffer zone within lower Nubia which they used to protect against what they saw as the Nubian military threat. The Nubian threat would continue to grow over the history of the two nations.

After the end of the 12th dynasty (1991-1786 BC), Egypt entered a second intermediate period where there was once again fragmentation of Egyptian society and internal conflict. Again at this point, Nubia was left to develop without interference and exploitation. But by the mid 1600s BC Egypt recovered from this period and a king by the name of Kamose the founder of the 17th dynasty, arose to begin the fight to dispel the Hyksos[9]. We notice in this period a return of the ancient Egyptian nationalism that had always reunited Egypt and would do so again in later times. The ancient Egyptians at certain points in their history had a sense of their national identity which made them want to push out those whom they saw as the foreign conquerors, who at this point in time were the

Hyksos from the near east. The Egyptians engaged the Nubians as skilful military allies, with whom they had a common cause. We have already pointed out the contribution made to this effort by Nubian military men. Again at the close of the second intermediate period it is the loyalty or otherwise of the Nubians to their African neighbours that could hang the freedom of Egypt from foreign dominance in the balance. During the reign of Kamose the Hyksos at one point controlled all of Egypt from the delta almost to Asyut (along the Nile between Abydos and El Armana) and the ruler of Kush at the time (whose name is unknown to us) controlled the whole of Nubia as far north as Aswan (between Abydos and Abu Simbel along the Nile).

The Nubians engaged in trade with the Hyksos, but did not side with the Hyksos against their Egyptian neighbours[10]. It is said that the Hyksos ruler Aawserre Apophis tried to persuade the ruler of Kush/Nubia to side with him against the Egyptians. It is said that the Egyptians stopped the Hyksos leader's messenger before he could pass the message on to the Nubians[11]. However, in hindsight, there would be no advantage for the increasingly powerful Nubia to side against the Egyptians, as this would leave them vulnerable to domination by a Hyksos state, more culturally remote from the Nubians than the Egyptians. At least both the Egyptians and the Nubians believed in the same God, Amun[12], the hidden one and shared many common religious and philosophical beliefs and cultural traditions.

In the 17th dynasty Kamose was succeeded by Ahmose I who is called the founder of the New Kingdom[13] – an era in Egyptian royal history of great wealth and military power. Though there was military hostility towards Nubia from Egypt from time to time, the people still interacted as two peoples having family connections. Nubians had fought in the Egyptian army, under Kamose, in their war of liberation from the Hyksos[14].

The part played by Nubian soldiers in the Egyptian war created more trained Nubian military personnel. After the war of liberation Egypt became so insecure about the growing military threat from neighbouring Nubia, that it created a buffer zone within Nubia which was occupied with Egyptian troops[15]. This situation is a repeat of events taking place in the period of Egypt's 12th dynasty, when there was also a threat to Egypt's southern border. Though the Egyptians inhabited Nubia/Kush they did not militarily defeat the Nubians until the accession to the throne of Thutmose I who started the pacification of Nubia, which was eventually completed by Thutmose III[16].

By 1400BC the Hyksos were defeated and pushed out of Egypt. The re-conquest of Egypt happened under Thutmose III, who was titled the "Royal Son of Kush". Thutmose III expanded the Egyptian empire south to include Nubia. Unfortunately, whilst we can speak of Kamose, Thutmose and Apophis of the Hyksos, we do not even have the name of the Nubian rulers at the time. The expansion of Egypt's empire brought great wealth which can explain the great opulence of Egypt in the 18th dynasty.

Thutmose III started his campaigns against the Nubians while still sharing his throne with his aunt, Queen Hatshepsut, who could have (but its seems had not) prevented him launching such campaigns[17]. This calls into question the view that Thutmose III and his aunt were bitter rivals rather than collaborators, on some level. Thutmose III continued the expansion of the Egyptian empire to the area of Syria and Palestine. Thutmose's Egyptian empire reached as far as the River Euphrates as well as encompassing Nubia[18].

By 1300BC the region had a radical change in climate. As a result of deforestation, the region received less and less rainfall and witnessed the encroachment of the Sahara desert. This led to the migration of people to the more fertile south and the rise of the province known as Dongola. This shift in population also meant a power shift from the North to the south.

The Egyptians intensively mined Nubia for gold[19]. Inscriptions from the 18th dynasty evince the mining of large quantities. Gold was the most prized commodity of this ancient world and gave Egypt leverage in negotiation with other nations. In the period of the 18th and 19th dynasties, the Egyptians continued to exploit the resources of Nubia for their own benefit. They mined its gold and produced monuments to their occupation. An example of this is the temple of Rameses at Abu Simbel. Nubia (Kush) would again come under the control of the expanding Egyptian empire. Later on, the Nubians would historically turn the tables of power on the Egyptians and accede to power as the 25th dynasty of rulers of Egypt.

References

Chapter Three - Nubia: The Relationship with Egypt

1. Closed minded historians say African people never established any sophisticated civilizations, but forget about Nubia and Egypt, two of the earliest civilizations in the world.
2. By researchers of the Oriental Institute of the University of Chicago. See Williams, B., *The Lost Pharaohs of Nubia*, in Van Sertima, I. (ed.), Egypt Revisited, Transaction Publishers, London, 1989, p. 90-104.

3. The Palermo Stone, in the Palermo archaeological Museum, Sicily.
4. Chandler, W., *Of Gods and Men*, in Van Sertima, I. (ed.), Egypt Revisited, Transaction Publishers, London, 1989, p.154-158.
5. Taylor, J.H., *Egypt and Nubia*, British Museum Press, London, 1991, p.6.
6. Payne, E., *The Pharaohs of Egypt*, Landmark Books, Random House New York, 1964, p.76 and Gill, A., *Ancient Egypt*, Harper and Collins, 2003, p.33.
7. Morkot, R., *The Black Pharaohs - Egypt's Nubian Rulers*, Rubicorn Press, London, 2000, p.1-2.
8. Watterson, B., *Ancient Egypt*, Sutton Publishing, 1998, p.44-45 and Taylor, J.H., *Egypt and Nubia*, British Museum Press, London, 1991, p.18.
9. Watterson, B., *op. cit.*, p.53.
10. Save-Soderbergh, T., *Temples and Tombs of Ancient Nubia*, Thames and Hudson, London, 1987, p.36.
11. Morkot, R., *The Black Pharaohs - Egypt's Nubian Rulers*, Rubicorn Press, London, 2000, p.69.
12. Taylor, J.H.., *Egypt and Nubia*, British Museum Press, London, 1991, p.40.
13. Clegg, L.H., *Black rulers of the Golden Age*, in Van Sertima, I. (ed.), Egypt Revisited, Transaction Publishers, London, 1989, p.245-247.
14. Payne, E., *The Pharaohs of Egypt*, Landmark Books, Random House New York, 1964, p.76
15. Morkot, R., *The Black Pharaohs - Egypt's Nubian Rulers*, Rubicorn Press, London, 2000, p.69.
16. Ibid., p.72.
17. Ibid., p.73.
18. Watterson, B., *op. cit.*, p.65-66.
19. Save-Soderbergh, T., *Temples and Tombs of Ancient Nubia*, Thames and Hudson, London, 1987, p.36.

Chapter Four

Egypt (Kemet)

Manetho wrote that the first king of Egypt who lived 3,200 years BC or (5,200 years ago) was Menes who came from Thinis in southern Egypt. He ruled the kingdom of Egypt for 62 years and it is said that he died from the wounds of a hippopotamus. As Wayne Chandler has noted, Menes was the first known Water Engineer[1]. Some writers say that he

Figure 2. Menes - First King of Dynastic Egypt. Courtesy Wayne Chandler.

masterminded Egypt's irrigation programme, ensuring that in the arid landscape of Egypt, where rain was in some parts scarce, there was always sufficient water to enable the Egyptians to grow the crops they needed to feed their growing population.

This included crops like lentils, and copious varieties of vegetables such as cabbage, cucumber, water melon, and pumpkins (of which the seeds were roasted and eaten). This diet of vegetables was complimented with very little meat, taking the form of beef (very rarely) and also goat meat and fish[2]. The majority of Egyptians lived from the land. They were indeed one of the earliest nations of farmers.

It seems that the Egyptian society of those days was very class conscious. There were royals and nobility made up of the relatives of the pharaohs and their descendants, there were tradesmen, scribes and philosophers, builders and labourers.

The early Egyptians were African people who were small in stature by modern standards - no more that 5½ feet in height. Cheikh Anta Diop refers to them by name as the "Anu"[3]. Diop was convinced that the ancient Egyptians were Negroes, even if they grew steadily lighter as the centuries passed. To convince other Egyptologists he merely pointed to the portraits of pre-dynastic and new kingdom negroid Egyptians. Wyatt MacGaffey noted that: *"Such pictures have been a source of some embarrassment to Egyptologists"*. In response to this, as MacGaffey goes on to relate, some then stressed that people in Egyptian art that looked like negroes were really something else[3A].

Like traditional Africans the ancient Egyptians believed in reincarnation. They believed that each person is accompanied by a spiritual guardian or double in this life and into the next, which they called the Ka and traditional Africans in various languages call this spiritual double the Chi, Kla, Ori, etc[4]. The Egyptians poured libation to their ancestors, just as traditional Africans do. They also followed the tradition of divine kingship and indeed queenship as traditional Africans do till today. Myth has it that Osiris (wsr) was the first king of Egypt. The fact that Osiris is a god or divinity is an indication of the tradition of divine kingship. The King or Queen in Egypt was seen as the link between God and the people.

It has been claimed that the themes of the Holy Bible are to be found in the much earlier texts of the Egyptians. It is interesting to note the common aspects of the divinity of Osiris in comparison to Christ and also Lazarus. In a sense, Osiris is an ancient Egyptian Christ. Osiris, like Christ, is the intermediary between people and God. Like Christ and like Lazarus, Osiris was killed and rose from the dead after being embalmed inside a tomb.

The ancient Africans (Egyptians and Nubians), just as the traditional Africans, saw God, as a "life force". By this we mean that God was seen as a force that is continuously sustaining the Creation in existence. The Igbo of Nigeria relate in an old saying that "if God took away His/Her hand, the world would vanish " (*Chukwu wetu aka, Uwa a gwu*). If the King was ill this was a bad omen, because it meant the link of the people to the life force would be weak[5]. And the people would become weak and prone to disasters.

If we used the name the ancient Egyptians used for themselves as a nation and their land, rather than the name derived from a foreign language - the Greek *Aigyptos* - then we would use *Kmt* (pronounced

Kemet). Since the word *Km* referred to black (as in burnt black like charcoal), *Kmt* means something like "land of the Blacks"[7]. Some scholars argue that it means "Black Land" in reference to the soil. But this should be of no consequence because African languages commonly use the same word to refer simultaneously to the land and the people [7A]. In African languages, commonly, the people are one with the land or soil and the same word is used interchangeably for both. However, the Congolese Egyptologist and linguist, Theophile Obenga, is strict in his belief that the meaning of Kmt is unequivocally "land of the blacks"[7B].

Menes united Upper and Lower Egypt into a single nation. Thus he was known as the Lord of the Two Lands. Upper Egypt, that is, Southern Egypt and Lower Egypt (Northern Egypt) were at a point in history, separate nations, which Menes, the water engineer king, united into one nation[6], Kmt (Egypt).

Figure 3 Imhotep. Djoser's Prime Minister.
Courtesy Wayne Chandler

Various other interesting characters emerge in the history of Egypt after Menes. It is unfortunate the great passage of time means we don't know enough about such remarkable characters as Imhotep, an early renaissance man. He was at least an architect and a physician, among other things[8]. Imhotep is the first architect and physician in history to be known by name. As an official of the pharaoh Djoser of the 3rd dynasty, Imhotep designed and built the step pyramid at Sakkara around 2630-

2611 BC. Sakkara[9] certainly looks convincing as a prototype for what was to be one of the most massive building projects ever undertaken in the history of humanity: the Great Pyramids. He may also have been responsible for the first known use of columns in architecture. Imhotep also held religious office, being the high priest of the sun god Ra (the ancient Egyptian equivalent and predecessor of the Greek sun god, Apollo). Imhotep, is credited as the founder of Egyptian medicine and was worshipped by the Greeks by the name of Asclepius, the god of medicine and healing referred to in the Hippocratic oath[10]. The oath begins: "I swear by Apollo, Asclepius, Hygieia and Panacea to witness all the gods, all the goddesses, to keep according to my ability and my judgement, the following Oath".

The Great Pyramids

The idea that the Pyramids were merely tombstones for dead kings, seems a little simple, for these were massive building projects by any standard in any age. An alternative hypothesis is offered by the historical researchers Bauval and Gilbert (1994) that they were, rather, astronomical observatories for watching the star constellations; means by which the dead monarch's spirit could come into union with the heavens[11]. Most amazingly of all, the Ancient Egyptians recreated the very mapping of the heavens on earth as we see with the layout of the Great Pyramids built successively by the pharaohs, Khufu, Khafre and Menkaure. Bauval and Gilbert's study suggests that the Great Pyramids were a long term project. The project, would probably have been preconceived by Khufu and taken on by his successors and sons (or son and grandson), Khafre and Menkaure.

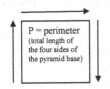
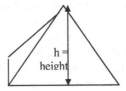

P = perimeter
(total length of
the four sides of
the pyramid base)

h = height

Diagrams showing the perimeter of the square base and the height of the Great Pyramid of Giza

Consider the following calculation to arrive at the mathematical constant Pi : P = Perimeter, h = height and   P/h = 6.28 = 2 pi   (The famous mathematical constant)

The great pyramid of Giza stands as additional evidence of the fact that from earliest times (2800 BC) the Egyptians knew of the Pythagoras theorem[12] and that the pyramids were a store of mathematical and astronomical information. This is further emphasized by measurements taken of the Pyramid of Giza shown above.

How the Egyptians built the pyramids is still not understood fully. It would have taken an estimated 100,000 men 20 years to build the Great Pyramid of Giza alone[13]. How could Egypt have amassed so much labour? Some accounts say that they used forced labourers, who were Hebrews in captivity in Egypt. But bible scholars will note that the Pharoah Rameses (c. 1291-1224 BC) was the Pharoah at the time of the exodus out of Egypt, according to dates given for the exodus. However, there is no apparent mention in Egyptian texts of the exodus, and yet there are so many Egyptian texts of that time[14].

The Great Pyramid of Giza was a remarkable building feat. The Great Pyramid consists of 2.3 million blocks each having a weight of 2 ½ tonnes. Each of these gigantic blocks was placed, somehow, without cranes or other modern means of mechanical lifting, within an accuracy of only a few millimetres in error. Their accuracy shows remarkable mathematical and technological skill for their time. The sides of Khufu's pyramid are aligned exactly true north. The base of the pyramid is exactly level, the lengths of the sides of the square base, vary by less than 5cm[15].

It was the pharaoh Khufu (2589 BC) who built the first of the Great Pyramids, the Great Pyramid of Giza. He is remembered as a ruthless pharaoh, who came to the throne as a young man in his twenties, and reigned for 65 years, according to Manetho. His cruelty is apparently the result of his frustration, because he fears that his dynasty will not survive[16]. He need not have feared, for at least in technical terms the 4th dynasty was a golden age in Egyptian history. Khufu had at least three children: his sons Djedefra and Khafre[19], his daughter Hetepheres II (named after Khufu's mother, Queen Hetepheres I) and also Menkaure his second successor, who some speculate may have been his grandson.

Khafre, son of Khufu, (2558 BC) is the builder of the second of the Great Pyramids. He is thought to have reigned for 26 years. Khafre built the Great Sphinx, which is supposed to bear Khafre's face.

The last of the Great Pyramids was built by Menkaure, who was either the son of Khafre or Khufu. It is said that Menkaure was kind natured and did much to alleviate the suffering caused by his grandfather (or father) Khufu's reign[19]. He had a tragic life, losing his only daughter whom he loved deeply to an illness suffered while still a child. He had her corpse kept inside a wooden bull until his own death[20]

The Egyptians became one of the first naval powers in history under the reign of Sahure of the 5th dynasty who ordered the building of boats in order to defend Egypt by sea against the invasive threat of the Persians.

In the time of Sahure we see the earliest attempts at the preservation of the Egyptian worldview documented in sacred literature recorded on the stone walls of the tombs of kings of the 5th and 6th dynasties at Sakkara[17],

Figure 4. Pharaoh Pepi I pouring ancestral libation.
Courtesy Wayne Chandler.

the location of Imhotep's step pyramid. These writings would later become known as the Egyptian Book of the Dead (Papyrus of Ani). These books were known collectively by the Egyptians themselves as the "Book of Coming forth by Day and By Night".

The early rulers of Egypt had very close links with Nubia and Pepi I was no exception to this tradition. It was Pepi I who raised the religion of Egypt to become a world system, explaining, not only the place of humans and God, but also the creation of the world. Pepi I shows the African nature of the Pharaoh's customs when he is shown in one sculpture offering libation to his ancestors[18], a custom which is uniquely

African. It seems that Pepi I expanded the Egyptian empire of his time. He ordered an expedition for the conquest of Nubia when it occurred that the Nubians in the north of their kingdom were blocking Egyptian trade with that region.

Pepi I married a lady by the name of Weretimtes. It proved not to be a perfect love match; for Weretimtes joined others in unsuccessfully conspiring against her husband. However, Pepi I survived to die a natural death in old age and was buried in Imhotep's step pyramid at Sakkara, along with other kings of the 5th and 6th dynasties[18A].

By the end of the 6th Dynasty we begin to see a temporary fragmentation of ancient Egyptian society with possibly several monarchs all ruling simultaneously. Egypt of that period was suffering. There was a great malaise in Egyptian society with contesting kingdoms and contesting warlords over the land. The uncertainty of the time is recounted in the poetic writings of this period,[19] the "intermediate period" (2500-1991 BC). The author is unknown, but due to the unbearable strain of living in this violent uncertain time the author, who contemplates suicide has a talk with his own soul, and through this he comes out of his moment of madness and reaches a more positive solution. In tune with the desperation of the times the 6th dynasty was ended by the suicide of the monarch, Queen Nt Aqrt (known in Greek as Nitocris) after her brother had been murdered by warlords. It heralded uncertain times in Egypt.

The 6th to the 11th dynastic periods in Egyptian history represent a kind of dark ages, with Egypt fragmented as well as under foreign influence. A people are more easily and peacefully governed according to institutions that they already recognise. In this context, the 11th dynasty Mentuhotep family who came originally from Southern Egypt, were able to bring back some much needed stability to Egypt. The last of the Mentuhoteps was Nebtowyre who was deposed in a coup by his powerful prime minister, Amenemhet I, who then founded Egypt's 12th dynasty[20]. Amenemhet married Nfrw (pronounced: ne-fe-ru) and their descendants included Kheperkare Senusret II, who along with his predecessor, Senusret I, led another period of the Egyptian colonization of Nubia[21], and also Nukaure Amenemhet and Nymare Amenemhet. The 12th dynasty ends after the succession to the headship of state of Nymare's sister, Sobkhare.

If the measure of the level of advancement of a society, is given by the social status of its women, then ancient Egypt, stands as one of the most advanced civilizations in the old world. It is fair to say the Egyptian nation was hundreds if not thousands of years ahead of its rival nations of the old world when it came to the status of women[22]. Nowhere else in the old world (outside of Africa) did we have women heads of state at this time. We will see that in the future of Egypt women will become more prevalent as heads of the culturally influential Egyptian state, and therefore powerful figures of the old world order. In contrast to the very visible Egyptian women, Greek women and Persian women were secluded from view as evinced by the absence of women in the artistic records of those cultures.

In contrast, the African women of Egypt, not only appeared everywhere in their pictures, but the women depicted openly and proudly displayed their African femininity, often wearing revealing dress that emphasized the feminine form. Dresses were worn, for instance, where the bust was revealed, yet the rest of the body was covered. This was not a uniform but apparently an attire of choice. In the same setting other women wore ankle length dress that covered their bodies from the neck line down. In Egyptian wall paintings and engravings a woman would be found playing musical instruments, dancing, enjoying the scent of a lotus flower alone or with her friends or husband, at the same time as freely embracing him, drinking wine and plaiting hair[23].

Egyptian women had equal property rights to men in marriage[24]. It seems that some Greek writers were so taken by this revelation that they may have chosen to exaggerate what they saw as alien: Diodorus says that part of an agreement entered into in Egyptian marriage is for the wife to have control over her husband, and that no objection should be made to her commands.[25]

The queens of Egypt wielded exceptional influence as advisers to the pharaohs and they had a significant political role. This was partly because the legitimacy of descent for monarchic rule was established through women. It is obvious that the Egyptians did this because this is the most reliable way of establishing descent. This custom was apparently handed down to traditional Africans.

It may well be that the issue of gender equality was raised as a topic of discussion by the Greek philosophers, as some commentators claim Plato does in his Republic.[32] But the Egyptians had a civilized society which had already put into practice some of the aspects of gender equality aspired to in Plato's republic. For instance, they had women rulers, and had done for over a thousand years before the time of Plato. At about this time, in 5th century BC, the Greek society could only aspire to this as an ideal through the writings of its philosophers – who were in any case persecuted for teaching doctrines regarded as foreign by the Greek establishment.

New Kingdom and the Re-establishment of Links with Nubia

With the defeat of the Hyksos in the 17th dynasty, Egypt began to emerge from its dark ages. In about the 1400s BC, the way was laid open for the advent of the 18th dynasty, the most opulent period in ancient Egypt's long monarchic history. It was Kamose who began the fight to rid Egypt of the foreign domination by the Hyksos.[27] Archaeologists believe that the Hyksos first conquered Egypt by filtering into Egypt by some of the many small rivers called "tributaries" that made up the Nile delta in the north of the country. Other accounts suggest that the Hyksos entered Egypt on horses as an invading horde that easily overpowered the unformed Egyptian army. The Hyksos ruled for 150 years, and like any other occupying army they were hated by the citizens of that country. The people's rescue came when the powerful prince Kamose of Thebes in Upper Egypt sailed downriver to attack the enemy capital. Kamose was killed in battle, but his brother Ahmes broke the power of the Hyksos and chased them out of Egypt across the desert and back to Syria. Kamose was succeeded on the throne by King Ahmose I, his brother, who founded the 18th dynasty.[28] Ahmose, in line with a custom continued by the Egyptian pharaohs from the beginning in order to keep the throne within the family, married his sister Ahmose-Nefertari. This incestuous form of marriage, however, may have led to birth defects in latter times as hereditary diseases would, most likely, be passed onto the next generation.

At this time the relations between Egypt and Nubia were complex. On the one hand there was, culturally, a genetic relation between the peoples of Egypt and ancient Nubia, Egypt being the daughter, and Nubia the mother. On the other hand there seemed to be an exploitative element to the daughter's relationship to the mother. For many centuries, Nubia was the source of much of Egypt's gold and natural resources. For instance, the rock used in building temple statues in the pyramid of Khafre (the second and second largest of the Great Pyramids built around 2600 BC) came from Abu Simbel in Nubia; and the great wealth in gold of the 18th dynasty derived from Nubian gold.[29] Even the name Nubia possibly derives from the Egyptian word for gold, nbw.

Sometimes there was military conflict between the two neighbours, and under Thutmose I, Nubia was colonised by the Egyptians. Thutmose I, it seems, gave himself the title, Royal Son of Kush.

Nefertari (1550-1500 BC) along with husband, King Ahmose, was founder of the 18th dynasty.[30] She is often regarded as the first significant woman ruler in history. There were earlier female monarchs such as Nit Aqrt (Netocris in the Greek) at the close of the 6th dynasty and Sobkaure, sister of Amenemhet in the 12th dynasty. Neither reign was as long or significant.

Nefertari is well known for her black complexion, pointing to a Nubian ancestry. A painting on the walls of the tomb at Deir el-Medinah, shows her complexion to be jet black[31]. Quite surprisingly, some Egyptologists insist that this black colour is used only ritualistically and is not an

27

indication of the race of the Queen[32], even though there were patently many Nubians of this complexion settled in Egyptian society.[33]

Hatshepsut (Maatkare) was the eldest daughter of Thutmose I and Queen Ahmose, who were known to have had one other daughter, who died while still a baby[34]. Thutmose had other children by his second wife Mutnofret, including Wdjmose, Amenose, and Thutmose II. As was common in Egypt in order to keep the throne within the family, Hatshepsut married her half brother Thutmose II. [35] On the death of Thutmose I, Thutmose II became pharaoh and Hatshepsut assumed the title of great Royal Wife. Thutmose II ruled Egypt for 13 years.[36] The

Figure 5 Queen Nefertari

Egyptians were therefore one of the earliest society of polygamists in the world [37]and probably handed on this custom to traditional Africans. Polygamy, as we know was common in precolonial Africa and is still alive on the African continent today. Polygamy probably arose in ancient Egyptian times because of the high frequency of infant and child mortality. It seemed almost to be the exception rather than the norm for children to survive into adulthood, and having many wives was a means of gaining more children and making it more likely for an heir to the throne to survive childhood illness.

On Thutmose's death the throne passed to Hatshepsut's nephew, Thutmose III who was in line for it. But as the boy was too young, Hatshepsut was announced as a temporary ruler in his place until Thutmose III was of the age to take the responsibility.

Hatshepsut set about re-establishing the trade networks that had been disrupted since the Hyksos occupation and she helped make preparations for a royal visit to the land of Nubia, which were vital for Egypt's trade relations. Hatshepsut was a strong military leader and had apparent success in military campaigns which the Egyptians fought successfully in Nubia, the Levant and Syria. She is credited with the erection of hundreds of grand building projects and monuments and was one of the great builder pharaohs. Her greatest acclaimed building was her mortuary temple at Deir al-Bahri[38] which is an example of a building of perfect symmetry and harmony, one thousand years before the Parthenon of the ancient Greeks. The temple was designed and constructed by her royal adviser and architect, Senmut on the West Bank of the Nile near the entrance to the Valley of the Kings.[39]

Hatshepsut became crowned as the pharaoh of Egypt and assumed all of the symbols of pharaonic power, including the head cloth, the Uraeus and the traditional false beard. Being black Africans, the Egyptian pharaohs did not grow beards as easily as the Asians, but nevertheless were culturally influenced by the fashion of wearing beards. So at a point, after the influence the Hyksos must have made on Egyptian culture, the false beard became a fashion.

Thutmose III (1479-1425 BC) assumed the throne at last, on the death of his aunt, Hatshepsut, to become one of Egypt's greatest pharaohs. Thutmose III was the son of Thutmose II and one of his minor wives, Isis (in Greek, or Ast in Egyptian). Many writers assume that Thutmose III resented his aunt, Hatshepsut, for hanging onto the throne for too long, but there is little evidence to support this view. On the contrary there is evidence of some mutual respect and collaboration between the two.[40] There is no evidence that Thutmose III ever tried to claim the throne whilst Hatshepsut was alive, and in all likelihood had a deep respect for her and would even appear to have modelled his own kingship on her example: building monuments, establishing trade and being militarily strong. Furthermore, he married Hatshepsut's youngest daughter Meritre[41], giving him yet more reason to regard her with respect rather than resentment. Despite the stories that Hatshepsut hung on to the throne to his disadvantage, he still managed to reign for at least 40 years. Later evidence that Hatshepsut's inscriptions were vandalised, were too late to fall in line with the theory that a resentful Thutmose had ordered the removal of her name on assuming the throne. Rather it is more likely her name was removed because she was a woman and that the office of pharaoh was still seen as the preserve of men[42].

Thutmose III was the most successful of the military pharaohs. He was an active expansionist ruler who is said to have conquered 350 cities in his rule, from his southern Nubian neighbours to the Euphrates River in the near east. In his reign he is known to have undertaken 32 military campaigns[43].

By the 18th dynasty, the colonization of Nubia by Egypt became more open exploitation. Egypt controlled Nubia's trade routes and Nubians had to pay annual taxes to the Egyptian state in the form of leopard skins, live animals, ivory, ebony and slaves.

It would seem that the Hyksos of Syria had their chance over 150 years to change the racial and cultural identity of Egypt's monarchic system. However, the reports of many historians disputes this. In fact the Hyksos could not succeed in ruling Egypt as foreigners. They had to adopt Egyptian titles, customs and culture in order to be accepted in their role[44]. This suggested that their rule and their influence could never be anything but temporary. It is likely that the Hyksos conquerors in their period of limited control over Egypt had little if any lasting impact on the Egyptian monarchic system racially or culturally; although the influx of foreign blood may have been enough to create a distance between the Egyptians and their relatives the Kushites to the South. However, in contradiction to this we see the Nubians and Egyptians appeared to cooperate to drive out the Hyksos[45]. We can point to a cosmopolitan Egyptian society in which Nubians were regarded as the pharaoh's citizens[46]. Whatever the case, it is implied that on some level, the Egyptians and Nubians recognised a common bond. The Hyksos threat continued, and fighting continued into the reign of Ahmoses's youngest son, Thutmose I, who became pharaoh in 1524 BC. Thutmose led his forces up to the upper Euphrates River to dispel the Hyksos threat, and erected a stone monument there to mark his success.[47]

Probably the greatest religious reformers in Egyptian history were the pharaoh Akhenaton and his Great Royal Wife Nefertiti (1353 – 1336 BC). Nefertiti was the niece of Queen Tiye, whilst it was well known that Akhenaton was the son of the pharaoh Amenhotep III and his Great Royal Wife, Queen Tiye[48].

According to Asa Hilliard III, in the volume edited by Ivan Van Sertima and titled *Egypt Revisited*, in all likelihood, the famous bust of Nefertiti to be found in Berlin Museum is not her. It has no royal inscriptions[49] and therefore should not have been assumed to be Nefertiti. Nefertiti's true likeness is to be found in a picture on the wall of her temple, and it looks radically different. She is certainly not pretty according to European aesthetic appreciation, unlike the bust, which may be the idealised creation of a Greek or Roman artist depicting the revered Nefertiti, or indeed an outright German fake.

Akhenaton was a religious revolutionary. He was not, however, as some claim, the originator of the concept of one God (monotheism) in Egypt[50]. This existed much earlier as shown by the text known popularly as "The Egyptian Book of the Dead", but known by the Egyptians themselves as "The Book of Coming Forth by Day and by Night". This text was in circulation by 2000-1900 BC. In this text it clearly refers to the idea that there is one and only one supreme being: "God is one and alone and none other existeth with him...", "...thou one, thou only one whose arms are many...thou one thou only one who has no second..", and many other examples.[51]

Figure 6 Amenhotep III, father of Akhenaton

Akhenaton, supported by his wife, the powerful and influential Nefertiti did, however, position the idea of one God at the heart of the ancient Egyptian religion[52]. It makes sense that Akhenaton and Nefertiti, being astute political rulers, also recognised the political advantages in doing this. It meant, essentially, that their subjects had allegiance to one God, personified as the sun god Aten, and one pharaoh. It served to wrest the power away from the traditional local priesthood, who made allegiances to various deities, varying from one region to another. The one God, Aten, would serve as both a centralising and a unifying force for the Egyptian state.

This point is amplified when we realise that Akhenaton proclaimed himself, as the pharaoh, to be the only channel between his people and God (Aten). Akhenaton shows us an early example of "divine kingship" in Africa, where the king or monarch is a living representation of God on earth. This is a tradition which was to be retained in Africa through out its history until modern times. The most recent example of this which we actually see in the African Diaspora is the deification of the Emperor Haile Selassie by the Rastafarians.

Although Tutankhamun is the most well known of the pharaohs because of his golden funeral mask at the Egyptian museum in Cairo, his reign was not of great significance compared to that of his half brother Akhenaton[53]. We note that Tutankhamun was born Tutankhaten, but changed his name to reinstate the cult of Amun[54], probably on the advice of his ministers. In the third year of his reign when he was still a young boy (perhaps 11 years of age) his name was changed by powerful priests who wished to reverse the revolution of Akhenaten, reverting to the revered hidden God, Amun.

Tutankhamun died whilst still in his teens. Studies in 2005 suggested that no foul play was involved[55], as had been believed for a long time[56]. Tutankhamun died of a rapid attack of gangrene after breaking his leg[57]. Like many of the pharaohs' skeletons, Tutankhamun was small in stature by 21st century standards, but at five and a half feet tall, he may have been tall for an Egyptian of his day. A lot of the pharaohs were of the height range five to five and a half feet tall.

Rameses II (1279 – 1213 BC) of the 19th dynasty is known as the pharaoh of the exodus, who held the Israelites in captivity, for his reign is about the time that Judaism became an established religion. Unfortunately, for those who put forward this idea, there are no written records of this by the Egyptians themselves. This throws doubt on this because the Egyptians were reliable at recording events in their written texts. It would be uncharacteristic for such a major event to go without mention.

The most important of Rameses' wives was Nefertari, namesake of Nefertari, wife of Ahmose I in the 18th dynasty.

Rameses was another successful military pharaoh. He sent expeditions into Israel, Lebanon and Syria. Rameses fought to resist Hittite rule in the area. The Hittites, an Indo European people of unknown origin, had conquered the Mesopotamian region and brought an end to the Babylonian Empire in the area of modern Arabian peninsula in 1600 BC.

Figure 7 Tutankhamun

Rameses also sent military campaigns into Nubia and his most well known monument is his temple at Abu Simbel. He was the longest reigning monarch in ancient Egyptian history.

References

Chapter Four – Egypt (Kemet)

1. Chandler, W., *Of Gods and Men*, in Van Sertima, I. (ed.), Egypt Revisited, Transaction Publishers, London, 1989, p.135. Chandler's powerful photographic data and scholarship (included in this chapter and beyond) have strongly influenced the way in which many view the ancient African past.
2. Romant, B., *Life in Egypt in Ancient Times*, Minerva, S.A. Geneve, Italy, 1986, p.55-56.
3. Diop, Cheikh Anta, Civilization *or Barbarism: An authentic anthropology*, Lawrence Hill Books, New York, 1991, p.121.
3A. MacGaffey, W., *Concepts of race in Northeast Africa,* in Fage, J.D and R.A. Oliver (ed.), Papers in African Prehistory, Cambridge University Press, 1970, p.99-115.

4. Kamalu, C., *Person, Divinity and Nature*, Karnak House, London, 1998, p.53.

5. See Payne (1964), Taylor (1991), Romant (1986).

6. Payne, E.,*The Pharaohs of Egypt*, Landmark Books, Random House New York, 1964, p.37-38.

7. Obenga, T., *Egypt and Black Africa*, Karnak House, London, 1992.

7A. Kamalu, C., *Person Divinity and Nature*, Karnak House, London, 1998, p.164.

7B. I put this point to Obenga at the 1998 conference of the Association of Classical African Civilizations in New York. His response was unequivocally that the term Kmt means "land of black people".

8. Finch, C., *The African Background to Medical Science*, Karnak House, London, 1990, p.77.

9. Chandler, W., *op. cit.*, p.158.

10.Ibid., p.72-75.

11.Bauval, R. and Adrian Gilbert, *Orion Mystery – Secrets of the Pyramids*, Random House, NY, 1995.

12.McLeish, J., *History that Counts*, Bloomsbury Press, London, 1992.

13.Hagen, R. and Rainer Hagen, *Egypt: Peoples, Gods, Pharaohs*, Benedikt Taschen, Cologne, 1999, p.35.

14.Tyldesley, J., *The Private Lives of the pharaohs*, Channel 4 Books, 2000, p.43.

15.Watterson, B., *Ancient Egypt*, Sutton Publishing, 1998, p.17.

16.Wikipedia

17.Budge, E.A.W., *Egyptian Book of the Dead*, Dover, New York, 1967, p.ix.

18.Chandler, *op. cit.*, p.176.

18A. Watterson, B., *op. cit.*, p.29-30.

19.Reed, B., *Rebel in the Soul*, Wildwood House, London 1978.

20.Watterson, *op. cit.*, p.39.

21.Ibid., p.39-44.

22.Romant, *op. cit.*, p. 104.

23.Ibid.

24.Ibid., p.7.

25.Ibid., p.7

26.Plato, *The Republic*, translated by F. Macdonald Cornford, Oxford University Press, London, 1979, p.144.

27.Watterson, *op. cit.*, p.53.

28.Ibid., p. 53.

29.Taylor, J.H.., *Egypt and Nubia*, British Museum Press, London, 1991, p. 32.

30.Ibid., p.28

31. Clegg, *op. cit.*, p.247
32. Ibid., p.246.
33. Morkot, R., *The Black Pharaohs - Egypt's Nubian Rulers*, Rubicorn Press, London, 2000, p.289.
34. Tyldesley, *op. cit.,* p.89
35. Hagen, R and Rainer Hagen, *op. cit.*, p. 122.
36. Morkot, *op. cit.,* p.72.
37. Romant, *op.cit.,* p.7.
38. Watterson, *op. cit.*, p.61.
39. *Ibid.*, p.61
40. Morkot, *op. cit.*, p.73
41. Wikipedia
42. Hagen and Hagen, *op. cit.*, p.123.
43. Wikipedia
44. Watterson, *op. cit.*, p.52.
45. Gill, A., *Ancient Egypt*, Harper and Collins, 2003, p.33.
46. *Ibid.*, p.31.
47. Watterson, *op. cit.*, p.59.
48. Clegg, *op.cit.*, p.251.
49. Hilliard, A. G., "Waset, the Eye of Ra and the Abode of Maat: The Pinnacle of Black leadership in the Ancient world", in I Vansertima (ed), *op. cit.*, p.234.
50. Kamalu, C., *Foundations of African Thought*, Karnak House, London, 1990, p.41.
51. *Ibid.*
52. Payne, *op. cit.*, p.119-132 and Watterson, op. cit., 72-75.
53. Payne, *op. cit.*, p.145
54. Watterson, *op. cit.* p.75
55. Handwerk, Brian, *King Tut Not Murdered Violently, CT Scans Show*, National Geographic News, March 8, 2005, p. 2.
56. Brier, B., *The Murder of Tutankhamen: A True Story.* Putnam Adult, April 1998.
57. Handwerk, B., *op. cit.*

Chapter Five

The Rise of the Kings of Kush and the Nubian Colonization of Egypt

In the 8th century BC, a powerful Nubian/Kushite kingdom emerged in the region of Napata and later became the foundations of the famous civilization of Meroe. This powerful line of Kushite rulers begins with Alara and the most famous of these is Taharka. The Nubians' culture is akin to that of the Egyptians, they are racially and ethnically connected[1] and have no hesitance in acknowledging Amun, the Egyptian God as their supreme Being[2]. The worship of Amun is as old as Egypt itself, possibly as old as the Nubians too. The Nubians and the ancient Egyptians were the most ancient of neighbouring black African nations.

The accession of the Nubian kings to the Egyptian throne was a return to original traditions[3]. The 25th dynasty ended about 700 years of chaos, mayhem and rule of Egypt by foreign rulers such as the Hyksos.

Kashta was the first ruler of this line to have left any inscriptions and secured control of Egypt as far as Aswan. He was succeeded by his son Piankhi (who reigned 741-712 BC). By the time Piankhi succeeded, lower Egypt had been in decline for over 500 years and it was torn by many internal conflicts. Piankhi's forces were so superior to any Egyptian opposition that they sailed up the Nile conquering towns at will. Like all the Nubian rulers, Piankhi was keen to preserve what they saw as the roots and essence of Egyptian culture.[4] It seems there was a sense in which to preserve Egyptian culture was to preserve their own identity and culture. Piankhi was sensitive to the decline that had taken place in Egyptian institutions and oversaw the restoration of damaged temples including one at Gebel Barkal[5].

Nubia itself is at this time an increasingly urbanised society and this advanced level of urbanisation was accompanied by a high standard of craftsmanship, and skill in areas like the working of bronze.

At the point at which Piankhi regarded the conquest of Egypt as complete, he returned to his Kush home at Napata[6].

Egypt was once again divided into a foreign dominated north and an African south. It was Kashta's successor the 21 year old Piankhy who began the war for the re-unification of Egypt and its liberation from the Asian king Tefnakt based in Sais in the north of the Egyptian delta. Piankhy sent a military expedition to defeat Tefnahkt (This is inscribed in the Temple of Gebel Barkal north of Dongola in Nubia on an erected granite stela).

The task of uniting Egypt was completed by Shabaka, the founder of the 25th dynasty in 700-750 BC. Many author's concentrate on the more military rulers such as Piankhi and Taharka, but Shabaka, appears to be more of an interesting man, being like all the Nubians conservative in preserving the Ancient Egyptian culture.[7] He was a man of high principles and it is said that he gave up the power of office for fear it would lead him to commit an injustice.

Shabaka brought about a cultural renaissance and sought to preserve Egypt's heritage.[8] Therefore he ordered the religion and philosophy of the Egyptians to be written in stone in the form of their accounts of the creation of the world now famously known as the Shabaka text. The stone became the famous Shabaka Stone and lies in the British Museum. This act of preservation showed that Shabaka was a highly sensitive ruler who valued Egyptian culture and heritage as if it were his own, cementing the idea of the close genetic connection between Nubia and Egypt. Shabaka's sister was Amenirdis I who held the position "God's Wife of Amun".[9]

Figure 8. Shabaka Stone, British Museum.

The Nubian/Kushite rule of Egypt was not to remain peaceful. In 671 BC the Assyrian leader Esarhaddon captured the Egyptian city of Memphis. The Nubian rulers of Egypt had a brief respite when Shabaka's nephew, Taharka, son of Piankhi, defeated the Assyrians in 699 BC and recaptured Memphis. As the king of Egypt, Taharka gave Egypt a breathing space from the domination of the Assyrians. Like his father, Taharka felt obliged to rescue Egypts temples from decay, rebuilding a temple at Kawa.

Memphis was to return to the Assyrians when Esarhaddon's son, Ashurbanipal defeated Taharka. In 661 BC the Nubians were finally driven out of Egypt by the Assyrian invaders, who burnt the library at

Karnak, the centre of Egyptian knowledge. Piankhy's line of rulers continued from Napata, the capital of Kush.[10]

References

Chapter Five - The Rise of the Kings of Kush and the Nubian Colonization of Egypt

1. Taylor, J.H.., *Egypt and Nubia*, British Museum Press, London, 1991, p.7.
2. Ibid., p.51.
3. Morkot, R., *The Black Pharaohs - Egypt's Nubian Rulers*, Rubicorn Press, London, 2000, p.208. Shabaka, at least, modelled his style of reign on that of the Old Kingdom pharaohs.
4. Goldman, P., *The Nubian Renaissance*, in Van sertima, I., (ed.), Egypt Revisited, Transaction Publishers, London, 1989, p.261-270.
5. Morkot, op. cit., p.15.
6. Taylor, op. cit., p.38.
7. Morkot, op. cit., p.208.
8. Ibid.
9. Ibid., p.19.
10. Taylor, op. cit., p.44.

Chapter Six

The Kingdoms of Kush and Axum

Rise of the Power of Kush

By 1370 BC, Za Besi Angabo founded a Kushite dynasty which would by 1000 BC give the world Makeda, the biblical Queen of Sheba.[1] It was Makeda's son Menelik who founded the line of the Lion of Judah which is reputed to have ended with the Emperor Haile Selassie.[2] Famous legend has it that Queen Makeda was so moved by the stories of the wisdom of King Solomon that she travelled to Judah to visit him with her entourage. It is fabled that when the two of them met they fell in love and the resulting child of their union was Menelik. This legend claims genetic connection between the monarchy of Ethiopia and the kingship of Israel[3] and the entourage who returned from Israel with Makeda are claimed to be the ancestors of the Jewish Ethiopian people whom are today known as the Falashas.

Like all history it is hard to separate fable from fact. But we do at least know that Makeda, was a Queen of Kush and we do know that the Solomonid line of rulers - those rulers from the blood line that starts with Menelik - existed at some point. Haile Selassie and his predecessors back to Tewodorus (when the lost Solomonid line was restored) are the evidence of this. Whether or not, the claim to the Solomonid line in their case is legitimate, they are the supporting evidence that there must have been such a bloodline. As Joseph E Harris points out: " The veracity of the legend of Sheba is less important than the fact that it influenced the structure of Ethiopian society and helped to entrench in Ethiopian traditions a focus of national identity and unity by legitimizing the Solomonid dynasty"[4].

A key aspect of the rise of the power of Kush is the establishment of a capital at Napata[6]. This had been the base from which the Nubians who conquered Egypt and formed the 25th Dynasty, launched their expedition.

The height of the Kushite civilization came with the movement of the capital of Kush to Meroe in the south. But the Noba repeatedly put the Kushites under attack and this led to the movement of the capital northwards to Axum.

The Civilization of Meroe and the Axumite Empire

When Taharka was defeated by Ashurbanipal he retreated to Napata to continue the line of Kushite rulers there. Kushite rule in Egypt properly came to an end with the rule of Tanutamun[6]. About 600 BC the capital of Kush shifted south from Napata to Meroe and gave rise to the flowering of the new and great civilization of Meroe.

Meroe was a significant civilization and had its own written script by 2nd or 3rd century AD[7]. However, till this day the script of that culture remains undeciphered, and this has been a major block to any further understanding of the civilization of Meroe.

With the reign of King Aspelta (593-568 BC) Meroe became an important religious centre. The religion of Meroe at the time was still akin to that of the Egyptians. At Napata, a temple of Isis (Ast) was built and this made Napata the centre of pilgrimage in this part of the world.

What led to the movement of the capital of Nubia/Kush from Napata to Meroe? Well Napata had suffered attack from the Egyptian Ruler of the Asiatic 26th dynasty, Psammeticus II. Meroe was less vulnerable than Napata, being south. Also there had been the change in climate and desertification and drought which caused the people of the city to migrate to a location with greener and heavier vegetation and hence greater rainfall.

As in Egypt, the Meroitic people believed in "divine kingship", that is they considered their monarchs to be intermediaries between God and the people. There was also a coincidence of the divinities worshipped in ancient Nubia and Egypt. For instance, the name of the divinity Amun was clearly known in ancient Nubia as shown by the Nubian names like Tanutamun. Another name which shows this is that of the Nubian/Kushite ruler Amenirdis I, the daughter of Kashta. The "Amen" in Amenirdis derives from the name Amun. Amenirdis was famous for beginning the move to establish a Kushite 25th dynasty in Egypt. As ruler Amenirdis's position was entitled something close in meaning to "Wife of Amun".[8]

To the outsider, Nubian/Kushite women had a high public status. Amenirdis, for instance was a woman of high office at a time in the world when this was rare[9]. It was unheard of among the Greeks, Romans and in ancient Middle Eastern societies. Kush was not however, at this time a monolithic unified state. There were, for instance, several queens of Kush ruling simultaneously by the 2nd century AD.

By the time Meroe was at its height, matrilineal succession was the custom as it was in Egypt. The throne would always pass from the king to the offspring of his sister. This specific indigenous tradition of matrilineal succession would later be continued in traditional West Africa and other African societies.

The relations with Egypt became very limited after the reign of Psammeticus II who attacked the Nubian former capital city of Napata. Relations with Egypt were re-established when the Greek dynasty of the

Ptolemys ruled Egypt and established trade outposts in the western Mediterranean, which increased the demand for Nubian goods such as ivory, spices, ebony, exotic animals and slaves, for which the traders of Meroe received food and manufactured goods. Conflict later broke out with Egypt, then under the control of the Roman emperor Augustus Caesar, over the control of Nubian goldmines in the area of modern day Wadi el-Allaqi. Caesar declared the area a protectorate of Rome and the famous city of Napata was ransacked.[10]

One major reason for the rise of the city and the civilization of Meroe was its production of iron. Iron weapons were harder than those made of copper and bronze. This technology had been developed inside Africa, because before the 1st century, as far south as Lake Victoria, Africans living on the shores were producing not only iron, but steel (a refined form of iron) of a very high standard. The ancestors of the Haya people of Tanzania are one of the ancient peoples of that region that have handed down this technology to their descendants in modern day Tanzania.[11]

Meroe was in the south of Nubia/Kush and more green and fertile in comparison to the increasing desertification of the more northerly region of Napata. This caused people to migrate and to populate and expand the city of Meroe.

By the reign of Nastasen 328-308 BC Meroe began to be less and less influenced by its past links with Kemet (Egypt).[12] New styles of architecture and art developed. But Egyptian hieroglyphs continued to be used on Royal tombs.

The new Kushites of the Meroitic period were eminent in trade. They traded north with Egypt, and west as far as Lake Chad. They traded east were they had ports along the shores of the Red Sea to trade with nations from the Arabian peninsula, other peoples of the east African region and with India and perhaps even China. The west African trade route forged the main route of dispersal of peoples from this part of north east Africa to West Africa.

In the meantime, Egypt was becoming the victim of new conquests. The Persians under Cambyses in 525 BC ended the Egyptian 26th dynasty. The Persians ruled Egypt for almost 200 years. Then their rule was ended by the Greeks under Alexander of Macedonia in 332 BC. On the death of Alexander, Ptolemy became Pharoah and this was followed by 300 years of Greek rule in Egypt by the Ptolemys. The Greeks even renamed the land with the original form of the name we use today: *Aigyptos*

Towards the end of Greek rule Cleopatra took the throne of Egypt. Cleopatra tried all means to stave off the Roman rule of Egypt, including having an affair with Anthony[13]. But on her death in 30 BC the Romans, under Augustus Caesar (the heir and adopted son of Julius Caesar), gained direct control over Egypt and Cleopatra had become a vassal ruler, who was bound by agreement to provide the Romans with an annual tribute. Augustus reigned until 14 AD.

In Nubia/Kush at about this time a powerful queen emerged of the name Kandake.[14] It is likely that this was the name of her title rather than her personal name. By some accounts she defended Kush against the armies of Augustus Caesar successfully. Other accounts say that the Romans did not even venture into her territory but sent two centurions to see if the kingdom was worth conquering. The Romans continued to rule Egypt until 642 AD when their rule ended with the coming of Islam into Africa in the form of an invasion led by the Arab general Amr Ibn Al As with 4000 soldiers.[15]

The decline of Kush as a force in the ancient world set in about 200 AD when its trade routes were obstructed by the nomadic people of the region, the Noba. Then, in the year 330 AD a King named Ezana scattered the Noba[16]. This did not prevent the final destruction of the city of Meroe in 350 AD and the end of the Meroitic civilization, although the Christian kingdom of Axum was to emerge.

Ezana converted to Christianity and a transfer of power in the region moved the centre of influence from Meroe in the south to Axum in the north. Ezana co-ruled with his brother Shaiazana. Their father had chosen the two of them as his successors.

Ezana's rule with his brother was remarkably peaceful without rivalry or territorial competition over the shared kingdom. The level of harmony is reflected in this poem by an ancient Ethiopian poet (Abreha and Asbeha are the names of the brothers Ezana and Shaiazana respectively; the latter names being their throne names):

> *Peace be to Abreha and Asbeha*
> *They in one kingdom did the sceptre sway;*
> *And yet in love and yet in accord still*
> *They lived as princes with one heart and will.*[17A]

It is said that the brothers who were kings and co-regents eventually both became Christians; although initially they followed the remnants of the pantheistic religion of the region that had derived from the Ancient Egyptian religion. They were both converted to Christianity by the efforts of two other brothers or two cousins by the names of Frumentius and Edesius, who preached Christianity discreetly to the Axumites at a time when their interest in the Egyptian religion had been waning. Frumentius, the better known of the two brothers travelled to the regional headquarters of the church at that time, in Alexandria in Egypt. His superior, Athansius, was presiding over a meeting of Bishops and was happy to receive him. Frumentius proceeded to impress his superiors with his plans to promote the advancement of Christianity in Kush. The Council of Bishops backed Frumentius's plan and decided to make Frumentius the first bishop of Ethiopia's Coptic Church at Axum. On return, Frumentius gained the whole hearted support of both kings Ezana and Shaiazana in his new role as an apostle to the Ethiopians, although the two Kings had at that time not yet publicly professed their belief in the new faith of Christianity. By 341 AD there were tens if thousands of Christian converts in the country and Christianity had become firmly established in ancient Ethiopia[17B].

Eventually, Kush/Nubia was split into 3 Christian kingdoms: Nobatae in the north, Makuria in the middle and Alwa or Alodia in the south.[17]

Egypt became Islamic under the Fatimids, but co-existed peacefully with the Christian kingdoms of former Nubia to its south. This changed, however, when the more radical Saracens took power in the 12th century. The three Christian kingdoms of the Axumite empire were thus effectively isolated from the rest of the Christian world, so that Africa's indigenous Christianity developed separately from that which developed in Europe.[18]

Axum reigned as the chief power in the region until the 8th century, trading as far as Ceylon, Arabia and India. Greek was used as the official language, but it was replaced eventually by the home grown language of Geez.

Of the three Christian kingdoms, Makuria was famous for its capital at Dongola.[19] The 3 Christian kingdoms were ruled through the Roman emperor Julian at Constantinople.

At this time Africans were rarely found among the clergy, although St Augustine in Alexandria, Egypt, who was probably the first African bishop, was an exception. Augustine, who lived in the 5th century, was also a philosopher and theologian of historical importance to the development of the church. He was a prolific writer who wrote mainly on theological subjects. Among many things his writings include a theory of time, a philosophy of history and his theory of salvation.[20]

Islam came to Egypt in 639-642 AD. The way was made easier for the Arab invaders of Egypt as Egyptian resistance had already been damaged by the preceding Persian invasion in 619-629 AD. These events led to the three Christian Kingdoms uniting to protect their faith in the face of the invasion by Islam onto the African continent. Abdullah the Arab governor of Egypt led the attack on the kingdoms, but was defeated in 643 AD.[21] But the Arabs attacked again and captured Dongola. This led to the peace treaty of 652 AD which called for the payment of 360 slaves every year. Although this led to some level of incursion of Islam into ancient Ethiopia, Ethiopia retained its indigenous orthodox Christianity and was never (as we shall see even in modern times) to be conquered or colonised by outsiders from the African continent.

References

Chapter Six - The Kingdoms of Kush and Axum

1. Hansberry, L., *Pillars in Ethiopian History*, Howard University Press, Washington, 1981, p.41.
2. Ibid., p.33-34.
3. Ibid.
4. Ibid., p. 35.
5. Taylor, J.H.., *Egypt and Nubia,* British Museum Press, London, 1991, p.38.
6. Ibid., p. p.44.
7. Ibid., p.50.
8. Morkot, R., *The Black Pharaohs - Egypt's Nubian Rulers,* Rubicorn Press, London, 2000, p.19.
9. Taylror, *op. cit.,* p. 40.
10. Ibid., p.48.
11. Shore, D., Steel making in Ancient Africa, in Ivan Van Sertima (ed.), *Blacks in Science: ancient and modern*, Transaction Books, New Brunswick and London,1985. p157-162.
12. Taylror, *op. cit.,* p. 45.
13. As implied in Hagen, R. and Rainer Hagen, *Egypt: Peoples, Gods, Pharaohs*, Benedikt taschen, Cologne, 1999, p.52.
14. Taylor, op cit., p.48
15. Williams, C., *The Destruction of Black Civilizations*, Third World Press, Illinois, 1976, p.142.
16. Taylor, *op. cit.,* p.59.
17. Ibid., p.62.
17A. Hansberry, L., *Op. cit.,* p.68.
17B. Ibid., p.69-70.

18. Davidson, B., (and editors of Time-life books) *African Kingdoms*, Time-Life Books, Amsterdam, 1966, p. 129.
19. Williams, op. cit., p. 139
20. Russel, B., *History of Western Philosophy*, George Allen & Unwin, London, 1946, p.335.
21. Williams, op. cit., p. 142-144.

Chapter Seven

African Medieval Empires

Ghana

At the time of the battle of Hastings in England in 1066, a great Arab Geographer, Al Bakri of Cordova compiled his book of Roads and Kingdoms.[1] Al Bakri talks about the court ceremony of the King of Ghana. Each evening the King gave an audience to his people to listen to complaints and generally participate in open debate. Al-Bakri's account has in one sense been confirmed by the statistics given in his book, because the distances given between locations can be confirmed as accurate.[2]

As in the case of the ancient African civilizations of Nubia and then Egypt, visitors were amazed by the liberal state of gender relations and also the highly developed sensitivity of Africans to injustice. Both of these characteristics point to the sophistication of civilisation in Ghana. Ibn Battuta was upset by the freeness of relations between men and women, pointing to the comparative conservatism of other cultures in regard to gender relations when he says "The women there have friends and companions outside the women in their own families, and the men in the same way have companions amongst the women of other familes."[3] In his opinion "Of all peoples, the Negroes are those who most abhor injustice".[4]

The historian Ibn Khaldun wrote that Arab traders (the Umayyads) crossed the Sahara as far as the Sudan in the 8th century.[5] New connections were being made between the Sudan and the Mediterranean and the Arab world, establishing the important trans-Saharan trade route.

The vast area of the Sudan, which in those times included most of West Africa south of the Sahara, was governed by an emperor by the title of the Tunka Menin, emperor of Ghana. The Ghana of old covered a much greater space than the Ghana of today and was a diverse ancient African society. The subjects of the emperor included African, Arab and Berber populations.[6] What was known as the Ghana Empire in those days, referred to most of West Africa from Djaka on the west coast of the river Niger to the Atlantic Ocean, and north to south, from the Sahara to the edge of Mali. Ghana was the first of the three Great West African Trading Empires. Its life spanned the period A.D. 700-1200 and its wealth was mainly founded on the region's wealth in gold.[7]

Ghana was followed by the empire of Mali. Before its fall Ghana was attacked by the Umayyads, but it was successfully defended. It used to be supposed, but is no longer, that the Almoravid Arabs finally succeeded in conquering Ghana in about 1076, ten years after the battle of Hastings in England. We will recall, this battle saw the death and defeat of the English King Harold who tried to defend the English against the Normans under William the Conqueror. No empire in Europe at the time, including William's Norman Empire, could compare to Ghana in wealth and size.

Mali

It is now supposed that by 1240 AD, instead of the empire of Ghana being usurped by the Almoravides, it broke up into competing chieftaincies which led to its disintegration[8]. This was followed by an attack by Sundiata Keita, which Ghana was unable to resist. Keita founded the Mali Empire.

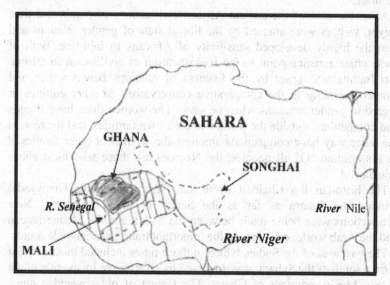

Figure 9 The Three Great West African Trading Empires

The origins of Mali are recounted in the epic legend of Sundiata, "Lord Lion"; although Sundiata was a real historical figure. In the legend, Mali is formed when the decline of the Ghana Empire allows the evil magician Samaguru to take control of the region. Sundiata, also a powerful magician, leads the chiefs of the Mande people to victory over Samaguru and his armies to found the Mali Empire[8A].

Sundiata was a divine king in the same tradition of divine kingship that is exhibited throughout the history of Africa. Like Ghana, its rulers, even when they later adopted Arab Islamic names, were predominantly followers of the traditional African religion, with Muslim merchants having an important role in the commerce and administration of the empire. Sundiata himself had the title "Master of lands" which was an acknowledged authority among the Mande speaking agricultural society. He was also a guardian of the ancestors, clearly defining him as a custodian of the African religious traditions. Sundiata did not care for Islam, although his successors were to become attracted to it. African traditional religion was still the chief influence in the spiritual life of the emperors of Africa's great medieval trading empires[8B].

But Mali represents a turning point at which Islam gains greater influence. Sundiata's son, Mansa Uli (who ruled 1255-1270 AD) was more receptive and made the pilgrimage to Mecca. Nevertheless, the African traditional religion remained a powerful influence in the background. No *Mansa* (emperor) could ignore the divinities, rituals and religious festivals that were central to the lives of the people, regardless of the emperor's religious persuasion[8C].

The Mali Empire turned out to be far greater than Ghana, covering a larger region and inheriting Ghana's international reputation. The empire of Mali stretched from Gao (east of Timbuktu, which lies on the northern bend of the Niger) to the Atlantic and from the Sahara to the tropical rainforest[9]. Ibn Khaldun writes that the emperor of Mali reigned over the entire Sahara.

At Khaldun's time the emperor was Mansa Musa. He made a celebrated pilgrimage to Mecca (1324-1325 A.D.) carrying so much gold that it depressed the regional gold market for 10 years[10]. It was Mansa Musa who built the University of Sankore in Timbuktu which Musa ensured was equipped with a rich library[11]. Musa's empire had commercial and diplomatic relations with Morocco, Egypt, Portugal and Bornu.

Mansa Musa was succeeded by Suleiman Mansa. The might of the Mali Empire was such that it was called upon for military assistance by besieged neighbours such as, on one occasion, El Mamer, the King of Morocco. There were even attempts by the resourceful people of the empire to reach America by boat before Christopher Columbus, as Mohamed Hamidullah recalls.[12]

Mali declined due to the strife between rival chiefs and also the incessant periodic pillage by Mossi horsemen and also Tuareg nomads, who took the city of Timbuktu in 1433. This pillaging drained the strength of the empire, which broke up into small chiefdoms[12A].

Songhai

Existing simultaneous with Mali there was a third great trading empire in West Africa: Songhai. The Songhai empire extended from east of the Niger as far as the Atlantic ocean, and from the head of the Niger River on the borders of modern day Sierra Leone and Guinea to Teghazza on the Tropic of Cancer line of latitude.[13]

Songhai inherited the fame of Mali. The era of the Songhai Empire began when Sunni Ali Ber (1464-1492 AD) drove out the Tuareg from Timbuktu who held that city after the Mandingoes[14]. After continued massacres and pillaging of the city, the people called for help from Sunni Ali to free the city. It is said that the Tuareg fled at the sight of Sunni Ali without a fight, when he entered the city on 30th January 1468.[15] The Tuaregs became vassals of the Askiyas whose family ruled the empire until its decline and fall.

Despite his Arabic-Islamic first names (Sunni Ali), Sunni Ali Ber did not care for the Islamic religion and its scholars in Timbuktu. On Sunni Ali's death he was succeeded by Muhammed Ture, who was a devout muslim and founded the dynasty of emperors known as the Askiyas (1493-1592 AD). Principally, being a muslim emperor facilitated the trans-saharan trade with the Arab settlers and Islamic Berbers to the north of the Sahara. Like Mansa Uli and Mansa Musa, his predecessors of the Mali empire, he also made his pilgrimage to Mecca in 1496 AD.[15A]

These African empires were cosmopolitan in character, with residing foreigners alongside indigenous people[16]. At about the same time, Islam was arriving in West Africa, having reached the north and northeast of Africa. The Islamic influence on these empires was significant and these states inherited Islamic traditions from the invading and settling Arabs. However, tensions continued to exist between Arab Islamic and African traditional religious tendencies.

Mwenemutapa

At the beginning of the first millennium AD, Stone Age hunter gatherers related to the San or Khoisan people moved in to inhabit the region just south of the Zambezi River which flows along the common border of modern Zambia and Zimbabwe. It is possible that these same people once inhabited the Sahara when it was green and fertile from about 6000 BC up to 600 BC.

Later on Iron Age peoples also migrated from the north and began to work thousands of small goldmines.

About the 9th and 10th centuries, Shona speaking people began to migrate into the region and intermingled with the Bantu-speaking people already there. They established the empire we know today as Mwenemutapa which dominated the area until the late 19th century.[17]

The living remnants of Mwenemutapa, the great temple of Zimbabwe, consists of a complex of huts, shrines, granaries and stone-walled passageways which are mostly in ruins today. Inside the temple is a conical tower which has mystified archaeologists. What was it used for? Most likely, this temple was the centre of a great African empire, which distinguished itself from the West African trading empires in that its impetus was entirely indigenous.

From about the eleventh century onwards the region of Zimbabwe was ruled by the Mwenemutapa, a title given to the ruler of the Vakaranga, one of the Shona speaking peoples of the region. The capital of Mwenemutapa lay about 100 miles north of the modern capital, Harare, and 300 miles north of the Great Wall of Zimbabwe. The Vakaranga were eventually forced to move due to the exhaustion of their salt mines. In those days, salt was a very valuable commodity.

Military expeditions by the Portuguese in the 16th century brought the Mwenemutapas into treaty with the Portuguese. It was the continuous invasion by the Portuguese that brought the Mutapa Empire into rapid decline by the beginning of the 17th century.

References

Chapter seven - African Medieval Empires

1. Davidson, B., *African Kingdoms*, Time-Life Books, Amsterdam, 1966, p. 80.
2. Ibid.
3. Ibid., p.82
4. Ibid., p.82
5. Diop, C.A., *Precolonial Black Africa*, Lawrence Hill Books, 1987, p. 89.
6. Ibid., p. 89-92
7. Ibid., p. 104.
8. Collins, R.O. and J. M. Burns, *A History of sub-Saharan Africa*, Cambridge University Press, Cambridge, 2007, p.83.
8A. Ibid., p.83-84.
8B. Ibid.,
8C Ibid., p.84.
9. Davidson, op. cit., p. 81.

10. Diop, op. cit., p. 92.
11. Karenga, M., *Introduction to Black Studies (second edition)*, University of Sankore press, *L.A., 1993, p. 94.*
12. Diop, op. cit., p. 94 and 208
12A Collins, R.O. and J. M. Burns, op. cit., p.84.
13. Davidson, op. cit. p.81.
14. Diop, op. cit., p. 96.
15. Ibid., p.96.
15A. Collins, R.O. and J. M. Burns, op. cit., p.87-88.
16. Ibid., p.99.
17. New African Yearbook 1981-2, IC Magazines, 1982, p. 386.

PART TWO

MODERN AFRICA AND AFRICAN PEOPLES - A BRIEF HISTORY

Chapter Eight

The Slave Trading Era

In the 1540s, the people of coastal West and South West Africa could not have foreseen the three hundred years of horrors that lay ahead for themselves and their future generations. What started as a low level trade in slaves for domestic and other jobs became ravaging mass enslavement. Africans were forced to provide labour to work the new lands acquired by the Portuguese and Spanish traders, who sailed to the so called "new world" of the Americas. Slave captives were not only sent to work on plundered land in the Americas, but also to England, where having African servants was a sign of status.

Over the next few hundred years, the lands of the Native Americans from the Caribbean to mainland America, were violently stolen from them by the new European immigrants for the purpose of growing tobacco, sugar and cotton and their populations were decimated. Later on, the Native Americans on the mainland were confined to barren land in so called "reservations". There was an explicit policy of forced removal and relocation of Native American peoples. This was implemented through the United States Congress's Indian Removal Act of 1830[1]. The United States President, Andrew Jackson, called for the killing of Bison to exhaust the food source of Native American families, starving them into the reservations. Tens, maybe hundreds of thousands died, not only from such indirect acts of killing and direct massacre, but also by diseases brought from Europe. The first Native American people to encounter Columbus, the Arawaks, numbering 1 or 2 million in 1492, were victims of outright massacre and starvation and had no resistance to these new diseases. By 1550 they were virtually extinct[2].

The violence and brutality had an economic foundation. By about the 1650s in England, for instance, tea, coffee and chocolate, all of which have bitter tastes without added sugar, were the popular drinks[3]. Thus came about the high demand for sugar. Sugar production promised vast profits for those "enterprising" enough (brutal and callous enough) to acquire the large resources of land and slaves required to grow it. However, this increased acquisition of land, increased the requirement for cheap labour in order to realise the huge level of profits.

Owning a plantation in the new world was a popular way for an English gentleman to boost his fortunes. By about 1750, individual European slave merchants were earning clear profits of £40,000 to £50,000 a year from the trade. [4]

Some of the most prominent benefactors of the slave trade are well known, household and high street names. They included people like the composer and former slave trader, John Newton[5], who is famous as the composer of the hymn "Amazing Grace" apparently inspired by his spiritual awakening to the evil of slavery, which he later renounced. Benefactors also included David and Alexander Barclay[6], who were engaging in the slave trade in 1756 and who used the profits to set up a well known high street bank, of the same name. One Mr Lloyd made a name for himself in a similar vein[7], using his profits from slave trading to first set up a coffee shop, which eventually grew to become another well known high street bank. Then there was the pioneering inventor, James Watt, whose steam engine opened the Age of Steam Locomotion and its huge consequential developments, all initially financed by the profits of slave plantation owners[8].

Even the church was not to be left out of the profits from the slave trade. It had from the beginning supported the trade. The Catholic Spaniards saw it as a chance to convert the heathen races. As well as the Catholics, the Jesuits, Dominicans, Franciscans and Baptists all owned slaves. Till the bitter end the Bishop of Exeter retained his 655 slaves for whom he received £12,700 compensation in 1833[8A].

Initially, the English were content to use their own citizens to meet the demand for labour in the Americas. At one point in the 17th century the demand in England for people to work in the new world became so great that it led to the kidnapping of children. Kidnapping was common in towns like London and Bristol. Adults would be plied with alcohol whilst children were enticed with sweets. The kidnappers were called "spirits", defined as "one that taketh upp men women and children and sells them on a ship to be conveyed beyond the sea".[9] Some sources claim that the very use of the term "kidnap" (deriving from ""kid-nab") in the English language began in this period, when child stealing emerged as a new and frightening development, resulting directly from the greed for profits in the new American colonies.

The English justice system also provided labour for plantations in the Americas through a system of punishment which included the sentencing of petty offenders to transportation to the plantations of the New World for hard labour. By 1745 someone in England could face the penalty of transportation for hard labour for the theft of a silver spoon.[10] It was not uncommon for judges in those days to be plantation owners, so that it was in their personal interests to increase the labour supply for their ventures through the penal system.

But great areas of land had been stolen from the Native Americans, creating a demand for labour that the English population alone could not continue to meet. The first instances of slavery across racial lines in the

New World (the Americas) involved the indigenous people of the region.[11] Christopher Columbus misnamed them as "Indians" due to the fact that when he stumbled upon the New World of the Americas in 1492, he thought he had landed in India. Instead of sailing east he had travelled west and therefore coined the term "West India" to name the land he encountered. Following the enslavement of Native Americans, Africans were enslaved. This enslavement of Africans became exclusive to Africans once the African captives showed more resilience to hard labour and more immunity to diseases brought by the European settlers than the Native American population.

A key fact to understand contrary to what we might expect is that the enslavement of Africans (and Native Americans) was not engendered by racism. Rather racism was a product of slavery. As the late Walter Rodney emphatically points out: The Europeans "enslaved Africans for *economic* reasons so that their labour power could be exploited..." [12] just as Africans had sold slaves among themselves and even to Arab traders for purely economic reasons. As Rodney continues: "...it would have been impossible [for the Europeans] to open up the New World [the Americas] as a constant generator of wealth had it not been for African labour. There were no other alternatives: the American ('Indian') population was virtually wiped out and Europe's population was too small for settlement overseas at that time. Then, having become utterly dependent on African labour, Europeans at home and abroad found it necessary to rationalise that exploitation in racist terms ..."[13]. Thus as Rodney has explained, the moral conscience of Europeans led them to justify what was clearly a debasement of their own humanity by denying that Africans were in fact humans. Africans were instead regarded as sub-human. Only in this way could their brutal treatment in the interests of European profit be seen as just. Thus racism was the product of enslavement, not the cause.

Eventually the rapidly increasing demand for slaves turned the attention of European traders to Africa in search of labour for the New World plantations. Trading with West Africa and along the South West African coast had already been long established by the Portuguese. By the 17th century, the English were also to turn their attentions towards African labour. It was the case that early European profiteers arrived on African shores in search of gold, but then came away with slaves[13A]. Thereafter, the demand fuelled the trade.

The prospect of riches in gold had long attracted Europeans to African shores. From the times of the great West African trading empires, the global fame in the old world of their great wealth, particularly in gold had long ago made trade with Africa an attractive prospect to Europeans. The story, for instance, of Mansa Musa the emperor of Mali, and his great display of wealth on his pilgrimage to Mecca in 1324 AD, was well known and had spread wide and far[13B].

The cruelty of the slave trade is well documented, yet no account is as revealing as the first hand account of an African ex-slave. Olaudah Equiano recounts his life and culture before being captured. The following very lengthy quotations from Equiano's life story[13C] give salient parts of Equiano's account, giving us, first hand, an insight into a life without material wants and needs experienced in his homeland before the colonial era. Equiano, born in 1745, relates his life as the life of

"neither a saint, a hero, nor a tyrant. I believe there are few events in my life which have not happened to many. It is true the incidents of it are numerous; and did I consider myself an European, I might say my sufferings were great: but when I compare my lot with that of most of my countrymen, I regard myself as a particular favourite of Heaven, and acknowledge the mercies of Providence in every occurrence of my life".

Equiano explains that he hails from West Africa in a kingdom then named Essaka, which is part of the Igbo-speaking region in modern day Nigeria. He describes the surroundings of African traditional life in which he grew up:

"In our buildings we study convenience rather than ornament. Each master of a family has a large square piece of ground, surrounded with a moat or fence, or enclosed with a wall, made of red earth tempered: which, when dry, is as hard as brick. Within this are his houses to accommodate his family and slaves; which, if numerous, frequently cause these tenements to present the appearance of a village. ...

As we live in a country where nature is prodigal of her favours, our wants are few, and easily supplied; of course we have few manufactures. They consist, for the most part, of calicoes, earthenware, ornaments, and instruments of war and husbandry. But these make no part of our commerce, the principal articles of which, as I have observed, are provisions. In such a state, money is of little use; however, we have small pieces of coin, if I may call them such....

Our land is uncommonly rich and fruitful, and produces all kinds of vegetables in great abundance. We have plenty of Indian corn, and vast quantities of cotton and tobacco. Pineapples grow without culture; they are about the size of the largest sugar loaf, and finely flavoured. We have also spices of different kinds, and honey in abundance. All our industry is exerted to improve the blessings of nature. Agriculture is our chief employment; and everyone, even children and women is engaged in it. Thus we are habituated to labour from our earliest years. Everyone contributes something to the common stock: and as we are unacquainted with idleness we have no beggars."[13D]

Figure 10. Olaudah Equiano

Equiano goes on to relate how as a child of 11 years old he and his sister were captured by African people from a neighbouring community whilst playing. He describes the manner of his eventual separation from his sister and the great sorrow that this caused him. He first became a slave in African households, where he was not unkindly treated. Indeed the last of the households treated him almost as a member of the family. But this only served to make what was to follow more terrible, by contrast, as he was delivered to a European slave ship. Equiano's account of the hellish conditions on the slave ship is harrowing. The account is narrated from the point at which Equiano, aged 11 years, is taken along with others to the coast to board the slave ship. Coming from in land, the young Equiano had never seen the sea or a ship in his lifetime:

"The first object that saluted my eyes when I arrived on the coast was the sea, and a slave ship, which was then riding at anchor, and waiting for its cargo. These filled me with astonishment, that was soon converted into terror, which I am yet at a loss to describe and much more the then feelings of my mind when I was carried on board. I was immediately handled and tossed up to see if I was sound, by one of the crew; and I was now persuaded that I had got into a world of bad spirits, and that they

were going to kill me. Their complexions too, differing so much from ours, their long hair, and the language they spoke, which was very different from any I had ever heard, united to confirm me in this belief. Indeed such were the horrors of my fears and my views at the moment, that if ten thousand worlds had been my own, I would have freely parted with them all to have exchanged my condition with the meanest slave in my own country. When I looked round the ship too, and saw a large furnace or copper boiling and a multitude of black people, of every description, chained together, every one of their countenances expressing dejection and sorrow, I no longer doubted of my fate; and, quite overpowered with horror and anguish, I fell motionless on the deck, and fainted. When I recovered a little I found some black people about me, who I believed were some of those who brought me on board, and had been receiving their pay: they talked to me in order to cheer me, but all in vain. I asked them if we were to be eaten by these white men with horrible looks, red faces and long hair. They told me I was not...

Soon after this the blacks who brought me on board went off, and left me abandoned to despair. I now saw myself deprived of all chance of returning to my native country, or even the least glimpse of gaining the shore, which I now considered as friendly; and I even wished for my former slavery, in preference to my present situation, which was filled with horrors of every kind, still heightened by my ignorance of what I was to undergo. I was not long suffered to indulge my grief. I was soon put down under the decks, and there I received such a salutation on my nostrils as I had never experienced in my life: so that with the loathsomeness of the stench, and with my crying together, I became so sick and low that I was unable to eat, nor had I the least desire to taste anything. I now wished for the last friend, death, to relieve me, but soon, to my grief, two of the white men offered me eatables, and, on my refusing to eat, one of them held me fast by the hands, and lay me across, I think, the windlass, and tied my feet, while the other flogged me severely. I had never experienced anything of this kind before, and although, not being used to the water, I naturally feared that element the first time I saw it, yet nevertheless, could I have got over the nettings, I would have jumped over the side, but I could not; and besides the crew used to watch us very closely , who were not chained down to the decks, lest we should leap into the water. I have seen some of these poor African prisoners most severely cut for attempting to do so, and hourly whipped for not eating. This indeed was often the case with myself. In a little time after among the poor chained men, I found some of my own nation, which in a small degree gave ease to my mind. I enquired of these what was to be done with us. They gave me to understand we were to be carried to these white people's country to work for them. I was then a little revived, and thought *if it was no worse than working, my situation was not so desperate. But I still feared I should be put to death, the white people looked and acted, as I thought, in so savage a manner; for I had never seen amongst any people such instances of brutal cruelty: and this is not only shown towards us blacks, but also to some of the whites themselves. One white man in particular I saw, when we were permitted to be on deck, flogged so unmercifully with a large rope near the foremast, that he died in consequence of it; and they tossed him over the side as they would have done a brute."*[13E]

Olaudah Equiano's first hand account is worth a thousand text book descriptions. His life story, as we see from the above description, is a testament to the suffering experienced by Africans who were captured and sold into slavery. Yet as Equiano admits, he was the most fortunate of them.

There were many instances of slave rebellions on slave ships often quelled with savage brutality. The case of the ship known as the *Amistad* in 1839 stands out as a successful rebellion where the slave captives managed to take control of the ship. Slave trading continued long after its legal abolition in 1807. The Amistad was owned by a syndicate who were carrying their human cargo of 53 African slaves along the north Cuban coast. A revolt led by a man known as Cinqué was sparked when the chef on the ship had joked that the captives were to be slaughtered and salted as meat for the white men. Cinque broke the slave irons and threw the captain and his crew overboard. The owners of the ship were ordered to sail back to Africa, but they instead arranged to sail the ship off course and docked at Culloden point, New York, where the ship was seized and the slave captives were arrested and taken to jail in New Haven. Employing the assistance of ex-President John Quincy Adams and abolitionists Joshua Levitt and Lewis Tappan, the 53 captives, led by Cinqué, successfully fought in the courts for their right to be freed and sent back to Africa. (They landed in Sierra Leone.)[13F]

It was an era in which, in addition to the depletion of West and South West African populations by slave trading, there would be sown the seeds of wars between the neighbouring West African kingdoms of Dahomey, Yoruba, Asante and other kingdoms[14].

Slave trading was without doubt a major factor in halting the development of Africa. In the 15th century Europe was not technologically far ahead of the rest of the world, but it had the distinct advantages of long distance boats and a new technological invention from China that had started to make an appearance on the scene: guns. Possibly, there never was an invention whose role in effecting the course of human history has been so understated as that of the gun.

Gunpowder was invented by the Chinese in 850 AD[15], quite by accident. It is said that at this time, Chinese alchemists experimenting with sulphur and other compounds were trying to create an elixir of eternal life. Instead, the unfortunate experimenters created an elixir of death and sustained serious injuries in the accidental explosion. By 919 AD gunpowder was used as a military weapon and by 1116 AD the canon had been invented for use in warfare. Gunpowder reached Europe in the 13th century. By 1290 AD the Chinese had made the first gun, later discovered in Manchuria[16].

We see from these dates that guns must have been available in Europe by the start of the 14th century at the earliest. Unlike Europe at that time, West and South West Africa, which first received European visitors in search of trade, had no access to trade with the Chinese. If Africans had had access to guns, this would have afforded them greater protection and reduced the need to trade in slaves, which at a point were often exclusively traded for guns[17]. The massive level of trade in African slaves could have been avoided; for those kingdoms desperate to acquire firepower to establish greater security for themselves from rival kingdoms, would not have needed to do so. West Africa would not have seen the level of trade in slaves by the Yoruba or Dahomean kingdoms, for instance, which were strongly motivated by the need to acquire firearms to either survive or gain advantage among their rival neighbouring kingdoms.

Had the trade in firearms taken place with China it is more likely that Africans would have been producing their own weapons. Otonti Nduka notes that Africans had developed great skill in working metals from an early stage and notes that this makes the lack of skill in producing firearms perplexing. Plainly, the skilful production of the art of the Benin Bronzes or the Ife sculpture shows that Africans had acquired great skill in the working of metals, surely more than enough skills to fashion firearms; and yet these skills were not put to the test[18].

By the 15th century, Europeans had developed long distance ships and could now reach the distant African coastal areas. The Portuguese in particular had established trade links extensively with Africa, being present along the East coast and trading with Mozambique, along the south west coast with Angola, along the west coast, and also with the various West African kingdoms emerging from the former trading empires.

In some cases Europeans took over trade links and routes that had been established by Arab traders, centuries before. The Arabs colluded with the European escalation of slave trading, although their own slave trading had been on a smaller scale than was to come with the establishment of the European trade in slaves. African slaves sold to Arabs were mainly domestic helps and soldiers[19]. They were a sign of status. The exception to the rule, however, was 19th century Zanzibar and Egypt, under Muhammed Ali, which in both cases exploited African labour on plantations to mass produce profitable crops[20]. This may also have applied to date palm production in Arabia. By this time, Europeans had been exploiting African labour to mass produce for profit for 300 years, and they were able to take over the established trade routes of the Arabs easily.

The above observation draws no moral distinction between Arab and European slave trading, but European slave trading signalled a point at which mass slavery of Africans led to the possibility of mass production of agricultural products and hence massive profits on a level never known before and on a scale which could finance massive European strides in industrial and technological development over the short space of a few centuries.

For centuries before, Europe had been in stagnation, technical progress had been minimal. Indeed, at the time of Mansa Musa's 1324 pilgrimage to Mecca, Africa was technologically rivalling Europe. Diop, with the support of Arab writer Muhammad Hamidullah, tells us that Emperor Kankan Musa of Mali's predecessor, who vanished at sea, made two attempts to explore the Atlantic[20A]. Africa had the technology, at least a millennium before, to produce the finest steel in blast furnaces with temperatures that would not be reached in European blast furnaces until the 19th century[21]. Africans of ancient Ghana had already established cities that were the envy of European and Arab travellers. By that time the Dogon of Mali knew about Sirius and its invisible companion, Sirius B, which was not to be discovered in America until 1862[22]. They knew, for instance, that Sirius B is highly dense. They also knew that Sirius B orbits the star Sirius once every 50 years. How they knew this is a mystery, as the Dogon have no telescopes.[23]

When Europeans arrived on the African coast line they met established African kingdoms which were related by complex ties and rivalries which Europeans exploited in order to divide and conquer them, but only over some period of time. It has to be said that this could not have happened without the cooperation of the Africans themselves who were prepared to provide their own peoples and the peoples of neighbouring kingdoms as captives to satisfy the growing European demand for slave labour to work on the vast areas of colonised territory in the Americas.

References

Chapter Eight – The Slave Trading Era

1. Encyclodaedia Britannica online
2. Ibid.
3. Fryer, P., *Staying Power: The History of Black people in Britain*, Pluto Press, London, 1984, p.14.
4. Thomas, H., *The Slave Trade: The History of the Atlantic Slave Trade 1440-1870*, Simon and Schuster, New York, 1999, p.352
5. Fryer, op. cit., p.39.
6. Ibid., p.46.
7. Ibid., p.46.
8. Ibid., p.16
8A. Williams, E., *Capitalism & Slavery*, Capricorn Books, N.Y., 1966p, 43.
9. Williams, E., Op.cit.,, p.11.
10. Ibid., p.12
11. Rodney, W., *How Europe Underdeveloped Africa*, Bogle-L'Ouverture, London, 1972, p. 47.
12. Ibid., p.99.
13. Ibid., p.99-100.
13A. Thomas, H., *Op. cit.*, p. 23
13B. Diop, C.A., *Precolonial Black Africa*, Lawrence Hill Books, 1987, p.92.
13C. Equiano, O., *The Life of Olaudah Equiano*, Dover, NY, 1999.
13D. Ibid., p.15
13E. Ibid., p.31-32.
13F Thomas, H., *Op cit*, p.718
14. Ibid., p.124-134.
15. Britannica Online
16. Ibid.
17. Rodney, op. cit., p.129
18. Nduka, O., *The roots of African Underdevelopment*, Spectrum Books, Ibadan, Nigeria, 2006, p. 16.
19. Rodney, *op. cit.*, p.158.
20. Ibid.
20A. Diop, C.A., *op. cit.*, p.208.
21. Shore, op. cit., p. 157.
22. Adams, H. H., "African Observers of the Universe", in Ivan Van Sertima (ed.), *Blacks in Science: ancient and modern*, Transaction Books, New Brunswick and London,1985. pp.27-46.
23. This knowledge they express in the context of the ritual known as the Sigui ceremony performed every 60 years and for each of which a Sigui mask is created. In a cave in Mali, 13 of these masks were discovered and radiocarbon dated back to the 13th century, proving that the Dogon have had this knowledge before the time of the Mali Empire.

Chapter Nine

The Slave Trade and Post-medieval African Kingdoms

It is a truism that the extent to which African kingdoms of the era contributed to the enslavement of their citizens has to be measured by their level of involvement in slave trading. African kingdoms which existed side by side often did not co-exist peacefully and the profits to be made (as well as the firearms to be acquired in most cases) from the trade in slaves were a means of gaining both economic and military advantage over neighbouring rivals. It could mean military and economic survival for a kingdom under siege.

The principal product gained from the exchange of slaves was guns, of which Europeans were the only suppliers. Guns were often offered exclusively for slaves, simultaneously intensifying slave trading and proliferating guns and warfare among African kingdoms.

Some African kingdoms like Dahomey had leaders who wanted the slave trade to increase their personal fortunes; whilst other kingdoms wise to the disastrous effect the trade was having on their own people, still found it difficult to resist being involved in the slave trading economy without jeopardising their own survival. At a point, the demand for slave labour, prompted some kingdoms, either out of greed or perceived necessity, to forcefully obtain slaves by selling their own people or making slave captives of other peoples through kidnapping from neighbouring provinces. This appears to be the predicament which some kingdoms - notably the Yoruba and the Dahomeans - found themselves in. Although, to their credit, others like Benin and Ndongo in Angola (under Queen Nzingha)[1] managed to resist slave trading, at least for some of the time.

Some kingdoms, like Amazulu in Southern Africa and Rwanda were free of slave trading, but this did not preclude conflict[2].

Ndongo – Angola

In 1622, Nzingha, sister to the king of Ndongo in Angola was acting as a diplomat for her country. The king would on occasion use her in negotiations with the Portuguese[3]. As an experienced diplomat, she had acquired great skill in dealing with the Portuguese, who wished to maintain their profitable supply of slaves from vassal chiefs in the region, for export to Brazilian plantations.

The Portuguese set up a model for the European exploitation of the African continent. In the beginning, Europeans would trade to acquire slaves for use on their plantations in the America's. For thousands of years, from ancient Egyptian times, Africans freely traded in slaves among themselves and later they sold slaves to Arab and then European traders. In the 15th century this was common practice the world over. At the time of the Renaissance the merchants of Venice and Genoa in Europe sold Christian slaves to Muslims in Egypt and the Middle East[4]. But as the demand for slaves grew, Europeans then used force to make African regional chiefs vassals, who had to provide slaves and other commodities in the form of a tribute or tax. Despite initially resisting vassal status, Nzingha eventually succumbed and was reported to have provided slaves for Dutch traders.

On her brother's death Nzingha became Queen of Ndongo and moved to oust the Portuguese from the region. Chancellor Williams says that in 1624 she declared all territory in Angola "free Country", so that any slave who reached this region was considered "free"[5]. Nzingha's spies infiltrated the forces of the Portuguese who forcibly recruited indigenous Africans to fight for them. Her spies stirred up unrest and influenced the men to mutiny[6].

Many of the vassal chiefs had had enough of the Portuguese sucking dry their human and material resources. The chiefs rebelled. The Portuguese recognised that Nzingha was at the centre of this regional rebellion. This caused them to attempt to put a lackey in her place by the name of Philip of Ndongo, who proclaimed himself to be the true king of Ndongo[7], and agreed to provide the Portuguese their tax of 100 slaves every year.

Nzingha, as Williams relates, was pursued by the Portuguese and to keep a step ahead she spread the news of her own death. In 1629 the Portuguese were in for a shock when Nzingha burst upon them "from the grave"[8]. But Nzingha was unable to defeat and force out the Portuguese invaders and agreed to a treaty with them, after a life-time of battle.

Yoruba

Oyo, the Yoruba state located in the region now known as western Nigeria was one of the most established and advanced African states at the time of European arrival on the West African coast in the 15th century. In the 14th and 15th centuries it made important artistic achievements, although this declined afterwards[9].

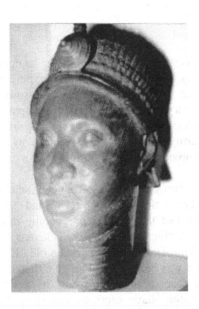

Figure 11. Ife Brass head of a ruler, Ife Nigeria. The brass sculpture is an example of the widespread expertise in pre-colonial Africa in the working of metals.

Oyo was situated in a slave trading area and attempted successfully for some time to stay free of slave trading, only to give in to it in the 18th century[10]. Oyo was already an important outlet for cloth before the slave trading era and continued to be afterwards. It was connected with the Western sudanic trading zone where Oyo traded with traders across the Sahara desert to the north of Oyo. It was through the trade from the north that Oyo gained its horses that equipped its highly respected and powerful army.

By the 19th century, Yorubaland, including Oyo had begun to export a considerable number of slave captives to European traders in the Americas. They were obtained as captives from wars with rival kingdoms and also through kidnapping and slave raiding in neighbouring provinces. Like other kingdoms, the effect of slave trading together with the security threat from the Islamic north led to the fall of the Oyo Empire by about 1830. Slave trading led to infighting among the Yoruba, and Ife, the Yoruba ancestral home, was destroyed, as its citizens became refugees. However, the resourcefulness of the people in this part of Africa, was such that they were within a short time able to rebuild the new states of New Oyo, Ibadan, Ijaye, Abeokuta and Ijebu, centred on towns with successfully managed agricultural lands[11].

Dahomey

Dahomey was essentially a military state, sometimes described by historians as a "Black Sparta". It was the eastern neighbour of Asante and was heavily involved in slave trading, which to a great extent increased its aggressive military character. Its preoccupation with war was reflected in its societal structure. Boys as young as 11 years old were recruited into the army as apprentices. Even the art of Dahomey of this period reflected its preoccupation with military glory.

According to statistics presented by Rodney, Dahomey had a stagnant or declining population throughout the 18th and 19th centuries almost certainly due to the fact that it had an economy that depended almost exclusively on slave trading, even of its own citizens.

One cannot condemn Dahomey as Africa's old "Evil Empire" without understanding that it was in a sense a kingdom that had lost control of its own destiny, and that to a great extent it survived militarily and economically by selling slave captives, including its own citizens. In selling its own citizens Dahomey was in the active state of committing national suicide. It is not so surprising that Dahomey became the most dominant of the slave raiding nation states in West Africa at that time.

Although the old Dahomeans must be given responsibility for their national character, the destructive cycle had already been set in motion by the arrival of Europeans, which restricted the Dahomean economy and means of survival to slave trading. The principal product of exchange for slave captives was guns, exclusively supplied by European traders. The firearms gave the Dahomeans an economic and military dominance over their rivals which could not be relinquished without great loss. Thus the Dahomeans became a notorious slave raiding state, trapped in a cycle of destruction that was to diminish and depopulate the West African region as a whole. The slave raiding of the Dahomeans increased the bitterness of rivalry within the region and created increased levels of conflict.

Some leaders of the time personally benefited from slave trading and abused their positions for personal gain, even at the expense of their own people. We learn from Hugh Thomas that by 1750, King Tegbesu of Dahomey was making £250,000 a year[11A] from trading in slaves from his own and neighbouring peoples. Perhaps this figure is an exaggeration. Thomas claims Tegbesu was only selling up to 9,000 slaves a year implying an average of £27 per slave, which is higher than the top price of £10 paid for slaves as late as 1848. However, this does show the high rate at which slaves were captured and sold and that the king of Dahomey was surely making an astronomical sum for that time[11B].

The kingdoms around old Rwanda in the 14[12] and 15[12] centuries were disunited and not a single political state[12]. They later became a single state in the 17th century. The kingdom of Rwanda (which includes the region now occupied by the modern states of Rwanda and Burundi) was headed by a ruler known as the "Mwami"[13]. He was a divine king in that his powers were thought to be linked to the power of God. He was God's representative on Earth. His powers emanated from God and he ruled by divine right. This is a further case of the tradition, which is widespread in Africa, and known as "divine kingship" (although it was not limited to male rulers in the case where there was a queen).

The three prominent ethnic groups present in old Rwanda were the Twa, the Hutu and the Tutsi. The Twa, who were comparatively the smallest in stature, were probably the original inhabitants of the region and were originally hunter gatherers. After the Twa came the Hutu, who were farmers and whose stocky build was sustained by an agricultural diet. Finally, they were followed by the Tutsi, who came to the region from East Africa, possibly Ethiopia, in the 15th century. In keeping with the physiology associated with higher altitude East African regions, the migrating Tutsi were originally very tall and slender in stature[14].

The migrations from east Africa of this period were probably not such an uncommon occurrence over a long period of time, and serve to highlight the manner in which Africans, before Africa's partition into its modern boundaries by the European powers in 1885, would have avoided the unnecessary evils of drought and famine through continued migrations to areas of greater soil fertility and rainfall.

Although this freedom of movement guaranteed some relief from drought and famine, it did not reduce the possibility of human conflict. Movement to more habitable areas inevitably might mean moving to areas that were already inhabited and a competition for scarce resources, in terms of habitable land.

Why the migrating Tutsi should have almost immediately assumed a higher social status over the Hutu on arrival in the 15th century, may have been a cultural phenomenon brought about by elements in both the cultures of the arriving Tutsi and the Hutu inhabitants of old Rwanda. The Tutsi, coming from Ethiopia where a feudal system of societal organisation operated were able to force their way up the social scale due to their superior wealth in terms of cattle[15]. They maintained a monopoly in military organisation which helped them keep the Hutu in a subservient position. They exploited this position and exacted rent from the Hutu in the form of forced labour on the soil.[16]

Colonialism merely severed to heighten the bitter divisions and subservient role of the Hutu in comparison to the Tutsi, who were favoured by the German colonials (1890-1916) and later the Belgian colonials (1916-1962) who gave them a monopoly in education through the Belgian missionaries.[17]

Amazulu

Just as Rwanda had enjoyed a period free of slave trading, Amazulu, which lay south of the river Limpopo had been free of slave trading.[18] The Khoi Khoi herdsmen were early inhabitants of this region. Who were later displaced by Bantu speakers. When European (Dutch) ships arrived in the 15th century it was a scattered collection of homesteads, but within a few years the population increased as did the region's political organisation.

Many will have heard the story of Shaka, born in the year 1787. He is regarded alongside Napolean, Julius Caesar and Hannibal as one of the greatest ever military strategists. He is credited with building the Amazulu into a formidable and highly disciplined army and developing their strategies for war. A famous tactical invention attributed to Shaka is the strategy know as the Bull Horns formation whereby the enemy forces are encircled from the left and the right whilst a reserve force followed later from the centre to support the encircling regiments.[19] It is a variation on the "pincer movement" used by modern European armies. In 1876, the Amazulu inflicted upon the British one of their most resounding military defeats in relatively modern times at Isandlwana.[20] Despite the overwhelming firepower of the British, the Amazulu were able to inflict defeat armed only with spears and a large number of fighters deployed with superior military strategy.

The Zulu army at the time was a remarkably disciplined educational institution rather than merely a fighting machine. It cut across clans and could be considered as truly national. Promotion was therefore based solely on merit. Because Shaka's vision was political as much as military, he not only forged a Zulu army, but a Zulu state which encompassed the regions now known as Natal, Lesotho and Swaziland under one ruler[21].

It is clear that if the armies of Shaka and the Amazulu had had guns, the British and the Dutch would never have overcome the military strategy of Shaka's descendants. This was really more a case of plain bad luck than one might imagine. Let us not forget that the invading Europeans were not using their own technology to annihilate African opposition. The gun was the invention of the Chinese, and it was indeed fate alone that determined the fact that whilst the Europeans had access to the gun through trade with its Chinese inventors, the Africans did not. Had this single detail in history (an accident of location one might say) been different, Africans would never have been subject to mass enslavement and subsequently colonial domination. It is a fact that all over Africa from west to east and to the south, Africans were formidable opponents of European invaders, even without the modern weapons of the era. With firearms they would surely not have been defeated on their own soil.

Apart from the resistance led by men like Shaka and his successors, there were many instances of African resistance to European incursion and domination led, notably, by African women, and we have not had the space and correct context to allude to them all here. That of Nzingha we have noted. But we also have the resistance of Nehanda of old Zimbabwe in 1896, Yaa Asantewa of the Asante kingdom against the British in 1900, and Amina (1533-1610), a military leader of the region now encompassing modern Nigeria. All of these women leaders led resistance against European incursions.

Benin

South east of Yoruba, on the fringes of the Niger River delta was the kingdom of Benin. According to the Yoruba, Benin was once ruled by one of the sons of Oduduwa, a descendant from heaven and mythical first ruler of Ife. In the Benin legend Oduduwa's son set about the political development of the kingdom some time in the 14th century.

The Benin Bronzes (in fact made of brass) evinced the high artistic and technical achievements of the Benin civilization.

In the middle of the 15th century, Benin had expanded, becoming a more militaristic and imperialist state under the warrior ruler Ewuare (c. 1450-1480)[22].

The rise of the Benin kingdom's militarism, quite predictably, coincided with its emergence as a slave trading economy. According to Hugh Thomas, although the king of Portugal had a licence to trade with Benin in slaves in the 1480s, the Oba (king) of Benin tried to completely cease the harmful trade in 1550, and Benin instead traded in cloth, pepper and ivory. The Portuguese tried but failed to convert the Oba and his subjects to Christianity. As Thomas is correct in observing, the determination of the Oba of Benin to avoid slave trading showed the degree to which some African kingdoms were able to avoid slave trading when their leaders had the political will to do so[23]. It should be added that some were more able to do this when they were able, as in the case of Benin, to revert to some alternative form of trade to survive outside the slave trading economy of the region. At the same it cannot be denied that there were African rulers (like the king of Dahomey) who were simply greedy and continued the trade because it was personally highly profitable.

References

Chapter Nine – The Slave Trade and Post-medieval African Kingdoms

1. Williams, C., The *Destruction of Black Civilizations*, Third World Press, Illinois, 1976, p.259-272.
2. Rodney, *How Europe Underdeveloped Africa*, Bogle-L'Ouverture, London, 1972, p.126-146.
3. Williams, C., op. cit., p.259-272..
4. Davidson, (and editors of Time-life books) *African Kingdoms*, Time-Life Books, Amsterdam, 1966, p.106.
5. Williams, C., *op. cit.*, 259-272.
6. Ibid.
7. Ibid.
8. Ibid.
9. Rodney, W., *op. cit.*, p126.
10. Ibid.
11. Ibid., p.130.
11A. Thomas, H., *The Slave Trade: The History of the Atlantic Slave Trade 1440-1870*, Simon and Schuster, New York, 1999, p.352.
11B. Ibid., p.725.
12. New African Yearbook 1981-2, IC Magazines, 1982, p. 281.
13. Rodney, *op. cit.*, p. 138.
14. Ibid.
15. Ibid.,
16. New African year Book, op. cit., 281.
17. Ibid.
18. Rodney, W., *op. cit.*, p.141.
19. Ibid., p.143.
20. Ibid., p.142.
21. Ibid., p.144.
22. Collins, R.O. and J. M. Burns, *A History of sub-Saharan Africa*, Cambridge University Press, Cambridge, 2007, p. 134-136.
23. Thomas, H., *Op. cit.*, p.358-359.

Chapter Ten

African Cultural Influences on Renaissance Europe

Meanwhile, in Europe, as Portuguese ships were alighting on African shores for the first time, Africa's cultural past was continuing to make an impact on European development. Europe was about to embark on a period of enlightenment and renaissance that would lay the foundations for an intellectual and cultural revolution on a scale and with a rapidity never before seen on the planet. The roots of this renaissance could be traced to two important traditions exported from African soil: (i) that of the Ancient Egyptians and (ii) that of the Moors of North Africa in the region of modern Morocco. The first in a complete sense was an indigenous African tradition, whilst the second was a hybrid of Mohammedan (Arab Islamic) and African culture.

Influence of the Moorish Tradition

It is simplest to start with Moorish tradition. After the death of the Prophet Muhammed in 632 AD there was an outreaching of Arab Muslim culture to the rest of the world known as the Hegira. It had reached North Africa in the 7th century from which the Moors, a people of mixed Arab and African descent, launched their conquest of much of Europe, meeting little resistance.[1] By the 8th century they had conquered most of Spain and part of Italy and had established the centre of their empire at Constantinople (Istanbul in modern Turkey).

This Muslim empire which embraced part of Europe and all of north Africa and encroached on West Africa, included Persia, Syria and even reached as far as India. Without doubt Africa, like the rest of the old world, benefited from the influence of Islamic learning and organisation, most notably in the formation of the Mali and Songhai empires, and to a certain extent in Ghana. The formation and establishment of Ghana, was indigenous and only in the later stages of the Ghana empire do we come across signs of tension between indigenous African and Islamic traditions. Mali and Songhai, however, were more definitely influenced by Islam, with several emperors becoming converts to the religion. Nevertheless, there were still the forces of African tradition at play. At times these aspects of African indigenous character were asserted. The change from traditional African to Arab Islamic traditions is best illustrated by the change from a matrilineal to a patrilineal mode of inheritance of power and property, particularly in west Africa.[2]

There is some difficulty surrounding the identity of the Moors. Certainly many accounts refer to them as being of a mixture of black African and Arab descent. Diop does not give much thought or time to this problem, failing to comment on the Moors where we would have expected some comment from him (in *Precolonial Black Africa*).

Despite the short period of time between the Arab Muslim conquest of North Africa in 642 AD and the conquest of Spain in 711 AD (about 70 years), some scholarly contributors to the book *The Golden Age of the Moor* edited by Van Sertima, appear to argue that the Islamic conquest of Europe was predominantly an indigenous African initiative. This would have required a massive adjustment for the conquered Berber society, who only in 642 AD had been defeated by the Arabs despite their gallant resistance under their queen, Daya Kahena, Queen of the Magherawa Berbers, who organised them to resist the Saracen Arab invasion[2A]. Within 70 years the indigenous Berbers of the region, including the queen's relation, General Kaiseila had been converted to Islam. They must have either embraced the religion with such fervour or been so effectively colonised by the Arabs as to soon join the Arabs in the conquest of southern Europe, in their mission to spread the religion of Islam.

The Moors, who inhabited Morocco (hence the name), were often identified with the North African Berbers. Much of the debate on Moorish identity centres on the complex issue of what a "Berber" is; which cannot be done any justice in the limited space available here. But broadly speaking, the Berbers are agreed by many to be a people of mixed African (negroid) and Caucasian descent with disagreement confined mainly to the time at which some authors believe original north African negroes (the Garamantes cited by Wayne Chandler and others) became mixed with other groups. Some suppose this mixing happened with the invasion of Arabs after the Hegira. Some like Chandler believe this mixing happened early on with an ancient and indigenous Caucasian population known as "Libyans", existing in the time of Menes[2B]. Diop believed this mixing took place in the era of Rameses in the ancient Egyptian 19th dynasty (about 1300 BC).[2C] Others like Dana Reynolds see this mixing taking place later on when millions of slave captives from Europe were procured by the settling Arabs, often as tributes exacted from conquered European provinces[2D].

Diop apparently saw the Berbers as originally foreigners rather than indigenous peoples and considers the Moors to be the descendants of Arab settlers who invaded after the Hegira. Diop's position was a disappointment to African-centred scholars such as Van Sertima and others, who believed him, particularly on the point of Moorish identity, to have been uncharacteristically mistaken.

However, Diop's assertions are not easy to refute, as it is unlikely that the term Moor was used in the same vein before the time of the Hegira. Brunson and Rashidi, look at the meaning of the word Moor from antiquity and observe that the word became a terminology used to refer to people with dark or black complexion. This, however, did not guarantee that "Moor" was always used exclusively to describe Africans; although this was certainly the case in the time of Shakespeare and the European Renaissance[2E]. The term Moor was used by Europeans to describe the African, African-Arab and Arab people who invaded Spain. Later, its usage became even more diverse in meaning referring to any people who resembled these invaders. Hence the term was used diversely to refer to black people or people of a dark complexion in comparison to Europeans, as well as to people from the same region the invaders were perceived to have come from (mainly Morocco). The term was even used to refer to people practicing the same religion as the invaders practised (principally, but apparently not exclusively, Islam).

One can see that Diop must have made his assertion that the Moors were the descendants of Arab invaders whilst assuming the term Moor to be synonymous with being a Muslim. Had this been the case, then his argument would have to be correct; for there would then be no such thing as a Moor before the incursion of Islam into North Africa. Reynolds encourages us to believe Diop to be wrong when she argues that there are non-Muslim Moors and pre-Islamic Moors. However, because the meaning of the word "Moor" changes with time, we are unable to know if a Moor really existed in the same way before and after the Hegira. The term Moor after the Hegira might be a reference to a different set of people altogether from those meant in the sense of the word before the Hegira.

It has to be said that reading popular accounts of the Moorish conquest of Spain will hardly give the reader any sense that the Moors were anything other than Arabs, with Berber accomplices; although Lane-Pool writing at the end of the 19th century, acknowledged that the forces that conquered Spain under Tarik, were almost entirely Berbers, including Tarik himself[2F]. One will not find, in popular literature, much analysis of the origins of the Berbers or the term "Berber". There is not even the recognition that modern day Berbers are a diverse group ranging in appearance from negroid to being indistinguishable from Arabs. Invariably, black Africans are portrayed in the Moorish European Empire in the position of slave guards, or common slaves to invading Arabs.

This view of the Moorish empire is strongly challenged by the work of the authors in Van Sertima's collation of scholarship on the subject.

Wayne Chandler records that the Moorish army was often led into the conquest of parts of its empire by black generals often leading predominantly black troops. Of the 7000 troops led by Tarik-bin-Zaid to make the initial conquest of the Spanish coast in 711 AD, 6,700 were native Africans (including Berbers) whilst only 300 were Arabs[2G]. Chandler quotes Dubois who says "Spain was conquered not by Arabs, but by armies of Berbers and Negroids, [at times] led by Arabs."[2H]

The point should be made, that a predominance of black African troops does not in itself guarantee the Moorish conquest of southern Europe was an indigenous African as opposed to Arab Islamic initiative. Despite the predominance of African troops in the Moorish conquest cited by Chandler, we cannot forget that the Force Publique, which the Belgium colonials used to brutalise the Congo were cadres of indigenous Africans; but employed effectively against their own people to facilitate the colonisation of central Africa in the late 19th and early 20th century. Nor need we be reminded of the West African Frontier Force and other forces of indigenous African and African Caribbean soldiers that bolstered the British war effort in Africa and beyond during the first and second world wars.

In the end, we see that the terms "Berber" and "Moor" defy being pinned down and clearly defined. In the literature, the term "Moor" was used conveniently by Europeans to describe diverse groups they had never encountered before in terms of their own familiar experience. Thus a Moor could mean an Arab, a black African or a Muslim, an inhabitant of north Africa or Morocco, a person of dark complexion. In scholarship on Africa, the term "Berber" (whether indigenous or not) served to provide a barrier between sub-saharan Africans and any cultural achievements on the continent. Instances of cultural and technological achievement in Africa could be explained by the civilizing influence of an amorphous so called "hamitic race" or "brown race", identified with Berbers, who served, in effect, as an African race of Caucasians. The brown and Hamitic race myths had long been discredited by the close of the 20th century*.

African/Moorish Cultural Contributions

Whatever their origins or identity, the Moors (loosely defined as peoples of mixed African and Arab descent) acted as preservers of

---

* MacGaffey, W., *Concepts of race in Northeast Africa*, in Fage, J.D and R.A. Oliver (ed.), Papers in African Prehistory, Cambridge University Press, 1970, p.99-115.

ancient wisdom, facilitating its transmission to Europe, which up to that point had become mired in an age of intellectual and cultural darkness.

The Arabs had a great admiration for Greek philosophy, in particular Aristotle, but also Plato. As will be argued later, much of the so called Greek philosophy, pre-Socratics at least, was in fact ancient Egyptian.

Through the conquest of Egypt the Arabs came into contact with the philosophy of Plato and Aristotle. This is plain if one recalls that Alexandria in Egypt was for many centuries the centre of learning in the old world. It remained a centre of learning. Indeed, up until the time of St Augustine, one of the "Doctors" of the early Christian church and a voluminous writer of the 5th century, Platonic thought was influential in Alexandria. So when Egypt was conquered in 642 AD it is certain that this tradition of philosophy had been continued there. The invading Arabs, therefore served to preserve this knowledge, commentate on it and transmit it to Europe through the Moorish conquerors.

We say this bearing in mind that Platonic and other Greek philosophy preserved so well at Alexandria in Egypt was to a substantial extent, regarded by renaissance thinkers to be ancient Egyptian wisdom. That Egyptian thought was seen as the "original article" in comparison to Greek thought will be exemplified shortly in looking at its reception by renaissance European thinkers, like Giordano Bruno.[3] In support of the views of these thinkers we see that very little of the so called Greek philosophy actually goes on in mainland Greece. It happens in Africa, in Alexandria, over a period spanning more than one thousand years before the time of the Arab conquest of Egypt. This point must raise difficulties for those proposing Greek origins of philosophy by analogy to the modern world. It could not be conceived of, for example, that the western scientific tradition, which at present is the world's most advanced, makes its greatest discoveries in a university in Africa for instance. Yet those who would have us believe in the Greek origins of philosophy would have us believe that its greatest triumphs, like those of Euclid for instance and the pre-Socratic Greek philosophers, emerge from institutions in a foreign land in North Africa. This is odd: One would not have expected the British colonisers to set up the equivalent of Oxford or Cambridge in Kenya; yet this is equivalent to what the Greeks are supposed to have done; for Alexandria was indeed the centre of learning in the old world in the way that Oxford and Cambridge have been for hundreds of years. The proposed resolution of this oddity is the conclusion that ancient Egypt was indeed the origin of much so called Greek thought. One is not to deny the ingenuity of the Greeks in progressing this knowledge; however, the originators were the Egyptians and this is why Alexandria is based in Africa not in mainland Greece.

There was also an Asian contribution to the European cultural renaissance. It was the Arab Muslims in Persia who came into contact with India. The name Muhammad Ibn Musa Al-Kwarazmi is notable as that of the translator who made contact with India and translated many mathematical and astronomical Indian texts from the Sanskrit. He published a book in the 12th century called *Algoritmi de numero Indrum*.[4] It was, according to the 20th century English mathematician and philosopher, Bertrand Russel, from this book that the West first got its numerals 1,2,3,...etc.[5] Before this, one supposes that only the cumbersome Roman numerals were in use. This would have greatly facilitated the science of calculation. Although these are popularly called Arabic numerals they were in fact Indian in origin. Al-Khwarizmi was also the author of a book on algebra (in fact the word algebra comes from the Arabic "al-Jabr", meaning "transformation") which was in use as a text book in Europe until the 16th Century.[6]

Another important name from Cordova in Spain was the Moorish intellectual, "Averroes" (Ibn Rushd) who is credited with seminally influencing the Scholastic school of philosophy. Of his 32 commentaries 15 were translated from Arabic into Latin and widely read in 13th century Europe.[7]

The Influence of African (ancient Egyptian) Animism on the Early Development of European Scientific and Philosophic Thinking

The surprising role of ancient Egyptian belief systems in the development of European Renaissance thought is largely unknown and unacknowledged. A distinguishing feature of belief systems which are African is that they may largely be described as "animistic", deriving from the Greek word *anima* meaning "soul". Animism is the idea that everything in the universe has some form of life-force or consciousness. There have indeed been thinkers in western philosophy that could be out rightly described as animists. They may have been labelled, more politely, as "pan-psychists", like the well known philosophers Leibnitz, Schopenhauer or, more recently, A. N. Whitehead.[8] But whether we speak of animism, pan-psychism, vitalism or pantheism, we are broadly speaking of the same thing.

In eighteenth century England, the philosopher John Toland, a contemporary of Leibnitz, maybe described as a pantheist of the time, if we go by his 1720 publication "Pantheisticon", which he penned under the author name Janus Julius Eoganesius. Inis Eogain was the place of Tolands birth, whilst Janus Julius were the names by which Toland was christened and known.[9] The writer Sorley, at least, is convinced of Toland's adoption of pantheism:

"Toland thus began as a liberal or rational theologian, and ended with some form of pantheistic creed. ... there is no evidence that he ever accepted the cardinal point of what is commonly called deism – the idea of God as an external creator who made the world, set it under certain laws, and then let it alone." [10]

Of course, Toland did not emerge from a vacuum but was influenced by the philosophers of his time. Bernal claims that the original source of Toland's pantheism is ancient Egyptian and that in this vein Toland was deeply inflenced by Giordano Bruno: "Toland had absorbed many of Bruno's cosmological hermetic and Egyptian ideas of animate matter and a world spirit, ideas which led to pantheism and even atheism".[11]

To see the roots of western philosophical animism, we must go back to the Renaissance of the 15th century onwards. From Frances Yates, the late authority on renaissance history of the University of London, we learn that at the time of the renaissance there was a mood of veneration for Egyptian philosophy as the original source of Greek philosophy. In Yates' own words, we learn that: "Above all, it was the Egyptians who were revered in this age, ... The belief that Egypt was the original home of all knowledge, that the great Greek philosophers had visited it and conversed with Egyptian priests had long been current ...".[12] A figure by the name of Hermes Trismegistus, who was thought to be an Egyptian sage, was believed to have authored the Hermetic writings (so named after "Hermes") going by the titles of the *Asclepius* and the *Corpus Hermeticum*.[13] These writings in Greek greatly influenced renaissance thinkers and were thought to contain wisdom originating from the ancient Egyptians.

At the time of the renaissance, Egyptian philosophy was more highly regarded than Greek thought. The truth of this is shown by the story of the translation of the Corpus Hermeticum. Between 1450 and 1465 Cosimo de Medici began collecting Greek manuscripts. He ordered his secretary, Marsilio Ficino, to translate two manuscripts that had come into his possession: one was the *Dialogues of Plato*; whilst the other was the *Corpus Hermeticum*. On his deathbed Cosimo ordered that Ficino should leave the Dialogues of Plato, which he had already begun translating and proceed with the translation of the Corpus Hermeticum. A sense of urgency for Cosimo on his deathbed led him to give priority to the writings of supposed Egyptian origin. This can only point to the prevailing belief at that time that Egypt was the true source of philosophy. Cosimo died the following year.[14]

Science as we know it did not really exist in Europe before the start of the 16th century. In 15th century Europe, on the verge of the renaissance era, the practices of magic and alchemy were common. These practices had perhaps proved to be a fruitful avenue of discovery. It was the practice of alchemy, after all, in China that had led to the discovery of gunpowder and its subsequent development for military use. These developments were seen in the vein of "magic" and "alchemy" rather than "science" as we know it.

Yates has made an almost inevitable connection between Copernicus's heliocentric theory and the ancient Egyptian sun-power and demi-urge, Ra, the centre of the ancient Egyptian pantheon of gods. The Asclepius and the Corpus Hermeticum speak of the divinity of the sun and this apparently influenced Copernicus and his contemporaries.[15] One notes that although Copernicus's theory of the revolution of the sun around the earth (published in 1543) was proved by means of mathematical calculation, his own respect for ancient Egyptian thought led him to take the trouble. As Yates notes: "One can say that either the intense emphasis on the sun in this new worldview was the emotional driving force which induced Copernicus to undertake his mathematical calculations on the hypothesis that the sun is indeed at the centre of the planetary systems; or that he wished to make his discovery accessible by presenting it within the framework of this new attitude. Perhaps both explanations would be true, or some of each."[16]

This "new attitude" Yates refers to is one in which ancient Egyptian knowledge is regarded as the origin of true philosophy, anterior even to the Greeks. This is precisely the attitude that led Cosimo de Medici on his death bed to order Ficino to leave translating the Dialogues of Plato and instead work on the Corpus Hermeticum.

A notable feature of the Renaissance era and the new scientific spirit emerging, was the consideration of number as a key which could unlock mysteries of the universe. As a result of indirect Egyptian influence in the form of Pythagorean mysticism (with its apparent Egyptian origins), the manipulation of number was seen in the renaissance as a magical means of making the cosmos work in man's favour. This was highly relevant now that western scholars were adopting the Sanskrit numerals 1, 2, 3, ..., deriving from India and introduced by the Arab researcher, Muhammad Ibn Al-Khwarizmi in his 12th century best seller, Algoritmi de numero Indrum. These numerals would take the place of clumsy Roman numerals and were much easier to work with, greatly facilitating the advancing art of calculation. We learn from Yates the emerging power of number during the Renaissance:

"Thus Renaissance magic was turning towards number as a possible key to operations, and the subsequent history of man's achievements in applied science has shown that number is indeed a master-key, or one of the master-keys, to operations by which the forces of the cosmos are made to work in man's service."[17]

Thorndike acknowledges that the rudiments of western science lie in the principles of magic.[18] To fully see the extent to which the principles of science evolved from the principles of magic, one must make a comparative study of the two.[19]

The innovation introduced by the British mathematician and physicist, Sir Isaac Newton (1642-1727) was to do away with the vitalist or animist spirit of Aristotle's philosophy and replace the notion of living matter with that of dead matter.[20] Aristotle was without much doubt influenced by the vitalist/animist nature of ancient Egyptian thought. The prevailing spirit of thinking at the time of the Renaissance appeared to acknowledge this, as the behaviours of Cosimo de Medici, Copernicus and others suggests. Newton's theory of "dead matter" was not in line with much of the thinking of the time. Newton's thinking replaced the "living matter" of Leibnitz's popular and vitalist continental philosophy with "dead matter", which relied on an external force (God) for its motion. It is worth noting that this idea was more in line with the doctrines of the church, which demanded the recognition of God as an external creator.

Newton's direction of thinking is made more interesting when we consider his preoccupation with alchemy and magic at the time. Bronowski notes the surprise of John Maynard Keynes who bought a trunk full of Newton's papers, only to discover that "Newton spent as much time studying alchemy and numerology as he did formulating his laws of motion."[21]

Apparently, it is likely that Newton's thinking in regard to the dead or living nature of matter placed him in a dilemma, which he was eventually bound to resolve in accordance with political and religious considerations rather than merely scientific ones. According to Martin Bernal, Newton may well have privately hesitated on the question of whether matter was a dead or a living entity: "...Newtonianism was not merely scientific. It had a consequent political and theological doctrine which depended on the passivity of matter, with motion coming only from the outside. Otherwise, theologically, the universe would need no creator..."[22]

At the time of Newton, the idea of a universe which had no need for a creator would have been considered outrageous and blasphemous. Newton could have opened himself to the condemnation of the Church for such ideas. Thus there is the strong possibility that the direction of Newton's science may have had as much to do with his Christian beliefs and his concern not to upset the Church as with scientific reasoning. Only 50 years previously, Galileo had narrowly escaped being beheaded for blasphemy by proclaiming that the earth revolved around the sun. The Italian philosopher, Giordano Bruno, an ardent exponent of Egyptian philosophy, travelled throughout Europe teaching Hermeticism and heliocentric theory (the theory that the earth revolves around the sun) and as late as 1600, was burnt at the stake for heresy.

The African (ancient Egyptian) Source of Pre-Socratic Greek Philosophy

When Martin Bernal caused a storm by claiming in his book *Black Athena* that renaissance thinkers generally regarded Egypt to be the source of Greek philosophy[23], he was largely saying something that African scholars from the continent and in the diaspora had been saying for many years, but from a different standpoint. Rather than making the point directly that Greek philosophy is borrowed (or stolen) Egyptian philosophy as G. G.M. James had written in Stolen Legacy[24] and as latter day scholars like Cheikh Anta Diop and Theophile Obenga have maintained; Bernal was able to make the similar claim indirectly that actually, this is what the renaissance thinkers believed, only that later on, the phenomenon of race politics had created a climate in which it was almost a religious article to regard the Greeks as the originators of all thought.

Why is it that renaissance scholars such as Toland, Bruno and others should have believed that the original source of Greek philosophy was the ancient Egyptians? Bernal's book caused such a storm because it was a modern instance of the idea being put forward by a white scholar. Sadly but truly it was taken as a more credible case for this reason, and therefore seen as a more serious threat. Consequently there was a concerted counter attack on Bernal's work, by those wishing to maintain the thesis of Greek origin.[25] However, the work of the late Cheikh Anta Diop remained largely unchallenged.

It is not hard to see how Egyptian philosophy influenced Greek thought, as Bertrand Russell admitted. Consider the first known Greek philosopher. This is known universally to have been Thales of Miletus who lived about 585 BC. Indeed, Thales is the key to the whole conundrum about the true origins of Greek philosophy – the tool that will enable us to dispel centuries of untruths. Aristotle says that Thales is the founder of natural philosophy. But if Thales was taught Egyptian natural philosophy whilst in Egypt, then surely the source of Greek philosophy is Egyptian; since all Greek philosophy began with its founder, Thales. One cannot overturn the inevitable logic. If one accepts Aristotle is reliable in claiming that Thales is the founder of natural philosophy, then the truth of the Egyptian origin of Greek philosophy is as solid as Euclid's ancient mathematical proof that the number of prime numbers is infinite. One cannot avoid the conclusion: Thales was the first Greek philosopher ever. Thales was taught philosophy by the Egyptians. Therefore the original source of Greek philosophy is Egyptian. Indeed Thales is thought to have travelled to Egypt and thereafter to have brought the Greeks the science of geometry.[26] So in fact, mathematics as well as philosophy begins with the Egyptians.

We know that Thales' primary speculation was that water is the most fundamental of the elements. This idea is clearly reminiscent of the Egyptian idea of primeval water which is the origin of all things, which they named Nun or Nu. This idea is recurrent in many of their texts. It is an idea which survives in the cosmologies of traditional West African people to this day.

We might consider the other philosophical ideas of Thales for ancient Egyptian influence too. According to Aristotle Thales held the view that all things are full of souls and gods.[27] This is clearly early evidence of pantheistic belief; which is characteristically African and in particular ancient Egyptian. There is little doubt that Thales was merely teaching what he had learnt from the Egyptians.

Lastly, the Ancient Egyptian source of Greek thought is also clearly demonstrated by the speculations of Thales successors as a school of thinkers on all of the four elements, showing that the ancient Egyptian doctrines of the 4 original elements clearly influenced the beginnings of Greek thought on the questions of the fundamental element building or constituting the universe. It would appear that the Greeks were not agreed as to which of four elements was fundamental. They apparently had difficulty accepting that there were four of them rather than one. Thales thought it was water. Anaximander (c. 547 BC) thought air and fire were the fundamental ones. His junior, Anaximenes thought it was air alone; whilst Heraclitus (c. 480 BC) thought it was fire.[28]

By the time of the early kingdom the ancient Egyptians had clearly assigned roles to the four elements: air, fire, earth and water as the four fundamental elements of the Creation.[29] There is evidence that the creation scenario involving the 4 elements represented in the form of primeval ancestors, has been retained in African cosmologies from the times of ancient Egypt despite migrations to West Africa. In particular we see traditional West African cosmologies which are more or less well established systems of thoughts according to whether they are more or less well preserved. The Dogon of Mali represent the best instance of a systematically preserved, well established African cosmology, retained through a strict and meticulous oral tradition. Nevertheless, even in the other less well established West African cosmologies, we can still discern the pattern of 4 (or 4 pairs of) elements or original ancestors repeated again and again. The Igbo of Nigeria name Orie, Afo, Nkwo and Eke as their 4 original elements/ancestors. Like the primordial egg of the Dogon, the image the Ibagwa Igbo use to illustrate the beginning is a figure (a circle) divided into 4 corresponding sectors; one for each ancestor/element as both the ancient Egyptians and the Dogon do[29]. The Bambara creation emerges out of 4 fundamental elements: air, fire, earth, water. The Fon myth of creation includes the four cardinal points, and so on[30].

It is apparent that Dogon cosmology is derived from the cosmology of the ancient Egyptians. We see this when comparing summarised accounts of the creation in both traditions.[31] Both accounts refer to eight (four male-female pairs of) original elements or ancestors representing the elements air, fire, earth and water in an original primordial egg of the world. Both refer to a primeval moisture or water referred to respectively in ancient Egyptian and Dogon accounts as Nu (or Nun) and Nummo (water spirits). Whereas the Egyptian high god is Amun, the Dogon high god is Amma, even the similarities in names suggest the connection claimed of a transmission by oral tradition from Egypt. Whereas in the Egyptian version it is the demiurge Ra that emerges out of the egg, in the Dogon version it is the chaotic agent Ogo who emerges out of the primeval placenta before his appointed time.[32] The parallels again point to connections between the two traditions. The creation texts dating back to the inscriptionas on the walls of tombs at Sakkara must date about 2500-2350 BC. This is much earlier than Thales, the first of the Greek philosophers.

In conclusion, the fact that Thales, the founder of Greek philosophy and science, was fundamentally influenced by Egyptian philosophy and science is patently clear when one considers the Egyptian notion of primeval water (the Nun or Nu), alongside the fact that Thales is best remembered for maintaining that water is the most fundamental of the elements. There should be little doubt that the water of Thales is the primeval Nun of the ancient Egyptians. Theophile Obenga, an Egyptologist who has translated numerous Egyptian accounts of the creation certainly takes this view. Secondly, the Egyptian four fundamental elements which are represented mythologically by 4 (or 4 male-female pairs of) primeval ancestors was present in Egyptian texts 2000 years earlier than the first Greek philosophers. The Egyptians clearly influenced the speculations of the early Greeks on fundamental elements and were also the source of pantheistic doctrines amongst the Greek philosophers.

References

Chapter Ten - African Cultural Influences in Renaissance Europe

1. Moriaen, *Aurthurian Romance*, translated by J. L. Watson, 1907, No. 4, p. 29, 39, 41, 103.
2. Diop, C.A., *Precolonial Black Africa*, Lawrence Hill Books, 1987, p. 48-59.
2A. Reynolds, D., "The African Heritage and Ethnohistory of the Moors" in Van Sertima, I. (ed.), in Van Sertima, I. (ed.), *The Golden Age of the Moor*, Transaction Books, New Brunswick and London, 1992, p. 129-130
2B. Chandler, W., "Rebuttal to Letter of Dana Reynolds on the Tamahu" in VanSertima, I. (ed.), *Op. cit.,* p. 25.
2C. Diop, Cheikh Anta, *Civilization or Barbarism: An authentic anthropology*, Lawrence Hill Books, New York, 1991, p.121.
2D.Brunson, J. and R. Rashidi, "The Moors in Antiquity" in Van Sertima, I. (ed.), *Op. cit.,* p. 36.
2E. Chandler, W., "The Moor: Light of Europe's Dark Age" in Van Sertima, I. (ed.), *Op. cit.,* p. 161.
2F. Lane-Pool, S., *The Story of the Moors in Spain,* T. Fisher Unwin, London, 1896, p.52.
2G. Reynolds, D., "The African Heritage and Ethnohistory of the Moors" in Van Sertima, I. (ed.), *Op. cit.,* p. 94.
2H. Chandler, W., "The Moor: Light of Europe's Dark Age" in Van Sertima, I. (ed.), *Op. cit.,* p. 165.
3. Flew, A., *Dictionary of philosophy*, Pan Books, London, 1979, p. 49.
4. Russel, B., *History of Western Philosophy*, George Allen & Unwin, London, 1946, p.416.
5. Ibid.
6. Ibid.
7. Ibid., p.419.
8. Flew, A., op. cit., p. 261.
9. Sorely, W.R., A *History of British philosophy to 1900*, University Press, Cambridge, 1965, p. 148.
10.Ibid., p.149.
11.Bernal, M., *Black Athena, Vol. 1: The Fabrication of Ancient Greece 1785-1985*, Free association Books, London, 1987, p.175.
12. Yates, F., *Giordano Bruno and the Hermetic Tradition*, RKP, London, 1965, p.5.

13. Hermetica – *The Ancient Greek and Latin Writings which contain religious or Philosophic teachings ascribed to Hermes Trismegistus*, translated by Walter Scott, Shambala, Boston, 1985.
14. Yates, F., op. cit., p.12-14.
15. Ibid., p.154.
16. Ibid., p.155.
17. Ibid., p.146.
18. Thorndike, L., *The History of Magic and Experimental Science*, 8 vols. Columbia University Press, New York, 1923-1958.
19. Kamalu, C., *Foundations of African Thought*, Karnak House, London, 1990, p. 78-88.
20. Bernal, M. op. cit., p.175.
21. Bronowski, J., *Black Magic and White Magic*, in T. Ferris (ed.), The World Treasury of Physics Astronomy and mathematics, Little, Brown and Company, London, 1991, p.810.
22. Bernal, M., op. cit.
23. Bernal, M., Ibid.
24. James, G.G.M., *Stolen Legacy*, The African publication Society, N.Y., 1971.
25. Lefkowitz, M. and G Maclean Rogers (ed.), *Black Athena Revisited*, University of North Carolina Press, 1996.
26. Russel, B., *History of Western Philosophy*, Allen and Unwin, London,
27. Ibid., p.45
28. Russel, B., op. cit.,
29. Compare the Egyptian and Dogon figures of the four elements represented by figures divided into four equal sectors as below:-

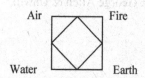

Air — Fire

Water — Earth

Figure (A) Egyptian Figure of Four Elements
(from G.G.M. James, "Stolen Legacy")

85

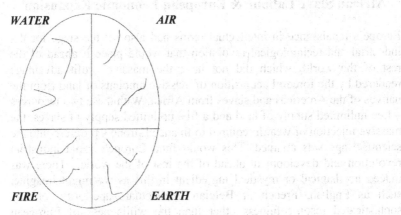

WATER   AIR

FIRE   EARTH

Figure (B) The Dogon Primordial Egg (from M. Griaule nad G. Dieterlen, "The pale Fox")

30. Kamalu, C., *Person, Divinity and Nature*, Karnak House, London 1998, p.107-143.
31. Ibid. See also   Kamalu, C., *Foundations of African Thought*, Karnak House, London, 1990, p. 120-126.
32. Ibid.

Chapter Eleven

African Slave Labour & European Economic Expansion

Europe's renaissance in intellectual terms had also set the stage for it's industrial and technological revolution that would place it ahead of the rest of the world, which did not have the massive profit advantage rendered by the forceful acquisition of massive amounts of land from the natives of the Americas and slaves from Africa. With these two resources – free unlimited supply of land and a free unlimited supply of slaves, the massive injection of wealth required to finance Europe's progress into the scientific age was attained. This would fund Europe's rapid industrial revolution and development ahead of the rest of the world. There was indeed no magical or mystical ingredient in this as we might imagine, such as English, French or Belgian intellectual superiority, or any sophisticated resourcefulness other than the willingness of European business men to use brute force and ruthlessly subjugate their fellow men and women for their own financial gain.

It cannot be denied that Europe's great technological revolution could not have happened so soon or so rapidly without the massive resources injected by the profits from slave trading. The industrialization of Great Britain, for instance, a giant among the European colonial powers required the establishment of an efficient transport network such as that provided by the railway network, and the lifeblood of this network was funded greatly by the profits of sugar plantation slavery, as demonstrated by the fact that the profits of sugar financed the Liverpool and Manchester railway and the Great Western Railway and James Watt's steam engine.

Too much emphasis cannot be placed on the role the development of British transportation technology played in industrialising and modernising Europe. One must not lose sight of the fact that the British railroad builders were technological pioneers, and their great achievements (massively financed by slave trading) led to them incurring, as Thompson notes: *"the price for technical experiments and mistakes that other countries were able to avoid. The opening of the Liverpool and Manchester Railway in 1830, using the steam locomotive, inaugurated the new era."*[1]

Indeed, the British model of transport created a blueprint for the new era which could be recreated all over Europe. It is a fact that almost all the railways built in Europe at that time were built using the experience and expertise of British railroad contractors. Russia began building its first railway in 1838. By that time there were already 490 miles of railroad in England and Wales and 50 miles in Scotland with their construction costing £13 million pounds - an astronomical sum for those times, which could never have been raised without the massive investments ensuing from the slave plantations of the Americas[2].

What we know today as mass production (producing or manufacturing things on a very large scale), properly started in known history with the mass forced labour of African people through the slave trade. The mass labour employed on a plantation scale in the New World of the Americas, enabled the creation of a level of wealth for individuals never before known on the planet. This new system, where individuals were able make huge profits from mass production, that they then invested in new schemes to make even further profits, was called *Capitalism*. Obviously, capitalism, whether one regards it as a good or a bad thing, did not have very attractive beginnings, for it began, most definitely with the Atlantic slave trade.

Once *mass production* appeared on the world economic scene, promising individuals a level of wealth hitherto beyond human imagination, there was no going back. The profits from mass production enabled investments into the creation of heavy machinery that would eventually take the place of many humans. Furthermore, this machinery would never tire or rebel and was cheaper to maintain, promising even more enormous scales of mass production and hence more enormous scales of profits for individuals. Already we see a pattern: We can see from this that what distinguishes the system known as *capitalism*, is that it concentrates more and more enormous levels of profits into the hands of fewer and fewer individuals.

One of the principal philosophers whose ideas justified this new attitude of materialism was Adam Smith[3] (1723-1790). More than anyone, Smith was the father of "free enterprise" unrestrained by government. He claimed that his philosophy based on the principle of self interest, was founded on observations of the nature of man. According to Smith the pursuit of self interest was in harmony with the increase of the public good and was therefore to be encouraged.

Some early American capitalists must have realised at some point what the future development of America had in store. In comparison to free men, slave captives would be relatively more expensive to keep. It was Adam Smith who once said slaves are less productive than free men. So it was inevitable that parts of America would move on.

The Civil War that broke out in America between the North and the South, over the Southern pursuance of slavery, was about this very fact: The richer more developed North was ready to move to the next stage of the development of capitalism,[4] from employing human beings to mass produce to employing machines (in conjunction with humans) to do the mass production, but the south was not yet ready to move on from a slave economy. No doubt, humanitarian arguments were factors in bringing along change more rapidly. But essentially, economics was a major motivating force, along with the determined resistance of African Americans. In the end, confirming Adam Smith's coldly calculated assessments, the resources expended in quelling rebellion made it uneconomical to continue the slave economy.[5]

As an economic historian might have predicted, the revolution in European transport which came with the railroads brought new demands for huge amounts of coal and iron. It created a parallel revolution in the heavy industries, especially mining and steel and iron production. Britain's coal output, which was 16 million tons in 1815 had almost doubled by 1835, and more than trebled by 1848. By the middle of the 19th century, half of all the pig iron produced in the world was from Britain. With the building of the railroads came mass employment on a scale never known before.[6]

In terms of the pioneering British economy, it was as much the Age of Cotton as it was the age of steam. Cotton was key in the expansion of British overseas trade. In 1830 nearly three quarters of the raw cotton imported into Britain was produced by African slave labour in the United states. By the middle of the 19th century, the textile industry in Britain employed over a million workers.[7]

The invention of the steam engine by James Watt, financed by slave profits, was applied to ships and the growth in shipping by steam and by sail was boosted by the growth in the shipment of cotton[8]. The astonishing progress was like a chain reaction or a domino effect. As we see today in the computer age, where technological progress is now exponential rather than step by step, we see that one significant step can lead to a whole chain of other developments. The mass enslavement of Africans was the reason for the prominence of the European world, financing the age of steam, developments of which would lead to the age of computers.

According to the late historian David Thompson: "By the 1850s Britain had established itself as not only the workshop of the world but also the shipper, trader and ... banker of the world"[9].

There were of course benefits directly accruing from slavery to other European countries. During the 18th century, the West Indies slave plantations accounted for 20 percent of France's external trade.[10] Rodney says that "The enormous profits of Portuguese slave trading enterprises rapidly passed out of the Portuguese economy and into the hands of more developed Western European capitalist nations who supplied Portugal with trade goods and capital investment. These suppliers included England, Holland and France." It goes without saying that the major cities of the U.S.A were built from the profits of slavery: cities like Boston, New York and Portland. In the 1830s about the time of the great European economic expansion, cotton produced by slave labour in America accounted for half of the value of all exports from the U.S.A.[11]

The colonial era marked a transition for European economic development, from a period where substantial profits came from the employment of African slave labour on American plantations to one where substantial gains could be made from territories occupied by the new European colonial powers. This exploitation of Africa is actually the source (as distinct from ongoing causes) of its current economic destitution. It is pertinent to review the division of colonial territory among the European powers. It is a natural progression that aside from Belgium which only won its independence from Holland in the late 1820s, the most prominent European powers in the colonisation of Africa were also the chief slave trading nations: England, Portugal, Spain and France. European gain from forced African labour continued after the abolition of slavery, when the expensive business of transporting Africans to plantations in the Americas was replaced by the more profitable alternative of forced African labour on African soil.

References

Chapter Eleven - African Slave Labour & European Economic Expansion

1. Thomson, D., Europe Since Napoleon, Pelican Books, 1966, p. 178.
2. Ibid.
3. Sorley, W.R., History of British Philosophy to 1900, Cambridge University Press, Cambridge, 1965, p.192.
4. Rodney, W., How Europe Underdeveloped Africa, Bogle-L'Ouverture, London, 1972, p. 98.
5. Karenga, M., Introduction to Black Studies (second edition), University of Sankore press, L.A., 1993, p.129, 134.
6. Thompson, D., op.cit., p. 179
7. Ibid.
8. Ibid.
9. Ibid., p.184
10. Rodney, W., op. cit., p. 96.
11. Ibid., p. 98.

Chapter Twelve

The Partitioning of Africa and the Advent of Colonialism

The massive profitability of slavery was not to last. At a certain point, it became more cost effective to employ Africans on their own land to produce crops for export than to ship them across the Atlantic to slave plantations where slave rebellions became common. Also, as already noted, this was the dawn of the machine age, and machines would soon be cheaper to maintain for the purposes of mass production than human beings. Capitalism evolved from its most extreme form at birth. Slavery became abolished, more as a result of economic change than moral change and a new stage in Europe's control of Africa began. All this did not diminish the efforts by the abolitionists, chief among whom were prominent African American freed slaves like Harriet Tubman, Frederick Douglass and others as well as the well known European campaigners like William Wilberforce in England and John Brown in America. Indeed, fierce resistance to slavery encouraged by the more radical abolitionists, contributed to making slavery less profitable with great costs being expended in quelling slave uprisings. In the end, the abolition of slavery in England in 1807 boiled down to hard economic realities. Economic reality rather than a reflection on moral conscience was in the end the chief factor behind change in the law.

Colonialism rapidly followed on the heels of slavery. According to Boahen[1], the imposition of colonialism came suddenly and unpredictably. There were no real signs of the coming catastrophe. African kingdoms were on the cusp of a new era, moving out of a period of economic reliance on slave trading into trade in natural products or "legitimate trade". At the beginning of the 19th century virtually the whole of Africa depended on slave trading to the Americas, and other destinations. In the first five decades of the 19th century the slave trade actually reached its peak. But by 1880 the slave trade had been suppressed to a trickle, with its abolition enforced by British naval patrols.

Perhaps Boahen is overenthusiastic about the changes in the 19th century, which he describes as "revolutionary". Certainly, as he points out, the cessation of the slave trade diminished the level of conflict between neighbouring African kingdoms. He remarks that this meant that the African was valued as a human being in his own right, rather than being a mere commodity to be sold. Rather the African became the seller of commodities. Africa began to recover from the collapse of kingdoms which were replaced by more centralised states. Also the population decimated by slavery increased from 104 million in 1840 to 120 million in 1880. But this was virtually cancelled out or even reversed by new diseases coming as a result of European arrival and atrocities visited on African populations. As many as 8 million or more were killed by King Leopold II in the Congo alone.

Certainly the period of "revolution" Boahen speaks of must have been a very brief window between the end of the slave trading era and the start of the colonial era. It is surprising if African kingdoms devastated by the effects of slave trading were able to recover so speedily as to enable the beginning of a "revolution" or renaissance.

At the very least, Boahen's discussion is useful because we might learn things from stopping to consider how Africa might have developed if it had not been colonised. Africa might have expected to further establish the lucrative trade routes of the Sahara and the east African coast and mainland. Indeed, slavery had so disrupted these trade routes that the eventual enforcement of the end of the slave trade, brought about, according to Boahen, a brief African economic renaissance[2]. Through Boahen's eyes we catch a brief glimpse of what might have been if Africa had been left alone to continue its economic development, with these chief trade routes as the lifeblood of its continued development.

By 1880 the European powers who had been active as slave traders in Africa, and even those who had not been, were squaring up to carve Africa up like a cake. In 1885 in Berlin, the European powers sat around a table and carved up Africa among themselves, taking no stock of the fact that the borders they set would lump diverse ethnic groups together and at times split one ethnic group among several of the newly created colonial territories. The Ewe, for instance, are seen to presently inhabit modern day Togo, Benin and Ghana. Those African borders were set without regard to traditional and natural boundaries leading to numerous violent border and territorial disputes in times to come.

The European scramble for Africa was a scramble for African resources and the powerful European nations vied with each other to grab as much of Africa for themselves as they could, in the hope this would lead to great economic gain for their countries. European historians and economists unanimously agree that the true aim of colonialism was not to "civilise", "enlighten" or "develop" Africa and Africans. Rather, as the economist J.A. Hobson writes: "...the basic motives were also the basest motives and that, whatever political, religious, or more idealistic excuses might be made, the real impulse was always one of ... greed for cheap raw materials, advantageous markets, good investments, and fresh fields of exploitation."[3] This is echoed by the French republican politician Jules Ferry when he says "The nations of Europe desire colonies for the following three purposes: (i) in order that they may have access to the raw materials of the colonies; (ii) in order to have markets for sale of the manufactured goods of the home country; and (iii) as a field for the investment of surplus capital."4

The great European scramble for Africa started in the 1880s. In 1881 France extended her colony over the area of Tunisia and in 1882 Britain controlled Egypt. In 1884 Germany established its first colony in South West Africa. It later controlled Togoland and the Cameroons in West Africa. Germany's success in gaining control of parts of Africa sparked France's jealousy. The French sent a force to seize unoccupied territory between Cameroon and Angola, which had been under Portuguese control since the 1600s. This territory seized by France became the "French Congo". The French later also took control of Timbuktu, Dahomey, Ivory Coast and Madagascar.

The snatching of African territories continued to provoke jealousies among the European powers and occasional conflict. France in 1898 upset Britain's plans for annexation in Eastern Sudan, which was given to British control. France compensated itself by then taking Morocco, leading to a dispute with Germany. This led to the calling of a colonial conference in Algeria in 1905, after which the dispute was settled and France and Spain gained control over Morocco. Germany later bought a piece of the French Congo from France. Italy had years earlier felt cheated and left out, as Britain and France's expansion pushed Italy out of the picture. So Italy, looking to the Horn of East Africa, decided to occupy Assab in 1882 and Massawa in 1885. In 1889 Italy colonised Somalia, which then became known as Italian Somaliland. Italy tried to colonise Ethiopia (former Abyssinia). But with British assistance the Abyssinians defeated them. Ethiopia was successful again in resisting colonisation by the Italians in the 1930s.

In 1876 the infamous King Leopold II of Belgium formed the so called International Africa Association, primarily to seize the huge territory surrounding the Congo Basin in central Africa. At the 1885 conference in Berlin, Leopold gained the approval of the other colonial powers to create Belgian settlements and form what was later called the "Congo Free State". The financial success of Leopold's International Africa Association led other European nations to promptly set up companies which would be responsible for exploiting the occupied territories. Thus we had the German and British East African Companies in 1888, Cecil Rhodes' South Africa Chartered Company to exploit the Valley of the Zambesi River in 1889, the Italian Benadir Company to exploit Italian Somaliland, the Royal Niger Company to exploit Nigeria in 1896. By these and other means the European powers consolidated and expanded their occupied territories.

Britain was well established in the Cape in the southern tip of Africa. She "appropriated" (stole) Bechuanaland (Botswana) in 1885, Rhodesia (later renamed Zimbabwe) in 1889, Nyasaland (Malawi) in 1893. Britain's expansion brought her into conflict with the Dutch (Boer farmers) who had arrived in the Cape region in 1652. They had set up the "Orange Free State" and the Transvaal. The direct result of Boer conflict with Rhodes was the Boer War, which began in 1899.

Following this insane scramble and subsequent partitioning and sharing of Africa, the European colonial powers proceeded to subjugate and "pacify", their African colonial subjects. The partitioning of Africa continued into the 20th century. Some colonies changed hands after the first and Second World Wars. Germany lost all of its territories, through defeat in the two world wars.

The Dawn of the Colonial Era

In every African state defined by the colonial boundaries of the 1885 Berlin conference, the history is of course unique. But the process experienced by the people of each country at this time was common: namely the redirection of their labour from African self subsistence to sustaining European business interests. By this we mean the experience of forceful acquisition, control and exploitation of African land and labour by the colonial powers for their economic benefit, through state owned companies. There is no more important case study of how this change took place than that of the Belgian Congo.

In 1891 an African empire existed deep in the heart of the Shaba province of the Congo (later to be known as the Democratic Republic of Congo, and also as Zaire). The empire was headed by a traditional ruler by the name of M'Siri. M'Siri is not the hero of our story; nor is he the villain. One can safely say he is closer to a villain than a hero in the unfolding history of colonial and post-colonial Africa; for his kind may represent a certain self-serving tendency in African leadership that not only led to the demise of Africa and its colonization by Europe, but continues till this day to sell Africa to European and American business individuals and organisations.

More of a hero at that time than M'siri in terms of African aspirations for freedom was the Ndebele leader Lobengula who in 1893 led Zimbabwe's first *Chimurenga*[5] (war of liberation) against the British South Africa Company established by Cecil Rhodes. To the chagrin of Zimbabweans in later times, the territory that Lobengula was forced to forfeit in his eventual defeat in 1897, was later named Rhodesia after Rhodes himself. A second Chimurenga was launched in 1896 in which former adversaries united and the Ndebele joined forces with the Shona.

M'siri was no African liberator, but he was without doubt a powerful and influential man. Gailey describes M'siri as a "crafty king who kept a variety of peoples pacified by means of his superior intelligence and firearms"[6]. He was born around 1830, the son of Chief Mazwiri-Kalasa. His father Mazwiri was engaged in the east African caravan trade between the mineral rich Katanga province of the Congo and the East Coast of Africa. M'siri inherited the Katanga trade of his father and extended his wealth greatly through trading in copper, ivory and slaves. He was not unusual in trading in slaves. As we have seen, many kingdoms through Africa of the past 300 years had been involved in trading in slaves with Europeans on a large scale, ever since the Portuguese first set foot on the West African coast. However, M'siri was a slave raider, and not just a moderate slave trader. This in particular made him a villain to the African cause. By 1856 M'siri had established his own kingdom. His accumulation of wealth in copper, ivory and slaves enabled him to buy guns and therefore to have an advantage in wealth and power over his rivals. Probably his most powerful rival was Kasongo Niembo, the chief of the Luba, who had been advancing their own empire southwards towards Katanga. But Msiri, who was in control of the Katanga province, halted them and Niembo was forced to pay him taxes[7].

So in 1891, when the Belgians had a jealous eye on Msiri's kingdom, which included the mineral rich Katanga, Msiri could not have known that his best days were behind him. He could have been excused for not seeing the signs, for the Belgians, in the deceitful manner typical of other European colonisers had first come with their Christian missionaries preaching the Bible and attempting to convert the natives from their African gods.

It had been six years since the European powers had sat around a table to share African territories among themselves, as if sharing pieces of a huge cake. In the years after the 1884-85 conference in Berlin, the conquest and colonisation of Africa was accelerated. It was an ominous period. All over Africa we can see that changes which were to have a catastrophic economic and social impact on the lives of Africans were taking place in the 19th and early 20th century.

The Portuguese accelerated their military conquest of Angola and in Kenya the British did not waste time in annexing as much African land as they possibly could. The first incursions of the British began through business interests represented by the British East Africa Company. Unlike the other Europeans who just grabbed the land, the British preferred to at least create the appearance of legality in their actions. The British East Africa Company obtained a trading concession from the Sultan of Zanzibar and agreed respective areas of influence with the Germans. The

British passed laws to give themselves African land in areas now occupied by the modern states of Uganda and Kenya; whereas the Germans were given Tanganyika. In a crafty ruse to break the economic power of the Sultan, the British liberated all slaves on the nearby East coast, so the Sultan could no longer gain the income from their labour[8]. After 1888, the British made efforts to seize further territory through trade with local chiefs in the name of the British Crown. In 1893 the British government took over the British East Africa Company in Uganda and declared the area a British protectorate (that is, a territory under "British protection") and declared Kenya a second protectorate. Kenya was eventually declared a British crown colony in 1920.

In Mozambique, as in other parts of Africa, the 19th century brought along the end of slavery and the shipping of masses of Africans to the American plantations, but heralded the beginning of the era of forced labour on African soil. The ruthless Portuguese regime ensured that each African man worked at least 6 months of compulsory labour per year[9]. In effect, this was still slavery, only on African soil.

In 19th century Namibia the British annexed Walvis Bay for their Cape colony in 1878, but the Germans got there first. By 1890 Namibia's present international boundaries were agreed amongst the European powers. Burundi and Rwanda fell under German control by the late 19th century.

In Nigeria in the 19th century there was an established Fulani empire under the autocratic rule of Usman Dan Fodio. This entrenched an Arabic and Muslim cultural influence in northern Nigeria, and was the last in a series of upheavals that revolutionised the Hausa kingdoms. The result was the replacement of the Hausa kings with Fulani rulers, and the establishment of the Sokoto Caliphate. The revolution led by Dan Fodio to overthrow the Hausa kings was fuelled by the resentment of settled Fulani whose economic grievances partly stemmed from the imposition of a market tax; whilst the cattle herders, the pastoral Fulani, suffered under the imposition of cattle taxes. The poor Hausa also rose against their hated leaders and joined the rebellion[10].

The slave trade on the Nigerian coast came to an end in the 19th century when Britain had become economically ready for the change from sugar based and slave based trade to an industrial economy. This economy created a market for manufactured goods. The Niger delta states like Oyo and Dahomey which were based on a slave economy and who were unable or unwilling to switch to the new industrial economy opposed the abolition of the slave trade. After the Berlin conference of 1885, through the Royal Niger Company, Britain set about the military conquest of Nigeria. There was strong resistance to British rule in areas of West Africa about the same time, including that led by Amina of the Hausa

Kingdoms and Yaa Asantewa of the Asante. In Nigeria, the north and the south of the country were separate protectorates in 1900 which were run through traditional rulers, who were conveniently made part of the colonial system. Lagos was made a separate colony but was united with the south in 1906. In 1914 the protectorates of the north and south were united to form Nigeria, named by the wife of Lord Lugard, the British Governor General of Nigeria (1914-1919).

The story of Yaa Asantewa is an interesting episode in the African resistance to British colonization of the Gold Coast (later known as modern Ghana). It all began during the scramble for Africa in the 1880s. The areas adjacent to the Gold Coast had been annexed by the French and the Germans. Britain felt compelled to grab the Gold Coast before its rivals did. Therefore in 1891 Britain offered a treaty of protection to the Asante and some of its neighbouring states. Prempeh I, the Gold Coast king rejected this offer once and then a second time when it was made again in 1895. Instead the Prempeh sent a high powered delegation to Britain to negotiate a treaty of friendship and cooperation. The British responded by launching an invasion of Asante and arresting Prempeh, even before his delegation had returned to the Gold Coast. Prempeh and his entourage were deported into exile. The Asante were at first unwilling to resort to arms and raised money to hire lawyers to fight a legal case for the release of Prempeh. Asante prisoners were kept in Freetown in Sierra Leone. The outbreak of the Yaa Asantewaa war led to the transfer of the Asante prisoners to the Indian Ocean Island of the Seychelles in September 1900. In 1896 the British rejected the legal case to free Prempeh. Instead the British were aiming to complete their conquest of the Gold Coast. They sought to destroy the will of the Asante people by demanding that the Asante give them their sacred Golden Stool, the supreme symbol of power of the Asante people. The British governor knew precisely what he was asking for. This deeply insulted the Asante who prepared for war. But it was the statement by the Governor that the Prempeh would never be repatriated that started the motion towards war. The British Governor's arrogant and blasphemous demand for the Golden Stool enraged the Asante: *"What must I do to the man, whoever he is, who has failed to give to the Queen, who is the paramount power in this country, the stool to which she is entitled? Where is the golden stool? Why am I not sitting on the Golden stool at this moment? I am the representative of the paramount power, why have you relegated me to this chair? Why did you not take the opportunity of my coming to Kumasi to bring the golden stool and give it to me to sit upon?"*[11A]

Yaa Asantewa became the driving force behind the Asante with her famous stirring speech. At the same time she defied the Governor Hodgson by refusing his demands for payment of interest: *"How can a proud and brave people like the asante sit back and look while white men take away their king and chiefs, and humiliate them with demand for the Golden Stool. The Golden Stool only means money to the white man; they searched and dug everywhere for it. I shall not pay one predwan to the governor. If you, the chiefs of the Asante are going to behave like cowards and not fight, you should exchange your loincloths for my undergarments"*[11B]

Figure 12 Yaa Asantewa

This moved the chiefs to swear the Great Oath of Asante to fight the British until the King Prempeh was set free from his exile. The British sent 1400 troops to crush the Asante resistance. When Yaa Asantewa was finally captured she was sent into exile to the Seychelles where she died in 1923.

In Ethiopia, as is well known, a literate culture which had been established since the days of the Axumite Empire in the 3rd and 4th centuries, continued. This was not the only writing systems that existed in Africa before the coming of Islam with the invasion of the Arabs. Egypt and Nubia had writing systems and common sense would dictate that there must have been later derivatives of these systems. Indeed they did exist, thanks to the necessity that long distance trans-Saharan trade provided to keep writing alive[11]. Diop in his work *Pre-colonial Black Africa* gave five different examples of scripts in Africa and also showed their genetic connection, in one instance, to ancient Egyptian. These included the Vai, Mande, Nsibidi, Bassa and Muom scripts[12]. Winters and Delafosse showed respectively that the Mande and Vai scripts are of ancient origins[13].

In the 19th century the descendants of Axum (ancient Ethiopia), the Abyssinians, continued a feudal social structure basically consisting of priests, warriors and peasant classes. At the top of the hierarchy sat kings claiming to descend from the line of Solomon (the Solomonid dynasty). This line is said to originate from the entourage that returned with the biblical Queen of Sheba, Makeda, from her visit to King Solomon of Judah about 1000 BC[14]. This dynamic institution ceased to function by about the mid 19th century, following a period of protracted civil conflict. The Solomonid throne was re-introduced, however, by Emperor Tewodros (1855-1868), despite the doubts that Tewodros was a genuine descendant of the Solomonid blood line. Emperor Menelik strengthened the Solomonid throne, and it reached its highest point during the reign of the Emperor Haile Selassie.

Italy tried to lay the basis of an Italian East African empire at the end of the 19th century in Eritrea (by 1885), and added Asmara in 1889. In the same year, Italy appropriated the coast of Somaliland and claimed a protectorate over Abyssinia. But in 1896, the Italians were soundly defeated by the Abyssinian forces at Adowa, with British assistance, and the world was made to recognise the independence of Abyssinia, later Ethiopia, the only African country to successfully resist colonization. This victory, no doubt helped to create the mythical and mystical status of the Emperor Haile Selassie and Ethiopia in the consciousness of the modern religious movement of Rastafarianism.

In 1845 the first European traveller to pass through Somaliland was an Englishman by the name of Richard Burton who was disguised as a Muslim merchant. Burton entered the walled city of Harar through one of its five gates, which like Mogadishu was a centre for Islamic learning.

The Somali's are originally a pastoral people who from early times developed a unique social framework. Like the Abyssinians the trade along the African east coast with traders from the Indian subcontinent and Arabia made their societies more cosmopolitan and consequently they share Asian and Arabic genetic influences in addition to their basically African heritage.

Richard Burton made the preliminary trip to Somalia and returned to describe the city of Harar to his countrymen, before the "scramble for Africa" led to Somaliland being partitioned between the British, the French and the Ethiopian empire of the 19th century. Although these 19th century boundaries were agreed, they were later subject to dispute and revision. The partition agreements were kept secret from the Somalis and the process of conquest of Somaliland lasted into the 20th century, being most forcefully resisted under the campaign led by Sayyid Muhamed Abdille Hassan, who is today recognised by Somalis as a pioneering Somali nationalist.

In Southern Africa the regime of forced labour also had consequences for the way in which the society was to become organised along racial lines. A brief look at the history of this region reveals how this racial structure develops. In 19th century South Africa, the Dutch East India Company, which was bankrupted by the transition from slave trading to industrial capitalism, drew its profits from forced labour of Africans on African land, and was made to hand over its south African colony to the British in 1806. In 1812 the British sent its military to drive 20,000 Xhosa off their land and declared the area a white settlement. In 1820 5000 British settlers recruited from the unemployed of the depression following the Napoleonic wars were settled on land in the Eastern Cape.

British rule diminished the influence of the Dutch settlers. The British used the same trick they had used on the Sultan of Zanzibar: They diminished the wealth and economic power of the Dutch settlers by abolishing slavery in the region. Slavery was abolished in the region in 1834 freeing 40,000 slaves and the Dutch objected. Possibly under Dutch pressure, the British introduced the Masters and Servants Ordinance; a law which gave former slave owners continued control over their former slaves. The forced labour regime was now beginning to take a particular racial form, which was unique to the region.

The Zulu, had continued to struggle for many years against colonization by both the British and the Dutch. The British military eventually overcame the resistance of the Zulu and proclaimed Natal a colony in 1843. Ultimately, spears were no match for the modern guns of the Dutch (Afrikaner) settlers and the Boers formed the Orange Free State and Transvaal colonies.

Boer rule was characterised by systematic control of black labour. The discovery of diamonds and gold in the 1860s and 1880s changed social relations even more towards a white/black and master/servant divide in the society. Black labour was now controlled towards the mining of these precious raw materials and the black Africans disposed of their land were now restricted to "reserves" consisting of the least fertile lands, insufficient for the Africans to sustain themselves and their families. They were forced therefore to work in the mines and on land appropriated by the whites (both Dutch and British). In addition, the African population in the reserves were subject to land taxes.

British supremacy in South Africa was being extended at that time. Spurred on by the German annexation of South West Africa, Britain extended its rule over Bechuanaland (modern day Botswana), and encouraged Cecil Rhodes' company to occupy the area north of the Transvaal and provoke the rebellion of non-Afrikaner white workers in the Transvaal. Rhodes encouraged Leander Starr Jameson to make raids into the Boer Republic of South Africa, but this failed. Conflict ensued between the British and the Boers, mainly over the control of cheap black African labour, which the Boers wanted to retain. This led to the Boer War (1899-1902) which ended the independence of the Boer republic of South Africa and the British gained overall rulership. The last of the wars of land dispossession from the Africans was won by the whites when a rebellion led by Bambata was overcome in 1906. The Union of South Africa was established in 1910, giving formal political control over a united South Africa to the whites and making conditions favourable for rigid control of black African labour. The 1913 Land Act legalised the restriction of black Africans to the reserves as well as the Pass Laws and the Master and Servants Laws, which restricted the movement of black Africans and penalised their desertion from their employers. Although slavery was supposedly abolished, these laws made black workers the property of their employers, and no better off than slaves[17].

One cannot know if Msiri, in 1891, would have been a changed man regretful of his slave raiding and self-interested past had he known the fate that was about to befall his region and indeed his fellow Africans all over the continent. Sadly, his past had shown him to be a man willing to sell his fellow Africans in the interests of his personal power and gain. There is no reason to think Msiri would have behaved differently, knowing all the facts. In this vein Msiri is no different from many of the African leaders today who continue to strive only in their self interests despite being faced with their own people's suffering and severe poverty. In that same year, 1891, Msiri was assassinated by a Belgian military officer and his empire was annexed to form King Leopold of Belgium's so called "Congo Free State".

Civilization or Barbarism? Belgian Rule in the Congo

At this point, if any economist and historian wishes to understand the prominence of Belgium as a European power in the 19th and 20th centuries, they need not consider any mystical "superiority" of the Belgians as a race. They only need to point to the consequent degradation and destitution of central Africa and its peoples. The twin relationship between *European advancement* and *African underdevelopment* is a dialectic of which we must be reminded again and again. To an extent these two things mean the same thing.

The presence of the Belgians in the Congo from 1876, following the exploratory expeditions of H. M. Stanley, in the footsteps of Livingstone before him, put them in a strong position to gain international recognition for their claim of the Congo. This claim was legalised at the Berlin conference in 1885[18]; but with the killing of Msiri and the annexation of his empire, Belgian colonization of the Congo began in earnest. As the constitutional monarch of Belgium, Leopold II became the sole owner of this vast territory in Central Africa[19]. When this area formally became a Belgian colony in 1885-1908 this part of Africa experienced one of the most brutal forms of exploitation in the colonial history of Africa.

From 1908 onwards, the Belgian presence in the Congo was characterised by barbaric "pacification campaigns" to subjugate the population under Belgian control. King Leopold's barbaric rule of the Congo enforced labour on its rubber plantations through acts of almost unbelievable cruelty. Hochschild gives an account in 1884 by an officer known as Fievez who describes the action he took against those who refused to produce their quota of rubber: *"I have made war against them. One example was enough: a hundred heads cut off, and there have been plenty of supplies ever since. My goal is ultimately humanitarian. I killed a hundred people...but that allowed five hundred others to live."*[20]

An account by another officer tells of how the Belgian colonial Force Publique went from village to village looting the poultry and grain, then kidnapping the women of the village and keeping them hostage until the required quota of rubber was produced. The women would then be sold back to the village for a couple of goats each[21]. Men who refused the demands for rubber had their wife or child murdered.

Africans dwelling in a rubber region needed permits to leave and had to wear a metal plate with a record of their individual rubber quota. Hochschild quotes the Governor of the Equatorial District of the Congo during the time of intense demand for rubber as proclaiming: "To gather rubber in the district... one must cut off hands, noses and ears."[22]

The letters of the American missionary, Joseph Clark, between 1893 and 1899 reported by Arthur Conan Doyle, describe the Congolese people's fear of the Force Publiqué (African conscripts led by Belgian officers). These were the state soldiers established by King Leopold II to carry out his reign of terror. Many families fled from their villages at the sign of their arrival and took refuge in the forest, where they went without food and their children died of starvation.[23] The Belgian soldiers along with their African subordinates were directly responsible for the barbarity. The Belgian soldiers would drive off with the young Congolese women and girls to do with as they pleased; whilst the protesting older women were tied up and burnt alive.[24]

King Leopold's reign of terror resulted in the first great genocide of the 20th century. Estimates of the number of Congolese people who died range from 5 to 15 million.

Any consideration of financial reparations by Belgium to the Congo in the modern era as recompense for this period of brutalisation would indeed be massive; for the Belgian missionary, Father Vermeersch, whose reports were related by Conan Doyle, estimated a revenue from the

Congo at the time of a staggering 8 to 9 million Francs per year in the late 1890s.[25] This of course does not include the vast profits Belgian companies extracted from the mines of Katanga during the Lumumba era and beyond.

References

Chapter Twelve - The Partitioning of Africa and the Advent of Colonialism

1. Boahen, A.A., *African Perspectives on Colonialism*, John Hopkins University Press, Baltimore, 1987, p.1.
2. Ibid., p.2-5.
3. Thomson, D., *Europe Since Napoleon*, Pelican Books, 1966, p.489.
4. Nkrumah, K., *Towards Colonial Freedom*, Panaf, London, 1973, p.3.
5. New African Yearbook 1981-2, IC Magazines, 1982, p.386.
6. Gailey, H., *History of Africa – from 1800 to present*. Vol. II, Krieger Publishing Co., New york, 1971, p.127.
7. New African Yearbook 1981-2, IC Magazines, 1982, p.370.
8. Ibid., p.144.
9. Seddon, D., *Popular Protest and Class struggle in Africa: An Historical Overview*, in L. Zeilig (ed.), Class struggle and Resistance in Africa, New Clarendon Press, Bristol, 2002, p.24-45, 27.
10. Gailey, H., Op. cit., p.2 and New African Yearbook 1981-2, IC Magazines, 1982, p.229.
11. Winters, C.A., *The Ancient Manding Script*, in I Van Sertima (ed.), Blacks in Science: ancient and modern, Transaction Publishers, New Brunswick, 1989, p.208
11A. Boahen, A.A., Yaa Asantewa and the Asante-British War of 1900-1, James Curry Oxford, 2003, p. 37.
11B. Boahen, A.A., Yaa Asantewa and the Asante-British War of 1900-1, James Curry Oxford, 2003, p. 118
12. Diop, C.A., *Precolonial Black Africa,* Lawrence Hill Books, 1987, p.188-9
13. Winters, C.A., op. cit., p. 208
14. Hansberry, L., *Pillars in Ethiopian History*, Howard University Press, Washington, 1981, p.43.
15. New African Yearbook 1981-2, IC Magazines, 1982, p.305.
16. Ibid.
17. Ibid., p.311.
18. Thomson, D., *Europe Since Napoleon*, Pelican Books, 1966, p.489.
19. Meredith, M., *The State of Africa – A history of Fifty years of Independence*, free Press, London, 2005, p.94.
20. Hochschild, A., *King Leopold's Ghost – A story of greed, terror and heroism in colonial Africa*, Macmillan, 1998, p.166.
21. Ibid., p.161.
22. Ibid., p.165.
23. Conan Doyle, A., *The Crime of the Congo*, London: Hutchinson and co., 1909, see chapter vi: "Voices from the Darkness", account by Joseph Clarke.
24. Ibid.
25. Ibid., see Chapter x.

Chapter Thirteen

African Struggles for Liberation I: Ghana and Nigeria at the Dawn of the Independence Era

In the period of African History covering the transition out of colonialism, it is more sensible to talk about the struggle for *African liberation* than for *African independence*. The term "independence" supposes that Africa is and was dependent on the colonial powers, without that dependence being reciprocated in any way. In reality the colonial powers, later joined by America, were and to a degree continue to be dependent on Africa for raw materials, markets and investment opportunities.

The next stage known as neo-colonialism was one in which the colonial powers and America, continued to derive benefits under the false disguise of "independence" for the former colonial territories. These remained firmly under the economic and military control of "the West", a term collectively describing the European powers and America. The hard won independence from former colonial masters in every case was only a "flag independence", with ties being maintained that did not give full freedom to African countries to choose between a market (or capitalist) economy and any other. The attempt, for instance, by Lumumba, the newly elected Prime Minister of the Congo, to take a "non-aligned" path, neither for nor against the market economy was met with moves by the Belgian and American governments to violently remove him from office. The Congo crisis was a measure of how free any African country really was to choose its own destiny when that newly independent country had great wealth in raw materials such as oil or precious metals. The tragedy of the Congo was the first example of what we call Neo-Colonialism; the next stage of control of African countries by their former colonial powers. After World War II this brotherhood of colonial powers was joined by America, with its now supreme military and economic might, used openly or secretly (through its Central Intelligence Agency – CIA) to force any country refusing to comply into submission.

In African countries the lead up to independence had been almost universally a protracted and often violent struggle for freedom from the control of the former colonial power. The British colonies (aside from Kenya and Rhodesia) underwent relatively peaceful transitions to independence, of which Ghana was the first followed by Nigeria in 1960.

**Figure 13 Kwame Nkrumah, first prime minister of Ghana,
being interviewed by a reporter (Library of Congress)**

Ghana at the Dawn of Independence

Ghana (formerly known as the Gold Coast) was one of the first countries in Sub-Saharan Africa to gain independence. Dr Kwame Nkrumah acceded to the presidency at independence in 1957. Nkrumah was the prophet of Neo-colonialism. In his writings in the 1940s he had long foretold of the emerging nature of European and American control of the continent of Africa. His prophecy of neo-colonialism materialised most completely in the crisis that was to emerge in the Congo in the 1960s and in southern Africa in the 1970s.

Nkrumah, born in Nkroful in the Gold Coast (modern Ghana) was a student at Achimota School in Accra and a Roman Catholic Seminary. In 1935 he left Ghana for USA and received a BA, an MSc in Education and MA in philosophy. He came into contact with the ideas of Marcus Garvey which deeply influenced him. As he often acknowledged they helped nurture his ideas on Pan-Africanism. Nkrumah returned to Ghana in 1947 and within 10 years he had served his political apprenticeship (so to speak) and formed the Gold Coast's most popular party, the Convention People's Party. In 1957 CPP won the elections and Kwame Nkrumah became the first president of Ghana (as it was renamed).

Nkrumah struggled to industrialise Ghana, taking on the massive challenge of building the Volta Dam, which promised to supply the new Ghana with unlimited electricity for all. But the project turned out to be highly expensive, almost bankrupting Nkrumah's government. Also the American contractors employed to construct the dam placed restrictions on the workings of the dam that effectively sabotaged its completion at a reasonable cost.

In 1966 whilst Nkrumah was on a state visit to China a coup plot supported by the American military and the CIA succeeded in toppling him. Nkrumah lived the remainder of his life in exile in Conakry as a guest of Sekou Toure. He continued to contribute to the pan Africanist cause through his writings. He died of cancer in 1972.

It was the vision of Nkrumah that helped further the creation of a framework and platform of ideas for a Pan-Africanist view of Africa as a single unified state free of the restrictions of colonial boundaries with a single centralised government that would manage the great resources of Africa for the benefit of its peoples. This was at least, the utopian vision of pan-africanists everywhere. It was Nkrumah's vision that led to the creation of the Organisation of African Unity (OAU) and the present day African Union.

Nkrumah was of course not the first pan-africanist. Pan-africanism as an ideology dates back at least to the dawn of the 20th century. The first pan-africanist conference in recorded memory took place in London in 1900. It was attended by the likes of W. E. B. Dubois and the composer Samuel Coleridge-Taylor. The conference was called by Sylvester Williams. It took a global view of the predicament of African people and its scope included "the treatment of native races under European and American rule". The conference petitioned Queen Victoria over the forced labour of Africans in South Africa and Rhodesia, and the Pass Laws which restricted freedom of movement for Africans. It clearly recognised the deceitful role played by Christian missionaries. After the conference, a pan-African Association was formed by Sylvester Williams, with various branches in the Caribbean, and many years later, in 1919, Dubois organised the First Pan African Congress. Nkrumah himself attended the fifth Pan Africa Congress in 1945, which hosted, among others, Amy Ashwood Garvey (Marcus Garvey's wife), Dubois, Jomo Kenyatta, George Padmore, CLR James and many others. It was at this conference that Nkrumah famously promised that he would return to the Gold Coast to liberate his people from the rule of the British. The Congress was a landmark in the history of African decolonisation, and helped gather the momentum towards African independence.

Ghana after Nkrumah

For a while after Nkrumah, Ghana was under military rule headed by a committee named the the National Liberation Council. In 1969 after a parliamentary election the Progress Party of Dr Kofi Busia won the largest number of seats. Busia was eventually elected Prime Minister in 1970.

In Busia's short time in office he was unable to control the country's spiralling inflation. The state of the economy eventually led to his overthrow in January 1972 in a bloodless coup led by Col. Ignatius Acheampong, who headed a committee called the National Redemption Council. This was later replaced by another committee named the Supreme Military Council (SMC). The government of Acheampong became mired in corruption and inefficiency. This led to Acheampong's arrest by his chief of staff, Lt. Frederick Akuffo, who replaced him as head of state, supported by a committee known as Supreme Military Council 2 (SMC-2). Akuffo's government was marked by the continued rampant corruption of its predecessor, and senior military officers were implicated.

On June 4 1979, Akuffo's government was overthrown in a bloody coup led by Flt. Lt. Jerry Rawlings. Rawlings led the new government supported by a new military committee known as the Armed forces Revolutionary Council (AFRC). Many of the former military leaders were executed including Akuffo and Acheampong. Special Tribunals tried many military officers and government officials for corruption, confiscating their property and sentencing them to long terms of imprisonment. The AFRC returned Ghana to civilian rule for a time but returned to remove the incumbent president Limann. The AFRC was replaced by the Provisional National Defence Council. Rawlings subsequently retired from the military and eventually became re-elected as Ghana's president, finally stepping down in 2001.

Perhaps the Rawlings revolution in Ghana is an example of a movement based on good intentions and the need to dispel corruption, but which apparently failed to eliminate it from government. Many Ghanaians might have been more tolerant of this failure had the Rawlings era not been inaugurated in such a bloody and self-righteous fashion. During the 1980s, Rawlings' revolutionary government had come into favour with the international financial institutions such as the IMF (International monetary Fund) and the World Bank, because he had accepted their policies. These policies, by and large, involved the provision of aid to African countries with certain conditions that promoted liberal access for western business operations in Africa, that were more advantageous for large multinationals than the impoverished African countries in which they operated. Rawlings is known to have later regretted his close relationship with these institutions.

Nigerian Independence and Beyond

Having been granted independence in October 1960 under a constitution for a British style parliamentary government, Nigeria went into the era of its First Republic, with the traditional tensions between the north and the south of the country balanced by the appointment of an Igbo and southern President, Dr Nnamdi Azikiwe and an Hausa and northern Prime Minister, Tafawa Balewa.

Other appointments in the new government included Obafemi Awolowo, finance minister, Hezekiah Oladipo Davies, federal minister and Jaja Nwachukwu, foreign minister. The three latter appointees and Azikiwe had all attended the 5th Pan-African Congress in Manchester, England in 1945. The congress was an important motivator in the movement for African independence when one considers that many of the conference participants went on to become the leaders of their respective countries.

The newly independent Nigeria allowed a level of self government for each of the three regions (north, east and west) associated respectively with the country's three major ethnic groups (Hausa, Igbo and Yoruba).

When elections were held in 1965, voting along ethnic lines led to tensions and disputed results led to civil unrest. In January 1966, a group of mainly Igbo officers, led by the young, charismatic and idealistic Maj. Chukwuma Nzeogwu, overthrew the government in a bloody coup which involved the assassination of Tafawa Balewa, the Sarduana of Sokoto, the premier of the western region and others. They had failed to locate the premier of the eastern region for assassination. This would lead to the coup being seen as an attempt to install an Igbo government.

The coup plot was eventually foiled and an Igbo General, Maj. Gen. Johnson Aguiyi-Ironsi became the new military head of state in a transition to civilian rule. The coup was popular as many hated the Sarduana, the premier of the western region and others who were seen as blatantly corrupt. Ironically, Ironsi was initially greeted like a hero, as if leading the change of government; whilst being the coup's abortionist!

His honeymoon with the people was not to last as his government drifted amid accusations of inefficiency and corruption and also his over-reliance on Igbo advisers. This only appeared to confirm suspicions that the coup had implanted a government intent on Igbo supremacy. A subsequent coup by mainly northern officers in July 1966 established Major General Yakubu Gown as Nigeria's leader.

Ethnic (and religious) tensions in the north erupted with attacks on Igbos leading to thousands of deaths and the return of hundreds of thousands of Igbo people back to the Eastern region. In May 1967 Lt. Col. Emeka Ojukwu emerged as the leader of an Igbo secessionist movement and declared the independence of the eastern region as the Republic of Biafra. As the eastern region contained significant oil wealth, the secession was unacceptable to the Nigerian federal government and also to Great Britain, its main supporter. By some estimates the war resulted in over a million deaths before Biafra was defeated in 1970.

Following the civil war, the country turned to the challenge of its economic development. The country's revenues increased sharply as the oil price rose in the period of 1973-74. However, the country continued to drift and Gowon failed to set a date for the return of Nigeria to civilian rule. So on 29 July 1975, General Murtala Mohammed and a group of officers staged a bloodless coup, sending Gowon into exile in Britain. The coup plotters accused Gowon of delaying the country's return to civilian rule. In contrast to Gowon's government, Mohammed set a date for civilian rule immediately and announced the programme for return to civilian rule, which his administration followed to the letter. He addressed corruption, forcing mass dismissals in the civil service, judiciary and the universities for corrupt practice. Most significantly the Mohammed regime pronounced Africa to be at the cornerstone of its foreign policy. Mohammed was advised by astute Pan-Africanist political scientists like Patrick Wilmot. Wilmot was later expelled from the country by the military regime of Ibrahim Babangida in 1988. Wilmot, a Jamaican-born intellectual who had married a Nigerian, had been settled in Nigeria since the 1970s.

In line with the mood of the times, Nigeria of the 1970s and 80s had a strong community of intellectuals who were pan-Africanist and ant-imperialist in their political outlook. That is, they saw the need for a struggle to breakaway from the neo-colonial relationship with the West. Wilmot taught at Ahmadu Bello University, Zaria, where another prominent intellectual and fearless critic of the era, Yusuf Bala Usman, also taught. Persecuted intellectuals from other parts of the continent resided in Nigeria as exiles (from South Africa and Uganda for instance). Okot P'Bitek, the poet and writer, was exiled from Idi Amin's Uganda and taught at the University of Ife.

At the time of Mohammed's government, Nigeria demonstrated its shift in foreign policy towards Africa with its stance on Angola, where Nigeria supported the role of Cuban troops in countering the South African forces hostile to Angola's MPLA government. This greatly angered the Americans, who wanted Cuban troops to pull out.

Murtala Mohammed was assassinated in an aborted coup attempt in February 1976 with suspected foreign involvement. Olusegun Obasanjo took over the reigns of government after the coup attempt was thwarted. He maintained the timetable set by Mohammed to move to civilian rule and the second republic came into being with the election of Shehu Shagari as president in 1979.

The second republic ended in December 1983 when Brigadier Muhammadu Buhari took the leadership of the Supreme Military Council and peacefully overthrew Shehu Shagari's government. This followed Shagari's re-election landslide victory in August 1983, which was nevertheless heavily disputed on grounds of widespread rigging and irregularities. The Buhari regime, jointly run by Buhari with his Chief of staff, Maj. Gen. Tunde Idiagbon, worked to address the collective values of contemporary Nigerian society with social awareness programs such as WAI (War Against Indiscipline), which were implemented with some visible results on societal attitudes. The regime became heavy handed and tolerated no dissent, press criticism or public debate.

The peaceful overthrow of the Buhari government followed in August 1985 led by Ibrahim Babangida. The religious violence that had plagued Nigeria sporadically from the days of Shagari's government continued. But rather than upholding the secular nature of Nigeria as stated in the suspended 1979 constitution, Babangida took Nigeria into the OIS (Organisation of Islamic States) in February 1990. Babangida had pledged to hand over power to a civilian government in 1990, but later he postponed the handover till 1993. Eventually, elections were held and in 1993, the Yoruba politician, M.K.O. Abiola won the majority of the votes in the presidential race. This was the same politician that had been accused in the songs of the nation's foremost musician, Fela Anikulapo Kuti, of colluding in the theft of the nation's riches via the American multinational company, I.T.T. (International Telephone and Telegraph Corporation, or in Fela's words "ITT, international thief thief"). Despite doubts about his honesty and past credentials as a potential agent for western multinational company interests, Abiola, a wealthy businessman, was widely deemed to have won a free and fair election. However, chaos was to reign when Babangida annulled the results of the election. The violence and protest unleashed as a result, forced Babangida to appoint an interim government with lawyer, Ernest Shonekan as Babangida's successor. However, Shonekan was unable to calm political tensions and the chaos was not abated until the Defence Minster Sani Abacha took over the reins of power and forced Shonekan to resign.

Abacha shutdown all the democratic institutions and replaced the civilian state governors with military governors. Abacha proved himself to be the most brutal of dictators in Nigeria's history. M.K.O. Abiola declared himself President on 11 June 1994 and went into hiding until his arrest 12 days later. Abacha rounded up Union leaders and military officers who had supported the campaign to release Abiola and accused them of treason. Several death sentences were given and former head of State Obasanjo and his former deputy, General Shehu Musa Yar'adua, were among the accused arrested. Both Abiola and Yar'Adua died whilst incarcerated. In 1994 Abacha set up the Ogoni Civil Disturbances Special Tribunal to try the Ogoni activist Ken Saro-Wiwa, who was executed, accused of responsibility for the deaths of 4 Ogoni politicians. Saro-Wiwa, a poet, had campaigned for the more equitable distribution of the nation's oil wealth to the Ogoni districts from which Shell extracted Nigerian oil. The government was unheeding of protests at the lack of environmental responsibility and health and safety provisions at Shell installations. Petroleum gas was allowed to burn into the open environment polluting the atmosphere of poor local communities with little educational or basic health care facilities. Uncovered pipelines were allowed to leak and contaminate the local agricultural land and groundwater; whilst the local communities remained without adequate schools, hospitals, clean drinking water or electricity.

Abacha died of heart failure in 1998, to the almost palpable relief of the nation that the days of a tyrannical leader had been numbered. An interim government was led by General Abdulsalam Abubakar to oversee a transition back to civilian rule.

In 1999, Olusegun Obasanjo, a former military head of state and former political prisoner of the Abacha regime, was elected as Nigeria's civilian president. Obasanjo's time in office was marred by continued religious violence and tension with several northern states adopting Sharia (Islamic) Law. The Niger delta continued to be a potential source of regional and national instability with great environmental devastation by western oil companies and poverty due to central government neglect continuing unabated in the region.

Bibliography

Chapter Thirteen - African Struggles for Liberation I

Arnold, G., *Africa – A modern History*, Atlantic Books, London, 2005.
De Witte, L., *The Assassination of Lumumba*, translated by A. Wright and R. Fenby, Verso, London, 2001.
Meredith, M., The *State of Africa – A history of Fifty years of Independence*, free Press, London, 2005.
New African Yearbook 1981-2, IC Magazines, 1982.
Nkrumah, K., *Handbook of Revolutionary Warfare*, Panaf books, London, 1968.
Nkrumah, K., *Towards Colonial Freedom*, Panaf, London, 1973. (Written in 1945).
Thomson, D., *Europe Since Napoleon*, Pelican Books, 1966.
McGreal, C., *Delta Force*, the Guardian, 10 May 2007.

Chapter Fourteen

Neo-Colonialism in the Congo

The Assassination of Lumumba

In the Congo we have the foremost case study of the transition from colonialism to neo-colonialism and the devastating effect on Africa. Despite its long history, it is the name of Patrice Lumumba that resonates in the story of the Congo, for his premature departure at the hands of European and American powers (and their Congolese collaborators) effectively changed the course of African history.

Lumumba was born in the Kasai province of the Belgian Congo and educated at a Catholic missionary school and government post office training school. He began his working life as a postal clerk, and became an active trade unionist. Like the other Congolese of his generation, Lumumba was stifled by the colonial establishment and not allowed to advance his education beyond a rudimentary school certificate. He managed, however, to qualify as a nurse, which in those days was one of the most advanced qualifications open to Congolese. In 1956 Lumumba was accused of stealing funds from the post where he worked as a clerk. This needs to be seen in the light of Renton, Seddon and Zeilig's observations on the situation: "The decision of the state to prosecute Lumumba should not be seen as an isolated action, but rather as one minor expression of a much greater process, a war of manoeuvre that was taking place between, young, educated Congolese, and their colonial overlords."

We become aware that the young Lumumba underwent a remarkable transformation over a short period, from a naïve youngster repeating, according to Renton and his co-authors, the same old "common sense" of his generation. They continue: "It took the experience of many personal defeats, the constant lies of the colonial foremen and masters, to teach Lumumba the need for a much more militant critique." Indeed the Lumumba of early writings in 1957, differs greatly from the radical Lumumba at the end of 1959, by which time he had been jailed once and had been put on trial by the colonial authorities. From talking of "Belgium, moved by sincere and humanitarian independence... to eradicate disease, to teach us.. and to eliminate barbarous practices from our customs" Lumumba moves to: "the ... earnest wish to make this continent of Africa a free and happy continent... from fear and from colonial domination."

Possibly encouraged by the success of his contemporary, Dr Kwame Nkrumah, Lumumba formed the Congolese National Movement (MNC) in 1958. He led a series of strikes and demonstrations calling for immediate independence of the Congo from Belgium. Lumumba was arrested, but after the people's mass demonstration and support the authorities were forced to release him.

20th century Congo had gone through many years of independence struggle before Lumumba's formation of the MNC. The Catholic missionaries were an effective aid to achieving the mental colonisation of the Congo people. It was ironic, therefore, that Christianity provided the framework for the first independence movements in the Congo. The resistance of the Congo people to colonization initially took the form of messianic sects which opposed the Belgian Catholicism that had been used effectively to colonise them mentally and physically. The new messianic sects preached a view of Christianity that opposed the abuse of Africans as unjust. In 1921 Simon Kimbangu led a messianic sect whose popularity provoked the response of the colonial authorities. Kimbangu was a charismatic leader whose followers believed that he was a prophet and that he could cure the sick. Kimbangu was jailed in Elizabethville, where he died in 1951 after thirty years of imprisonment. Whilst in jail Kimbangu continued to be regarded as a spiritual leader and a symbol of Congolese nationalism. His followers were persecuted by the Belgian authorities, but this only served to make the movement more radical. The sect preached an anti-colonial religious message with Christ being a symbolic liberator from colonial chains. In 1925 the Kitwala sect, emerging from Jehovah's witnesses and led by Bushiri, spread from Rhodesia (now Zimbabwe) and brought about an attempted peasant revolt in 1944. But the uprising failed and Bushiri and 73 of his followers were executed.

This early resistance laid the ground for the independence movement and the formation of political parties calling for the control of the country to be given to Africans. By 1956 ABAKO (Alliance des Bakongo) was calling for immediate independence. The late 1950's saw the emergence of new political parties, most of which supported one ethnic group or another. Lumumba created an exception in heading a political party that embraced all the ethnic groups of the region. It replaced ABAKO as the most progressive and radical party. Lumumba and his comrades represented the MNC at the All African People's Conference in Accra, Ghana, hosted by Kwame Nkrumah in December 1958. There he strengthened his belief in the philosophy of Pan Africanism, an idea that had become articulated most forcefully by Dr Kwame Nkrumah.

In late October 1959, Lumumba was jailed for six months by the authorities for inciting a riot in Stanleyville (now Kisangani). His release was delayed to prevent him from attending a Brussels conference on the independence of the Congo. However, those attending the conference demanded his release. The conference ended with the declaration of Congo independence and the date was set for 30 June 1960. Independence was indeed granted and Lumumba became the Prime Minister, whilst Joseph Kasavubu became President.

Lumumba's MNC formed the government by making an alliance with some of the ethnically based parties led by moderate leaders who supported continued links with the former Belgian colonial power. These leaders included Moi Tshombe of the Katanga based party Conakat, who would shortly become instrumental in the downfall of Lumumba.

Lumumba had taken note of Nkrumah's warnings of the dangers of neo-colonialism. He already knew that the European and American powers had designs for the continued exploitation of the mineral rich Katanga region. He therefore distanced himself from the western powers (Europe and America) and was willing to have relations with the Soviet Union. This was the era of the "cold war" when the world was largely divided into two camps: the Christian capitalist west and the communist east including the Soviet Union (USSR – United Soviet Socialist Republics), various eastern block countries like Yugoslavia, Romania, Czechoslovakia as well as China. Courting the socialist states like the USSR was perceived as a threat in the form of communist global expansion. More importantly, it was seen as a threat to western economic interests in the region. Lumumba's policy of non-alignment meant that he was willing to deal with any country that would enable him to negotiate for the best interests of his people. He intended, by all means to use the great wealth of the Congo for the development of the Congolese. Lumumba was seen as a dangerous communist who was a block to western economic interest in the region. At the least, this was a view of Lumumba that served to justify western interference in the newly independent territory.

What infuriated the Belgians to begin with was Lumumba's speech at independence. The retiring Belgian colonial masters had tried to sideline Lumumba at the independence ceremony by omitting him from the list of speakers. This did not prevent Lumumba getting up to speak uninvited and unscheduled, so that it came as a shock to King Badouin of Belgium and other present Belgian dignitaries and government officials.

Lumumba's speech, although strident at times was quite embracing of the Belgians as future partners in the Congo's development. Perhaps Lumumba had more cause to be infuriated given the manner of King Badouin's earlier remarks, even going so far as to praise his uncle King Leopold II for his "genius" and for conceiving the undertaking of the Congo's independence. Then he went on to add: *"Don't compromise the future with hasty reforms, and don't replace the structures that Belgium hands over to you until you are sure you can do better. ...Don't be afraid to come to us. We will remain by your side, give you advice, ..."*

Figure 14 Lumumba and Belgian Prime Minister Eyskens at Congo's independence ceremony, 1961 (Library of Congress)

Lumumba had to remind the audience that this independence was not magnanimously granted by the King's uncle Leopold, but won with the blood of Congolese nationalists:

"For this independence of the Congo, even as it is celebrated today with Belgium, a friendly country with whom we deal as equal to equal, no Congolese worthy of the name will ever be able to forget that is was by fighting that it has been won [applause], a day-to-day fight, an ardent and idealistic fight, a fight in which we were spared neither privation nor suffering, and for which we gave our strength and our blood.

We are proud of this struggle, of tears, of fire, and of blood, to the depths of our being, for it was a noble and just struggle, and indispensable to put an end to the humiliating slavery which was imposed upon us by force.

This was our fate for eighty years of a colonial regime; our wounds are too fresh and too painful still for us to drive them from our memory. We have known harassing work, exacted in exchange for salaries which did not permit us to eat enough to drive away hunger, or to clothe ourselves, or to house ourselves decently, or to raise our children as creatures dear to us. ...Who will ever forget the massacres where so many of our brothers perished, the cells into which those who refused to submit to a regime of oppression and exploitation were thrown [applause]?

All that, my brothers, we have endured."

Lumumba had high ideals about the future of the Congo and wished to make the Congo an example for the Black World:-

" The Republic of the Congo has been proclaimed, and our country is now in the hands of its own children

Together, my brothers, my sisters, we are going to begin a new struggle, a sublime struggle, which will lead our country to peace, prosperity, and greatness

Together, we are going to establish social justice and make sure everyone has just remuneration for his labor [applause].

We are going to show the world what the black man can do when he works in freedom, and we are going to make of the Congo the center of the sun's radiance for all of Africa

We are going to keep watch over the lands of our country so that they truly profit her children. We are going to restore ancient laws and make new ones which will be just and noble.

We are going to put an end to suppression of free thought and see to it that all our citizens enjoy to the full the fundamental liberties foreseen in the Declaration of the Rights of Man [applause].

We are going to do away with all discrimination of every variety and assure for each and all the position to which human dignity, work, and dedication entitles him

We are going to rule not by the peace of guns and bayonets but by a peace of the heart and the will [applause]".

In the remainder of the speech, Lumumba makes it quite clear he intends to use the Congo's vast wealth for the good of the Congolese and that he will trade or deal with any party which will offer the best for his nation:

"And for all that, dear fellow countrymen, be sure that we will count not only on our enormous strength and immense riches but on the assistance of numerous foreign countries whose collaboration we will accept if it is offered freely and with no attempt to impose on us an alien culture of no matter what nature [applause].

In this domain, Belgium, at last accepting the flow of history, has not tried to oppose our independence and is ready to give us their aid and their friendship, and a treaty has just been signed between our two countries, equal and independent. On our side, while we stay vigilant, we shall respect our obligations, given freely."

At this point it was already implied to the Belgians and Americans, by Lumumba's speech that he would scupper their policies in the Congo. According to Ludo De Witte, when Lumumba later proved that he was also a man of his word by beginning the Africanisation of the army, the western powers began their movements to eliminate him. Lumumba was undoubtedly a revolutionary leader of his day in so far as he knew that independence would not be enough to guarantee the freedom of the Congolese from the shackles of colonialism. As Renton and co-authors record, Lumumba held that the African continent should cease to be an economic colony of Europe.

Only days after independence, an army mutiny broke out over the question of the Africanisation of the army, now that Congo was to be handed over to the now independent Africans. The mutiny caused a panic among the Belgian settlers and the Belgian government used the issue of the protection of Belgian citizens as an excuse to send in Belgian troops.

The advantage Belgium had at independence was that Belgian officers remained in the Congolese army. The Belgian officer corps was the remnant of the brutal Force Publiqué, so infamous in carrying out King Leopold II's reign of terror. Established in 1886, it was established supposedly to fight slavery and prevent inter ethnic conflict. Instead they executed the barbaric "red terror", where the limbs of villagers were amputated if rubber collections by the Force did not meet the Belgian quotas. Hochschild's and Conan Doyle's accounts describe how hands were often amputated by members of the Force Publiqué and presented as proof that the soldiers had not wasted their bullets. So, according to the report of Roger Casement in Conan Doyle's "Crime of the Congo", for 6000 bullets used the soldiers had to bring back 6000 amputated hands. Thus 6000 used cartridges represented 6000 Congolese killed or mutilated. But according to Casement this implied many more than 6000 Congolese were killed or mutilated by the soldiers of the Force Publiqué, because children were killed by being struck with rifle butts. Children as young as 6 or 7 years of age had their hands amputated. Sometimes, to save bullets in killing the Congolese, the Belgian officers would order the line-up of several Africans and shoot a bullet through several bodies at once. Africans were recruited into the Force from a young age as apprentices. The Force Publiqué, with its brutal legacy was still in place at independence, controlled by Belgian officers.

In De Witte's account, just days after independence the army mutiny that broke out was caused by the Belgian Commander-in-Chief of the Congolese army, General Janssens, who provoked the mutiny when he wrote on the blackboard: "Before independence = after independence". Janssens let it be known that independence or not, there would be no Africanisation of the Congolese army. This immediately led to a rebellion by the Congolese troops, which was quelled when Lumumba's nationalist government removed General Janssens and allowed the troops to appoint black officers.

However, a hardcore of Belgian officers regrouped in Elizabethville, the capital of Katanga and backyard of Moi Tshombe, who was wary of the threat nationalist troops posed to his interests in the region.

With Belgian backing the next stage in the unfolding drama took place: Moi Tshombe, with the support of hired mercenaries and the Belgian mining company, Union Miniere, declared the secession from the Congo of the mineral-rich Katanga region. Thus, he declared himself President of Katanga, now separate and independent from the Congo. This would deny the Congo of Lumumba and his people the benefits of the mineral wealth of that region, should this secession become internationally accepted.

Given the background of Tshombe, this might have come as no surprise. Tshombe had always intended to retain control of the mineral rich Katanga province from which he hailed and which had been the power base from which he launched into a political career. Tshombe, the son of a wealthy businessman, was a few years older than Lumumba. He was educated at an American Methodist mission, and would later become an invaluable ally of big western business interests in the region. He later trained as an accountant. By 1951, when the struggle for freedom from Belgian colonial ties was reaching a high point; he was increasing his personal fortune and had taken over a chain of stores in Katanga. It is obvious that Tshombe had become nervous on seeing the direction in which Lumumba was taking the Congo with his non-aligned stance. It was clear that Lumumba favoured socialism. Tshombe had probably already calculated the immense fortune that American and Belgian mining companies in Katanga would add to his personal wealth. Renton and co-authors note that in breach of the pre-independence agreement Tshombe was paid royalties by the Belgians who ran Katanga's mines and Tshombe's administration. The payments enabled Tshombe to buy the services of mercenaries to oppose Lumumba's nationalist government.

The contrast between hero and villain could not have been more pronounced than the contrast between Lumumba and Tshombe. People enter into politics broadly for either of two reasons : as a vocation or as a career. Whereas Lumumba, from what we know of him in his time in office, saw himself undoubtedly as a servant of the people and therefore a vocational politician; there is no doubt that Tshombe was a self serving and ambitious, career politician, whose primary motivation was the increase of his personal wealth and influence.

The Belgian government sent troops to Katanga and installed a Belgian commander of the Kantangan army, even though no serious disturbances had been reported there in the wake of the mutiny. Belgian control of Katanga was total and the constitution of Katanga "was made in Belgium". The Katangan army, commanded by Belgian officers, would eventually be the killers of Lumumba.

Katanga was a neo-colonial state within Africa and the Belgian settlers there saw the mineral-rich Katanga region as virtually Belgian property. This is shown by an article in a Belgian newspaper (*De Standard*) at the time about scenes at Katanga airport:

At the airport we witnessed aggressive barracking by whites of blacks who had just arrived from Belgium or Leopoldville attacking the nationalist policies (of the Congolese capital). "Katanga is our country" said one woman to a black "our husbands must be allowed to finish their careers here."

The secession of Katanga was illegal as Lumumba was the head of a democratically elected government. He therefore pleaded that the UN should send troops to prevent the secession. The UN indeed sent troops but UN forces did not counter the secession as expected. On the contrary, the UN Secretary General Dag Hammarskjold appeared to do all in his power to support Belgian and American policy in the region, interpreting international law in a way that suited the consolidation of the Katanga secession.

The UN role was interpreted as one of non-interferance in the affairs of Katanga. This suited the Belgians and Tshombe's secessionist government in Katanga perfectly. The Congolese soldiers in Katanga were disarmed and the way was open for Tshombe, with the protection of Belgian troops, to disregard the authority of Lumumba's nationalist government in Leopoldville, the Congolese capital. At the same time as engineering the Katanga secession, the Belgian government went looking for suitable candidates to replace Lumumba.

The UN soldiers (the Blue Berets) set up camp throughout the Congo, except in Katanga, where Belgian troops were stationed. While the Belgians remained unhindered in strengthening Tshombe's regime in Katanga, the UN insisted that all aid to Lumumba's government had to go through the UN and would not be channelled through the Congolese government. Gizenga, Lumumba's deputy prime minister declared: *"The people of the Congo do not understand why we, the victims of [Belgian] aggression, we who are in our own country... are systematically and methodically disarmed while the aggressors, the Belgians, who are in our conquered country, still have their arms and all their firepower. ...The UN forces allow Katanga to consolidate secession and let the Belgians behave as they were in an occupied country under the smokescreen of a phoney Katanga provincial government, that we, the legitimate government of the Congo, have declared illegal."*

Hammarskjold was well aware of the illegal nature of Katanga as a state. He knew himself, if not through his assistant that Tshombe was *"a puppet manoeuvred by the Belgians, that he took no decision that was not inspired by the Belgians, that no official meeting was held without the presence of a Belgian and that without the Belgians he would never have come to power".*

As de Witte explains the UN leadership totally shared Belgian and American aims to destroy Lumumba personally and politically and hence snuff out the young life of the largest of Africa's early democracies. In short, Hammarskjold's behaviour pointed to sharing the same neo-colonial self-interests. As architect of the welfare state, Hammarskjold had spent his time building the western block's economic and social security and was committed to western interests.

Hammarskjold made it clear on which side of the lines of combat he stood. He was no neutral UN observer, although that was the impression he strived to present to the world. He stood firmly against the legitimate government of the Congo and in support of the illegal state of Katanga and its Belgian colonial masters. Lumumba declared his loss of confidence in the secretary general to implement the UN security council resolutions relating to the support of the legitimate government of the Congo. We borrow a quote of Lumumba's communication to Hammarskjold, from De Witte:

"After the adoption of the last resolution, you delayed your journey to the Congo for twenty four hours solely in order to engage in talks with M. Pierre Wigny, Belgian minister for foreign affairs, administrator for mining companies in the Congo and one of those who plotted the secession of Katanga. ...Completely ignoring the legal government of the Republic, you sent a telegram from New York to M. Tshombe , leader of the Katanga rebellion and emissary to the Belgian government. ... According to M. Tshombe ..., you entirely acquiesced in the demands formulated by the Belgians using M. Tshombe as their mouthpiece. In view of all the foregoing, the government and people of the Congo have lost confidence in the secretary general of the UN. Accordingly, we request the Security Council today to send a group of neutral observers to the Congo immediately. ...The task of these observers will be to ensure immediate and entire application of the Security Council resolutions."

Hammarskjold as the architect of the European welfare state and a political economist understood that the European post-war welfare state had to be buoyed significantly by the gains made from the European colonies. He was a thorough going and perhaps unapologetic neo-colonialist and he blatantly used his position at the UN to promote western economic interests in the Congo and in Katanga in particular.

Katanga, labelled by the Belgians as an "oasis of peace", was in fact an oasis of mineral riches the West greedily wanted to retain at all costs. The province was the domain of the Belgian mining company, Union Miniere and other European and American mining interests like Ryan and Guggenheim which had been established in the time of King Leopold. Union Miniere dated back to the time of King Leopold II, who owned huge interests in the company, in addition to his rubber fortunes gained through the killings and amputations of millions of Congolese at the start of the 20th century. The company exploited cobalt, copper, tin, uranium and zinc in mines which were some of the world's richest. Cobalt extraction from Katanga represented 75 per cent of the entire world production. All through the Congo crisis the main object of the West (Belgium, America and the UN) was to safe guard this neo-colonial treasure for the benefit of Belgian and American business interests. Katanga was undoubtedly seen as crucial for maintenance of Western economic, technological and military advantage. Therefore when we hear of CIA messages which state that *"...if [Lumumba] continues to hold high office, the inevitable result will ... pave the way to communist takeover of the Congo with disastrous consequences for... the interests of the free world ..."* we know that the Americans are not really talking about upholding freedom and liberty, but safeguarding their access to precious raw materials. In this instance, the phoney "cold war" was used by the Americans to justify one of the most callous breeches of a nation's right to sovereignty in world history. The Soviets were not intent on mounting a takeover of the Congo. The Soviets, for their part, made protests which were largely for domestic consumption rather than any real concern to save Lumumba.

The next stage in the removal of Lumumba came when in September Joseph Kasa Vubu, the President took the action of announcing Lumumba's dismissal as Head of the Government. Though this was probably illegal, as Lumumba was an elected Prime Minister, Kasa Vubu was boldly confident as he had the full backing of western governments and the support of the legally trained Secretary General of the UN. This was closely followed by a coup staged by Joseph Desire Mobutu. Lumumba was placed under house arrest, and later on when he eventually fell into the hands of Mobutu's troops, a list of charges were promptly devised in order to find Lumumba guilty and imprison him, such as inciting an army rebellion, and other alleged crimes.

Under house arrest Lumumba was surrounded by two cordons of soldiers. The inner cordon was formed by UN Blue Beret troops. The outer cordon was formed by Mobutu's troops, in whose custody Lumumba's life would be in grave danger. The UN guaranteed Lumumba security so long as he remained inside the UN cordon. Once outside this cordon, his safety would no longer be the responsibility of the UN. This was a ploy by the UN leadership to eliminate Lumumba politically. Lumumba still had considerable support and was a popular Head of State. In addition to this, Lumumba was a brilliant charismatic speaker capable of moving people to action. If he so much as broadcasted a speech to the nation, he could turn the situation around in a matter of hours. This is what the Belgians, the Americans and the leaders of the UN feared most. Inside the UN cordon, with no access to telephone or other communication to the outside world, Lumumba was powerless.

Furthermore, should he try to escape, his fate would be sealed, which was, in the end, what his arch enemies desired.

The US and Belgian governments had decided that Lumumba's elimination should not only be political, but physical. Kasa Vubu's Belgian aide, Georges Denis advised that *"...first and only problem was and is to eliminate one man: Lumumba."* During a meeting of the US National Security Council with President Eisenhower, the CIA chief Alan Dulles advised that *"Lumumba... remained a grave danger as long as he was not disposed of."* With the US President's approval the CIA set into motion a plan for Lumumba's assassination.

Lumumba's loyalists certainly did not succumb without a fight. The rule of law in the country seriously deteriorated whilst Lumumba was under arrest. There was fighting throughout the country with nationalist forces loyal to Lumumba gaining ground all the time.

At a meeting of the UN General Assembly in New York on the 24 November 1960, it could not be decided whether Lumumba's or Kasa Vubu's delegation should be accepted as the legitimate representatives of the Congo Republic. It was left to the western nations to engineer the vote in their own interests, and consequently the UN voted, by 53 votes to 24 (with 19 abstentions) to accept Kasa Vubu's delegation, formally recognising Kasa Vubu as the new head of the Republic of Congo. The vote was engineered with considerable pressure in the form of threats and inducements by the US, Belgium, Britain, France and others on vulnerable nations.

Basking in the glory of his delegation's recognition, Kasa Vubu made his grand entrance into the UN conference hall. Lumumba was able to witness the affair on television from his residential prison. Possibly, this final humiliation convinced him to mount an escape attempt.

In a fatal, but perhaps inevitable action, Lumumba escaped from his residence, and very nearly succeeded in reaching Stanleyville to set up a

Figure 15 Lumumba speaking with supporters whilst in struggle to reinstate his Government (Library of Congress)

nationalist stronghold there and regain control of the Congo Republic. Hiding under the feet of backseat passengers, he was smuggled past the two cordons of security in the car which each evening routinely took home the servants to his quarters. Lumumba headed for Stanleyville, where his former deputy, Gizenga, was organising the nationalist forces.

On news of Lumumba's escape, shockwaves were sent through Washington and the Belgian capital, Brussels. A real panic set in and Gilbert Pongo, Mobutu's assistant chief of security, was charged with hunting down Lumumba. Mobutu was given a European aircraft and a pilot skilled in low altitude flying to find Lumumba. Brussels was kept informed of every development on Lumumba's escape.

Lumumba and three others crossed the Sankuru River in a dugout canoe, while others, including Lumumba's wife and toddler son, Roland, waited on the river bank for the boat to return. Lumumba was on the way back to collect his family when he was captured by Mobutu's troops. Once in the custody of Mobutu's men, Lumumba and his companions were severely beaten. In a moment of lapsed attention, his driver managed to escape to a camp of Ghanaian soldiers serving with the UN force. The Ghanaian's, who witnessed the continued beatings, were ordered by their Lieutenant not to intervene as it was now not their responsibility to protect Lumumba once he had escaped the UN cordon. The Ghanaian soldiers rebelled against their commanding officer and managed to intervene to save 3 of his companions, but they were too late to save Lumumba.

Other than Lumumba, eight other nationalists journeyed to Stanleyville but only three reached their destination. Mpolo, Okito and Lumumba were arrested and taken back to Leopoldville, the Congo capital; whilst two others, Mbuyi and Mujanay, were killed in transit.

At this point, the UN could have intervened to save Lumumba's life. He was the democratically elected Prime Minister of the Congo. But the UN Commander-in-chief, General Carl von Horn issued the order from Leopoldville: *"No interference is to be made in the arrest of Lumumba by Mobutu's men."* Whilst the compassionate instinct of the Ghanaian soldiers was to rebel against their superior officer and take Lumumba into protective custody, they were given strict instructions not to intervene, and to leave Lumumba to his cruel fate. The fingers were pointed at Hammarskjöld in the affair. With full knowledge of the events leading up to Lumumba's arrest, Hammarskjöld had to lie to the UN assembly in order to save face, saying that the UN had no opportunity to protect Lumumba.

The Secretary General was denounced by the USSR as responsible for Lumumba's arrest. USSR also accused the western powers of being complicit and demanded Lumumba's release, his immediate restoration as the head of the Congo and the withdrawal of Belgian troops from the region. Predictably, this plea to the UN, which was not backed up by any intention of action, failed. Hammarskjöld, the political economist, lawyer and one of the architects of the welfare state in Europe, would the following year end his illustrious career as a casualty of the crisis. In September 1961, he and 15 other passengers were killed in a plane crash on his way to meet with secessionist president Moi Tshombe.

After his arrest, Lumumba was handed over to Gilbert Pongo. The triumphant Pongo with Lumumba and his military escort landed at Ndjili, Leopoldville's international airport. Lumumba appeared behind Pongo, with arms tied behind his back. He was then bundled into a lorry with a few other prisoners and taken to a camp near Mobutu's residence. Mobutu watched as Lumumba was thrown to the ground and kicked by surrounding soldiers. Pongo, who was hailed as a hero and later promoted for capturing Lumumba, shouted at the soldiers to kick harder.

A lot of violence towards Lumumba was filmed by the western media. The photos had shocked and caused outrage. People asked: how was it that the UN was able to protect Belgian settlers but not able to protect Lumumba?

Now Lumumba was back in custody, the Belgian government demand for a final solution was clear. Lumumba was to be eliminated. The call for *"elimination définitive"* was voiced by the government minister d'Aspremont Lynden. As Lumumba's time in jail dragged on, the opposition to his imprisonment in the country continued to grow and deep Congolese dissatisfaction had set in with the new regime led by Kasa Vubu. The situation in Thysville, where Lumumba was held, became almost unmanageable when soldiers were demanding a pay rise, a new government and freedom for Lumumba. Day by day it became more and more difficult to guarantee Lumumba's imprisonment.

The situation became so serious that Mobutu, Kasa Vubu and others flew to Thysville to visit Lumumba in his cell. They offered him a ministerial post in a government headed by Joseph Ileo; but Lumumba refused saying he would only accept freedom as head of government.

Meanwhile, fighting in the country continued between Lumumba's and Mobutu's forces. Mobutu's troops launched a New Year offensive on nationalist troops but the offensive failed. By mid-January 1961, forces loyal to Lumumba controlled half of the country. Neither Kasa Vubu nor Mobutu had Lumumba's charisma and popular appeal.

Lumumba was transferred from a jail near Leopoldville to one in the Katanga province. The transfer to Katanga had been ordered on 16 January 1961 by the Belgian government official D'aspremont Lynden in the knowledge that Lumumba would be killed in Katanga; for only in September the Interior Minister in Tshombe's Katanga, Godefroid

Munongo, had said: *"If he comes here, we will do what the Belgians couldn't do, we will kill him."*

Lumumba, aged 35 years, was executed by firing squad along with his nationalist colleagues, Maurice Mpolo and Joseph Okito on 17 January 1961. Belgian officers, Frans Verscheure and Julien Gat, were in command of the firing squad at his execution.

Three Belgian officers and Katangan politicians including Moi Tshombe were present at the execution. Later the Belgian military attempted to hide the truth of Lumumba's brutal murder. Renton and co-authors inform us that the Belgian police officer Gerard Soerte "exhumed the bodies, hacked them into pieces and dissolved them in acid". From De Witte we know that Verscheure kept a bullet from Lumumba's skull as a momento of the execution. He gave a bonus to the soldiers and policemen who took part.

The Belgians, the colonial forces, did all in their power to keep the truth from the Congolese people. According to Renton and co-authors nothing was said by the authorities for 3 weeks after Lumumba's death. Then followed the announcement of the death with an elaborate cover story. Nobody believed it, but compared to the student demos in various capitals of the world, the response of the Congo at the time was muted.

The Congo after Lumumba

Years later the flames of the Congo crisis had not died with Lumumba in Congo or indeed in other parts of the world. In America in 1964, just over two months before his own death by assassination, Malcolm X had linked the struggles of the Africans of the Congo with the struggles of African Americans and accused the American government of hiring Moi Tshombe to murder Lumumba and takeover the government of the Congo: *"Take Tshombe...He's a cold blooded murderer. He murdered Patrice Lumumba, the rightful prime minister of the Congo. ...They take Tshombe and they prop him up with American dollars. They glorify his image with the American press. ...He's a murderer, who has been hired by the United States government and is being paid with your tax dollars. ...And to show you what his thinking is – a hired killer – what's the first thing he did? He hired more killers. He went out and got the mercenaries from South Africa. And what is a mercenary? A hired killer."*

That same year Malcolm must have become familiar with the spectre of mercenary involvement in the Congo. He had gained new friends on an international level at the Cairo meeting of the OAU, where Julius Nyerere had championed his proposed resolution expressing OAU support of the 22 million African Americans of that time in their struggle for human rights in America.

Meanwhile, a new government compliant with Belgian and U.S. wishes had emerged in the Congo under Kasavubu with Moi Tshombe as the Prime Minister in place of Lumumba; but conflict between the two gave General Mobutu the excuse to stage a second coup in 1965, backed by the western powers. The crisis in the Congo and the brutal manner of Lumumba's removal from power had gained world-wide attention and opened eyes to the nature of western neo-colonialism. In order for Mobutu to come to power with western backing, forces loyal to Lumumba's legacy had to be crushed. At one point the international

**Figure 16 Malcolm X connected the struggles of Africans
of the Congo with that of African Americans (Library of Congress)**

Argentinian revolutionary Ernesto "Che" Guevara went to the Congo leading a Cuban contingent to try to support forces allied to Lumumba. However, he met with Congolese militants who did not impress him as disciplined freedom fighters. One of these was Laurent Kabila, who would (over 30 years later) oust Mobutu. Guevara's seven-month sojourn in the Fizi Baraka mountains of the Congo was disastrous. His small collection of Cuban troops encountered Mobutu's troops under the command of the infamous British mercenary, Captain "Mad Mike" Hoare, and were forced to retreat into friendly neighbouring Tanzania, then under the socialist government of Julius Nyerere. This was one of the first military conflicts in Africa where the West (Europe and America) avoided direct military involvement through the use of mercenaries. These mercenaries were often white ex-military from apartheid South Africa or retired soldiers from the British and other armies.

It is important to note that although the western powers were initially happy to support a Congolese government under Kasa Vubu, this changed very quickly when Kasa Vubu over-ruled Mobutu's objections and supported a UN resolution that would outlaw the use of mercenaries in African conflicts. This was seen by the US and other western powers as a sign that Kasa Vubu would not protect western interests.

Having taken control of Congo in 1965, Mobutu remained in power as president of Zaire (as the Congo was later renamed in 1971) until he was overthrown in 1997 by the rebels under Laurent Kabila. Whilst in power Mobutu concentrated more and more power in his hands becoming a dictator of the Congolese people. Nevertheless he was greatly favoured by European and US governments as a leader who would always serve their interests in exploiting the mineral wealth of the region, and was therefore maintained in power with western economic and military backing for over 30 years until his death. Under Mobutu, Zaire became a single party state. Mobutu made himself Head of State, Commander-in-chief of the Armed forces and Police, and in charge of foreign policy. His personal philosophy was called "Mobutism" or sometimes "authenticity" which he propagated through one of his country's research institutes.

In the rest of Africa the struggle of the former colonial powers and America to retain control of access to precious raw materials on African soil led to other instances of regime change and control, but the story of Patrice Lumumba remains the most potent example.

Bibliography

Chapter Fourteen – Neo-colonialism in the Congo

Arnold, G., *Africa – A modern History*, Atlantic Books, London, 2005.
Conan Doyle, A., *The Crime of the Congo*, London: Hutchinson and co., 1909.
Davidson, B., *Modern Africa – A Social and Political History* (2nd ed.), Longman, N.Y. 1983.
De Witte, L., *The Assassination of Lumumba*, translated by A. Wright and R. Fenby, Verso, London, 2001.
Gailey, H. , *History of Africa – from 1800 to present*. Vol II, Krieger Publishing Company, New York, 1971.
Hochschild, A., *King Leopold's Ghost – A story of greed, terror and heroism in colonial Africa*, Macmillan, 1998.
Malcolm X, *Malcolm X Speaks*, Pathfinder, New York, 1965.
Meredith, M., *The State of Africa – A history of Fifty years of Independence*, free Press, London, 2005.
New African Yearbook 1981-2, IC Magazines, 1982.
Renton, D., Seddon, D. and L. Zeilig, *The Congo: Plunder & Resistance*, Zed Books, London & NY, 2007

Chapter Fifteen

African Struggles for Liberation II

The Battle for Angola

The Angolan case must be seen in the context of Portugal's sudden demise as a colonial power and economic force in Europe. It is not coincidental that the other Portuguese territories of Guinea and Cape Verde, and Mozambique gained their independence along with Angola in 1975, in the wake of the final demise of the Caetano regime, brought about by a bloodless coup in 1974. This demise of the regime was preceded by the death of Salazar in 1970, whose policies Caetano continued.

The independence struggle for Angola presents, like the Congo crisis, an example of the western powers colluding on an international platform to destroy or prevent from emergence, a government that failed to protect western interests. Angola also stands out positively, however, as an instance, for once, where African countries have acted in concert to assert the right to self determination of a sister African state.

In Angola, after the acceleration of conquest that followed the 1885 Berlin conference, Portuguese citizens (including many exiled criminals) were sent to Angola to populate the territory with white settlers.. This increased sharply particularly after the coffee boom years of the 1950s when over quarter of a million Portuguese whites were settled in Angola. Angola's wealth which attracted continued Portuguese interest included diamonds which had been mined since 1920 and petroleum discovered in 1956.

However, the independence of Angola and other African territories under Portuguese control, like Mozambique and Guinea, came a step closer with the fall of the fascist regime of Caetano in 1974. At this point many of the Portuguese settlers fled these territories taking what they could and destroying what they could not take.

The movement towards independence in Angola was taken up by the MPLA (Popular Movement for the Liberation of Angola) which was formed in 1956 and also the UPNA (Union of the Population of Northern Angola) which was predominantly representative of the Bakongo ethnic group and later split to give rise to the FNLA (National Front for the liberation of Angola), which was to eventually form UNITA (National Union for the Total Liberation of Angola), an organisation that would in the future be the main opposition to the MPLA and also be the party in favour with the Portuguese and American governments who wanted a party that would maintain western interests in the region. The FNLA became the tool of Zaire under president Mobutu and covert western interference aimed at destroying the MPLA and any government that put the interests of Angolan peoples before the profits of western multi-national companies.

The MPLA was closely allied with the PAIGC in Guinea and Cape Verde under the leadership of Amilcar Cabral, since the two territories had in common that they were Portuguese colonial territories struggling for independence.

The MPLA, the most popular of the various parties contesting to lead an independent Angola, would have claimed to be the only force genuinely representing the interests of Angolans as opposed to those of western multinational companies seeking to profit from Angola's mineral wealth. The FNLA was led by Holden Roberto, a close friend and ally of Mobutu in Zaire (formerly the Congo); whilst the UNITA, led by Jonas Savimbi allied itself to the forces of apartheid South Africa in its desperate bid for power.

After the fascist government of Caetano fell in Portugal in 1975, a transition government was formed in Angola consisting of MPLA, FNLA and UNITA. However, this transitional government fell apart before the planned date of independence and projected elections. The country then moved into a war of liberation. Mobutu of Zaire moved his troops to the northern border of Angola to support his friend Holden Roberto and the FNLA. Covert military operations involving mercenaries and funded by the American CIA (Central Intelligence Agency) budget of 1975 were also started. Apartheid South Africa moved troops to Angola's southern border to support the forces of Jonas Savimbi's UNITA. Not only were South Africa supporting their ally in Savimbi, but their interests were directly involved, because MPLA had supported the efforts of SWAPO (South West Africa Peoples Organisation) in Namibia to resist South African control there (see section on Namibia, ahead). Meanwhile, MPLA besieged by these forces on all fronts accepted support from Cuba and Guinea Bissau, which sent small units of fighting forces, and also Mozambique, Nigeria and Algeria who sent equipment.

Throughout the late 1970s and 1980s the American government continued to portray the Angolan conflict as one in which the west supported anti-MPLA forces in order to prevent the expansion of communism in the region. In reality, this was a continued convenient misrepresentation of the real purpose behind American action in the region, which was to protect Western (especially American) economic interests. Chester Crocker, President Ronald Reagan's Under-Secretary of State for African affairs said in a speech in August in 1981: "We are concerned about the influence of the Soviet Union and its surrogates in

Africa". He then added the truth: that America needed South Africa's minerals. The continued play on the US public's fears of the spread of communism ensured continued support for apartheid South Africa. Meanwhile, African aspirations for freedom were relegated to being a "surrogate" cause, presumably masking the true aim of Africans (the MPLA), which was presumably to embrace and invite the spread of communism! Patently, western justification for interference in Africa was absurd and plainly dishonest and designed to confuse western public opinion.

In Angola the USA supported South Africa which continued to make incursions into the country, whilst also funding Jonas Savimbi's UNITA in its attempt to overthrow the MPLA government headed by Eduardo dos Santos. Meanwhile, American businesses still traded with Angola for its oil (mainly controlled by the ubiquitous oil company, Chevron).

The oil riches created a corrupt and wealthy ruling elite within the MPLA and the regime was divested of any genuine revolutionary credentials it might have had. Things were not helped by the fact that the countryside, which became increasingly remote from the MPLA leadership, was being destabilised by the actions of the US-funded UNITA rebels.

Angola continued to provide bases for SWAPO (the Namibian liberation movement) and the ANC of South Africa, tying the ongoing conflict to the wider liberation struggles in the region. For South Africa, its continued influence in the region and even its very survival now depended on defeating the Angolan forces, which now had substantial Cuban assistance. The war, particularly the heavy defeat the South African forces sustained at the battle of Cuito Cuanavale took a heavy toll and forced the South Africans into negotiations on Namibian independence. The US was still concerned by the presence of Cuban troops on African soil and Chester Crocker introduced the concept of the "linkage" of Cuban troop withdrawal from Angola to Namibian independence.

By the late 1980s South Africa was defeated in Angola and the Soviet Union, under Gorbachev, politically disengaged from the region, no longer supporting the Angolans.

By 1990 the MPLA of Angola formally abandoned Marxism-Leninism as its ideology, and a peace agreement was entered into with UNITA. A multiparty political system was introduced and in 1992 the country held its first ever multiparty elections. Savimbi was invited to participate, but lost the presidential election and thereafter returned to the bush continue his civil war and struggle for power. The war from 1992-1994 reached new levels of brutality in which 100,000 lives were lost. There were five years of peace; but the war resumed again in 1999.

Like the Congo (modern DRC), Angola became a region of perpetual conflict, kick-started by unrelenting western interference based on greed for regional wealth in raw materials. However, the death of UNITA's Jonas Savimbi on 22 February 2002 opened up the possibility of a renewed search for lasting peace in the region.

Nigeria's Role in the Angolan Liberation Struggle

Nigeria provided welcome direction to the African position on Angola at the OAU which was a reflection of the direction and purpose that Murtala Mohammed's government had brought to Nigeria. Ever since its independence, Nigeria, despite being called the "Giant of Africa" in economic and demographic terms, had never managed to have any real direction in foreign policy.

The role of Nigeria in the Angolan war of liberation was particularly important in effecting the outcome. Murtala Mohammed's Nigerian government strongly supported MPLA and rallied wavering African states into backing MPLA at the OAU (Organisation of African Unity) conference of January 1976. Despite Murtala Mohammed's assassination the liberation process had been set in motion. Nigeria's support for Angola helped to legitimise the use of Cuban troops against the threat from apartheid South Africa and mercenaries contracted by the western powers including the American CIA. The support of sister African states rallied by Murtala's government in Nigeria, ensured that the ploy of portraying the Cuban presence as an in road for communism, was frustrated. Rather, the Cuban presence was legitimised by the consent of African nations, who had called on their support in the interests of their Angolan sisters and brothers, under the auspices of the MPLA. The double standards of the western powers in calling for the withdrawal of Cuban troops whilst also supporting the South African military involvement, was exposed by Mohammed's government, and created a bargaining tool for the MPLA. Eventually, Cuban forces were withdrawn on the agreement of the simultaneous withdrawal of South African forces. However, the continued interference of the US and south Africa in later years would not allow Angola to emerge from the instability of civil war perpetuated directly by America's continued support of Jonas Savimbi's UNITA.

Cape Verde

The desperation of the Portuguese government as it clung onto its Angolan colony was repeated in the cases of Cape Verde and Mozambique where, in each case, the movements for independence were so violently resisted that the respective independence struggles had to be pursued through armed struggle, having exhausted peaceful means.

In Cape Verde in 1956 the intellectual, Amilcar Cabral, formed the Party for the Independence of Guinea and Cape Verde (PAIGC). Cabral and PAIGC peacefully attempted to articulate the wishes of the people for independence. But, Salazar's colonial authorities responded with brutal force, burning villages and killing their inhabitants. There were reports of villagers being sadistically burnt alive and drowned in local rivers by the colonial authorities. In 1959 after three years of frustration, the PAIGC took up the armed struggle for independence. On 3rd August that year, the massacre of 50 striking dock workers at Pidgiguiti, which left 100 wounded had been the final straw which tipped the balance for the PAIGC in favour of armed struggle.

The position of Cabral, however, was not that of blind condemnation of Portuguese actions. Cabral, a committed pan-Africanist, was in the school of thinkers like Nkrumah who explored and expressed the nature of neo-colonialism through his experience of struggle in the field, his writing and his speeches at the United nations and on lecture visits to America where he addressed African American audiences.

Notable are his famous speeches on "Identity and Dignity" (1972) and "National Liberation and culture" (1970), where he identified the critical role of culture in the liberation struggle against colonialism and neo-colonialism. Cabral made the observation that it was impossible for foreign domination to succeed, so long as it could not harmonise economic and political domination with the culture of the people. Cabral also observed that the redirection of African labour (or modes of production) from being applied to feed and sustain Africans to providing waged labour for European companies is the foremost factor in African underdevelopment.

Both Cabral and Nkrumah were deep and pre-eminent thinkers who were enormously influential in forging the pan-Africanist school of thought. However, they also represented a school of pan-Africanist thinkers that were an upset to the designs of the colonial and western powers. Moreover, they became dangerous because as pan-Africanists they saw their struggles as connected. Cabral held Nkrumah in the highest esteem for his clear articulation of pan-Africanism and as a personal friend, although he acknowledged W.E.B. Dubois as the father of pan-Africanism rather than Nkrumah. It was inevitable that they would both become targets of the western powers and that they would eventually both be either removed or eliminated. Cabral was assassinated by Portuguese agents on 20th January 1973, and Nkrumah's removal much earlier, initiated by the CIA, is well known.

Nevertheless, the wheels of liberation had been set in motion and the downfall of the Caetano regime in the Portuguese revolution in 1974 gave the people of the island of Cape Verde the confidence to come out in force and demand their independence from Portugal. This forced the Portuguese government to negotiate with the PAIGC and a transitional government was setup to steer the country towards independence on 5 July 1975.

Mozambique

Similarly, in Mozambique the harsh response of Salazar's colonial authorities to African aspirations for independence shifted the movement for self determination from peaceful protest to armed struggle when FRELIMO (Mozambican Liberation Front) launched its first military campaign in 1964. Its first president, Eduardo Mondlane was assassinated by Portuguese agents on 3rd February 1969. This did not halt Mozambique's momentum towards independence, which culminated in 1975 following the collapse of the Portuguese government. The independence of the country immediately led to an economic crisis created by the fleeing Portuguese settlers and also the international community, which withdrew its investments in the country overnight. Departing Portuguese settlers, having exploited the country for its mineral wealth and African labour for centuries, still took whatever they could and destroyed whatever they could not. Machinery and heavy vehicles were slipped across the border in to neighbouring South Africa, then still under the racist apartheid regime. Cattle that could not be taken were slaughtered. All these actions by the settlers led to a drastic fall in the agricultural production and food shortages in the towns. The currency of Mozambique fell sharply in value. FRELIMO, led by Samora Machel, were left with the challenge of building an economy to meet the needs of its people from this decimation and sabotage by the settlers.

Inspite of the flight of skilled Portuguese personnel and international investment from the country, Machel took on the task of rebuilding the country. Adopting Marxist-Leninism as the state ideology, he set about a revolutionary transformation of Mozambican society. Mozambique did not have the natural resources of the Angolans; so Machel had to concentrate his efforts on building the country's agricultural base. He attempted to establish agricultural cooperatives along the lines of Nyerere's Ujamaa villages, centralised the country's economic planning and nationalised businesses and all agricultural production.

On the international political front, Machel supported African liberation struggles in the region, providing bases for military opposition to the white ruled regimes of Zimbabwe (then named Rhodesia) and South Africa. These resistance movements had included ZANU and ZAPU in opposition to the Rhodesian government which fell in 1979, and the ANC military wing opposed to South Africa, which remained to be overthrown. However, South Africa, in turn, supported the rebel group RENAMO to attack Machel's government, causing widespread damage to the country's infrastructure and economy. The combination of the failing economy and the war with RENAMO forced Machel into accepting the Nkomati Accord in 1984. This was a mutual agreement with South Africa which involved both countries renouncing the provision of bases for rebel groups to attack one another. This agreement, which required Machel to give up support of the ANC through its provision of bases in Mozambique, was not kept by South Africa, which continued to support RENAMO. Eventually, Machel had to call on the help of Nyerere of Tanzania and the new government of Zimbabwe, led by Robert Mugabe, to fight the RENAMO guerrillas.

Following a meeting in 1986 in Malawi between the leaders of Mozambique, Malawi, Zimbabwe and Zambia that agreed to the removal of RENAMO bases from Malawi, Samora Machel was killed when the plane carrying him back to the Mozambique capital mysteriously crashed. The circumstances of the crash were never completely explained. Machel's Prime Minister, Joaquim Chissano, then succeeded to the presidency.

Namibia

Namibia was similar to South Africa in "racialising" the distribution and division of land and labour among white settlers and black Africans. The country suffered numerous atrocities and severe decimation of its population by the colonial powers in the course of its history.

In the 1884 scramble for Africa, Germany seized South West Africa. In 1897 a cattle plague devastated the flocks of the Herero. In desperation they sold their cattle to German settlers and also the land used for cattle pasture. The European settlers benefited out of the catastrophe whilst the Herero were left destitute; for they were a pastoral people dependent totally on their cattle for their livelihood. In 1904, this led to a Herero uprising against the German settlers, killing dozens of German men but, sparing the women and children. The German retaliation was extreme. The German emperor, William II selected General Lothar Von Trotha to lead the reprisal. He was ordered to put down the rebellion by "fair means or foul". So he proceeded to surround the Herero, leaving them only an escape exit that led to the Kalahari Desert, then he placed German guard posts to prevent their return. In the punishing sun with no water, 8000 Herero men perished together with their families and remaining cattle. Von Trotha then issued an "execution order" that any African caught in the German zone would be shot, so carrying out one of the 20th century's first genocides.

The Nama people of the region were next to rise up against the German settlers. But, eventually defeated, they were forced to work in labour camps where many of them died. A census in 1911 revealed that the population of the Nama reduced by half as a result of the harsh regime of forced labour over a ten year period.

At that time the Herero population was reduced by 80 percent over 10 years. Portuguese South West Africa had been the place of earlier atrocities against the Herero. In 1904 the Herero, led by Hendrik Witbooi, rebelled against the Portuguese; but paid the price in 1909 when 60 percent of the African population in the Police Zone (the southern two thirds of Namibia) were murdered. Fully 80% of the Herero were exterminated. The African population continued to decline under the forced labour regime which followed.

The First World War made the South Africans the new colonial masters. A South African military force made the Germans surrender in 1915 and the Treaty of Versailles confirmed South African occupation of Namibia under a mandate of the League of Nations, which was vaguely worded, but included: "...to promote to the utmost the material and moral wellbeing and the social progress of the inhabitants of the territory".

For 40 years traditional leaders led the opposition to South African rule including passive resistance to land removals. South Africa struggled for many years to hold on to Namibia, against the petition of Namibians for freedom from South African rule; but in 1967 the UN ruled that Namibia be a sovereign state. South Africa challenged the authority of the UN and began its illegal occupation of Namibia.

The main political organisation in Namibia, SWAPO (South West Africa Peoples organisation) came into existence in 1960, out of the former Ovambo Peoples Organisation which started in 1958 but soon grew to appeal to other ethnic groups as well as the Ovambo. SWAPO forces took up armed struggle against the South Africans by the 1980s. The war drained the South Africans' resources economically and militarily. SWAPO's forces were assisted in the war by Cuban troops sent by Fidel Castro, extending the role of support Cuba had given to African liberation movements. Some 2,500 South African troops died in the conflict by 1981, and the war was costing the south African government a billion dollars a year.

In 1988, South Africa's military effort collapsed and a cease-fire was agreed allowing for the simultaneous withdrawal of Cuban and South African troops. It is clear to see that the territories of Namibia and Angola for certain and perhaps also Mozambique and South Africa itself would not have become independent and African-ruled had Castro's Cuba not given military support to African liberation movements in the region.

In 1989 the UN supervised elections in which SWAPO won 59 percent of the vote. Sam Nujoma was elected as the president of Namibia, which formally gained its independence in March 1990.

Chimurenga: Zimbabwe's War of Liberation

With the fall of the fascist Portuguese government of Caetano in the revolution of 1974, the white government of Rhodesia (currently Zimbabwe) became more isolated as its regional neighbours and former Portuguese colonies, Mozambique and Angola, moved towards liberation and independence. The military liberation movements of Zimbabwe were inspired by the 19th century *Chimurenga* (wars of liberation) of their forerunners against the British. These liberation movements formed by the military wings of Zimbabwe African National Union (ZANU) led by Joshua Nkomo and Zimbabwe African Peoples Union (ZAPU) led by Robert Mugabe were gaining momentum. The two movements had formed a joint military command and also formed the Patriotic Front to put forward their case for black majority rule to the international community.

In 1923 Rhodesia officially became a self governing colony with the British government retaining powers in the colony. The Land apportionment Act of 1930 ensured that whites who made up only 5 percent of the population had 50 percent of the land containing the best, most fertile farmland; whilst the African population making 95 percent of the population were left the remaining 50 percent . The confining of Africans to the poorest, least productive land achieved the desired effect, forcing Africans (who were previously self-sufficient from the land) on to the labour market. At the same time the Industrial Conciliation Act of 1934 made it illegal for Africans to enter skilled employment. Thus Africans were forced to work as virtual slaves for pitiful wages for the white populace on white-owned farms, mines and in factories; instead of for their self subsistence on their own (now confiscated) land.

The main organisation to organise early resistance at the time of this new legislation impoverishing the black population, was the African

National Congress, formed in the year of the Industrial Conciliation Act. This gave way to its successor, the Zimbabwe African People's Union led by Joshua Nkomo. A breakaway faction of ZAPU became ZANU then led by Ndabaningi Sithole. By 1964 both ZAPU and ZANU were banned.

By the end of the 1970s white Rhodesians realised that their declaration of independence from Britain, made unilaterally in 1965, had not led to a more secure future. Besieged by the escalating guerrilla war, Rhodesia closed its borders with Zambia because of the rising level of guerrilla attacks coming from this region. Zambia, then under president Kenneth Kaunda redirected its trade outside of Rhodesia. It stopped sending its copper through Rhodesia and suspended currency dealings. It had by that time relied heavily on the then white-led South African government which began to disengage itself from Rhodesia's defence. By 1977 the head of the Rhodesian army, General Peter Walls, argued for negotiations with ZANU and ZAPU making it clear that the Rhodesian Army could not win the war. The Rhodesian government of Ian Smith then began to seek an internal settlement.

In April 1979 following a white people's referendum accepting the principle of majority rule (but without Patriotic Front participation) elections were held in which Bishop Abel Muzorewa became prime minister of Zimbabwe-Rhodesia. But the leaders of the African international group called the "Frontline States" (consisting of Nyerere of Tanzania, Kaunda of Zambia and Seretse Kama of Botswana) opposed the election, and international recognition of the election was withheld. Days later the UN Security Council declared the election illegal and called for imposition of sanctions, with the US, Britain and France abstaining. By 10 September the latest attempt to bring about a negotiated settlement began, overseen by the British Foreign Minister Lord Carrington, at Lancaster House in London. It was clear to the Thatcher government that a lasting settlement could not be made without the participation of the Patriotic Front (PF). The Lancaster house agreement, moving the country towards democratic elections based on one man one vote, swept Robert Mugabe's Zanu-PF to power with 63 percent of the votes. Joshua Nkomo's ZAPU-PF came second with 24 percent; whilst Bishop Muzorewa, perceived as a lackey for the whites, got less than 5 percent of the votes.

A key aspect of the Lancaster House agreement leading to Zimbabwean independence was the land question. It would come back years later to haunt Mugabe. Mugabe desired the redistribution of land to redress the inequality in land ownership between black and white Zimbabweans. However, the Lancaster House Agreement placed a limitation on how speedily this distribution could take place. Mugabe could only resettle Africans on white land that had been abandoned on a willing-seller, willing-buyer basis. Mugabe had agreed to abide by this agreement, and indeed did so to the letter.

After the first ten years of Zimbabwe's independence, the land question remained central. It represented an unresolved need to redress deep inequalities that still persisted in the Zimbabwean society. Despite the imposed limits, Mugabe had still managed to settle 52,000 African families on former white land. However, the redistribution was predominantly made to the families of ZANU party members.

Immediately after the war of liberation, much of Mugabe's energies were spent trying to resettle veterans fighters from the war. For the first 2 years these veterans were paid a monthly allowance. But they were left to fend for themselves after this period. By 1997, many of these veterans were destitute. Many of them took to the streets to protest at the government's neglect of their grievances. Under increasing pressure, Mugabe promised the veterans benefits, including land for resettlement.

Mugabe instituted a radical policy to resettle Africans on 12 million acres of land over a 5 year period. The move was immediately popular. As the economy continued to worsen and unemployment rose above 50 percent more than 70 percent of the population was living in severe poverty. The situation was ripe for a disgruntled population to reject Mugabe's government at the polls. However, the popularity of Mugabe was revived by the land resettlement programme, which eventually was taken into the hands of vigilante-style groups, principally consisting of destitute veterans of the liberation war, forcefully appropriating the white-occupied land. By 2002, ten white farmers had been killed in the ensuing violence of forceful appropriation.

The western media rage against Mugabe should have worked in the favour of the main opposition party, MDC (Movement for Democratic Change) led by Morgan Tsvingirai. However, MDC was unable to fully capitalise on its advantage due to the mistrust, by many, of its support base, consisting of powerful western politicians and businessmen, perceived to be working in their own interests.

In 2000, it was revealed by the London Observer newspaper that prominent British and American politicians and businessmen with energy and mining interests in Zimbabwe were behind the Zimbabwe Democracy Trust (ZDT), an organisation funded to oppose Mugabe and uphold western economic interests in the region. In April 2000, ZDT organised the visit to London of Morgan Tsvingirai, further tarnishing any credentials MDC might have had as a grassroots representative of opposition to the government. Without grassroots support, MDC was unable to mount any serious opposition to the government internally; although it had the advantage of western media sympathy.

Mugabe's handling of the land question turned out to be a successful political survival strategy. The re-allocation of land from the white farmers to disgruntled veterans assuaged long held feelings of injustice and inequality for Africans both inside and outside the country. Some hailed Mugabe as a hero for claiming back land appropriated generations ago by the whites, and saw him, almost as an African revolutionary. Of course, these were not literally the whites that had taken that land in the first place, and many had acquired the land after independence. But this fact did not diminish the symbolic justice for many of seeing white farmers chased off African land.

Although, there was a temporary respite for Mugabe's government, the country remained in a poor and deteriorating economic state.

The Struggle for South Africa

In South Africa we see similarities with Namibia in the management of forced labour along racial lines; although the system in south Africa is more comprehensively established.

After the years of the Boer wars between the English and Dutch (Boers) a focus was once more placed on the priority of extracting mineral wealth. By 1907 one third of all the gold in the world was being shipped out of Witswatersrand where the gold was found.

South Africa became a Union in 1910 giving political control to whites and creating conditions for the exploitation of black labour which characterised South Africa and its satellites like Namibia and Mozambique in certain ways. A system of labour emerged which channelled a steady stream of black workers from rural areas to urban areas. This was facilitated by the 1913 Land Act which enforced the restriction of Africans to barren and poor reservations, echoing the situation in Namibia, and even the appropriation of land by the English settlers in the Americas where native Americans where also placed in reservations, whilst the whites systematically stole the most fertile land. This forced labour created the growth of South Africa's economy. This formed the basis of racist practice that was to characterise the South African state.

The system left no place for blacks or so called "coloureds", who were not given the vote; whilst only whites could be elected to participate in governing the country. The apartheid system created a situation of psychological divide and rule whereby people who would in other places be considered as black, although of mixed race, were set apart as "coloureds". This marginalisation was emphasized in 1939 when the Natives Land Act was passed setting aside only 8 percent of the land for blacks. So whites held 90 percent of the land even though they only made up 20 percent of the population.

Black and coloured opposition began to come together and in 1923 the South African Native National Congress was formed and later became the African National Congress (ANC).

By 1924 the National Party came to power and Afrikaner nationalism gained a hold on the country. Afrikaner, replaced Dutch as the official language of the Union. The Afrikaner Broederbond, a secret Afrikaner brotherhood which formed in 1918 to protect Afrikaner culture soon became a significant ideological force behind the National Party.

In 1948 successive National Party administrations formulated the system known as apartheid, which totally segregated whites, blacks and coloureds to live separately, prohibiting intermarriage as unlawful. Families were severed with brothers and sisters sometimes being forced to live in separate areas according to race classification. "Coloureds" would be required to take tests including the "pencil test" to see if their hair was tightly curled enough to hold a pencil. Failing the pencil test might mean being sent to the native areas rather than being classified as a "pure" coloured and sent to coloured areas. On this basis families were split. Segregation was enforced by use of the Pass Laws which required black people over the age of 15 to present on request a form of internal passport or pass book, which stipulated where, when and for how long a person was permitted to remain in any province. Not holding a pass book was deemed an offence for which Africans were arrested and sent to rural areas.

In 1950 the ANC youth league influenced by young militants including Nelson Mandela, Robert Sobukwe and Walter Sisulu, called a general strike and in 1952 a campaign in defiance of unjust laws focussing mainly on the pass laws was launched. The authorities responded by arresting over 8000 people and introduced new laws to suppress protest such as the Criminal Laws Amendment Act and the Public Safety Act in 1953. In 1958 a group of Pan Africanists led by Robert Sobukwe broke away from the ANC to form the PAC (Pan Africanist Congress), who launched a defiance campaign against the pass laws in 1960. The ANC followed suit with a similar campaign. These campaigns ended with the sharpville massacres. On 21 March 1960, sixty-nine demonstrators against the pass laws were killed as police opened fire on a crowd of 300 peaceful demonstrators. Both ANC and PAC were banned and moved into exile to take up armed struggle against the apartheid regime.

In 1963, about 20 members of the ANC leadership and the ANC military wing were arrested and put on trial, including Ahmed Kathrada, Govan Mbeki, Nelson Mandela and Walter Sisulu. They were charged with treason and specifically with organising the military wing of the

ANC to overthrow the state. Mandela and Sisulu were the leading defendants of what became known as the Rivonia Treason Trial. Nelson Mandela, a lawyer by training, turned the trial into a defence of black ideals in South Africa, and brought the struggle to world attention. Mandela and his co-defendants were sentenced to life imprisonment on Robben Island.

In the late 1960s the vacuum caused by the movement of the ANC and PAC into exile led to the emergence of the Black Consciousness Movement, initially started by students and with the aim of liberating blacks from the psychological chains of the racism experienced on a daily basis. The Black Consciousness movement was led by Steve Biko, a medical student at the University of Natal Medical School. There he became involved with the National Union of South African Students (NUSAS). But the union, which was dominated by white students, did not represent the needs of black students. Biko resigned to form the South African students Organisation (SASO), which helped to service disadvantaged black communities, providing legal aid and medical treatment. Biko became the president of the Black Peoples Convention which was an umbrella organisation bringing together dozens of other youth, student and workers organsations. After being elected president of the BPC Biko was expelled from medical school. He was then detained and interrogated numerous times in 1975 and again in August 1977 under anti-terrorism laws. He was stripped naked and beaten during interrogation and sustained a head injury which later put him into a coma. Biko died on 12 September 1977 from brain damage. He was 31 years old. Biko's death attracted world wide attention and support grew rapidly internationally for the dismantling of the apartheid regime, whilst the armed struggle to bring down the regime continued.

Finally, in 1990 President F.W. de Clerk announced the unbanning of both the ANC and PAC and the release of Nelson Mandela after 27 years in jail on 2 February 1990, beginning the transition to black majority rule and democracy. Also released were Walter Sisulu and Ahmed Kathrada who had been jailed on Robben Island with Mandela. On 27 April 1994 the South African population voted the ANC into power and Nelson Mandela was inaugurated as South African President.

The South African government made world history in 1995 through an innovative and brave new model in national reconciliation. The apartheid years had been marked by brutal state-led assassination and torture of black and anti-apartheid activists. Rather than merely having a human rights trial of the perpetrators, the Truth and Reconciliation Committee (TRC) was established in 1995 under the chairmanship of Archbishop Desmond Tutu. It was controversial and many had expected it to address the justice for victims of the apartheid era. But TRC was concerned with reconciliation, it was not redressing injustices. The nation was invited to confess its experiences on both sides. More gruesome admissions of torture and assassinations emerged than had been expected.

Throughout De Klerk maintained that he was not responsible for the killings under his government. In 2007, accusations of de Klerk's involvement in assassination plots were made by former government and police officials charged with the attempted murder of Frank Chicane.

Despite universal popularity, Mandela managed to maintain a staunch commitment to his political principles and political allies of his days in the liberation struggle. For example, he refused to bend to US pressure to exclude Fidel Castro of Cuba from the guest dignitaries attending his inauguration in 1994; acknowledging Cuba's invaluable contribution to Africa and African liberation struggles. Mandela himself knew that he and South Africa might not yet have been released from the shackles of apartheid and colonialism had it not been for the sacrifices of Cuba, with the blood of its own citizens in the struggle for the liberation of Southern Africa. In another example of Mandela's loyalty to principles, he created a consternation in Daniel Arap Moi's government circles when on a visit to Kenya he asked to visit the widow of Dedan Kimathi. Mandela discovered that Kimathi's remains still remained buried within prison walls and demanded to know why, causing grave embarrassment for Arap Moi and straining relations between the two leaders. With the installation of Mwai Kibaki as President, the Land and Freedom Party moved from the status of a proscribed "terrorist organisation" to national heroes. On the 50th anniversary of Dedan Kimathi's execution by the British in February 2007, the Kenyan government unveiled a statue in his honour in a central district of Nairobi.

The Struggle for Independence in Kenya and British Colonial Land Policy

The forceful acquisition of land by the British in Kenya represented an important example of the brutal nature of colonial land-grabbing and the manner in which it led to regimes of forced labour or at the very least, the destruction of Africans' means of livelihood from the land, so that they would be forced onto the wages market where their labour would be exploited. The central position of land in the worldview of Kenyan peoples in particular and African people in general characterised the nature of the struggle for land and freedom in Kenya. Jomo Kenyatta himself was well aware of the central importance of land in the culture of the Gikuyu. For the Gikuyu, the struggle for the land was the struggle for the very soul of the Gikuyu people; for Gikuyu culture depended entirely on the land. Apart from supplying them with the material needs to sustain life, it was the means to perpetuate the communion with the ancestral spirits. As do many other African peoples, the Gikuyu consider the earth as their mother and the most sacred thing in their culture. The ferocity of Gikuyu resistance in particular and Kenyan resistance in general has to be seen in this light.

The forcible acquisition by the British of the best quality African land was proof positive that the reasons for colonisation were economic. The example of British colonial land policy in Kenya represents one of the worst cases of forceful dispossession of Africans of their land.

At the time, Kenyans, like traditional Africans generally, had in place their own systems of land use which they had been practising for generations before the arrival of Europeans. These systems included the technique of "shifting cultivation", moving from the cultivation of one plot of land to the next, allowing the soil of the previous plot to regenerate and grow wild vegetation. This cycle of cultivation continues always leaving some land to regenerate. Land left uncultivated to regenerate in this way is called "fallow". The British appropriated all land left as fallow and when the farmers returned back to the fallow plots to cultivate them, they found themselves to be "squatters" on their own land, forced to pay taxes to the British administration.

Land in Kenya was racially segregated from the beginning of the 20th century. Europeans wishing to settle in Kenya were given generous amounts of fertile land. Racial segregation of land, by this time, was made law by the 1915 Crown Lands Ordinance which prohibited Africans and Asians from "the white highlands" - land appropriated by the British colonial administration for its settlers.

Along with the forcible acquisition of land the other fundamental character trait of colonisation was forced labour. The acquisition of large amounts of land for settlers meant there was now a great demand for labour to work on these farmlands. To meet the demand for labour, the colonial administration introduced "hut" and "poll" taxes to force the African agricultural population onto the waged labour market. These policies mainly affected the Masai, the Gikuyu and the Kalenjin peoples of Kenya.

In the 1920s the aspirations for independence were articulated most forcefully by the Kikuyu Central Association, which later became the Kenya Africa Union (KAU), of which Jomo Kenyatta was the representative.

In the years 1947-51 the "forty" age grade built a network of freedom fighters, demanding the return of African land. In Africa it was customary to form age grade societies consisting of people of the same age group. The armed movement of the forty age grade was led by Dedan Kimathi. In 1952 the British flew in troops to crush the rebellion and all the major nationalist Kenyan leaders were detained, including Jomo Kenyatta. In 1954 the British launched Operation Anvil screening the entire Gikuyu population and removing 24,000 Kenyans to detention camps. By 1956 the armed rebellion was defeated and Dedan Kimathi was captured and executed.

The Kenya Africa Union was reformed in 1960. Kenyatta was released in 1961 and won elections in that year. Kenya gained its independence in 1963. Despite rising to power by means of advantage gained through the armed struggle of the Land and Freedom Movement led by Kimathi, Kenyatta later renounced Kimathi and the movement as terrorists. The Land and Freedom movement became a proscribed organisation.

By 2007 a previous visit of Nelson Mandela to see Dedan Kimathi's widow restored the contribution of Kimathi to the Kenyan liberation struggle to the national consciousness. A statue unveiled in Central Nairobi in February 2007 helped revive Kimathi's heroic national status

Bibliography

Chapter Fifteen - African Struggles for Liberation II

Arnold, G., *Africa – A modern History*, Atlantic Books, London, 2005.
Biko, S., *I Write What I like*, A. Stubbs (ed.), Heinemann, London, 1978.
Cabral, A., *Return to the Source: Selected Speeches..*, Monthly review Press, New York & London, 1973.
Davidson, B., *Modern Africa – A Social and political History* (2nd ed.), Longman, New york, 1983.
Freund, Bill, The *making of Contemporary Africa: The Development of African Society since 1800*, Macmillan, London, 1984.
Fryer, P., *Staying Power: The History of Black people in Britain*, Pluto Press, London, 1984.
Gailey, H., *History of Africa – from 1800 to present, Vol.II*, Krieger Publishing Co., New York, 1971.
Grogg., P., *Cuba-Africa: Decades of assistance and Cooperation*,
Inter Press service, 2004 http://www.aegis.com/news/ips/2004/IP040703.html).
Mattera, D., *Gone with the Twilight – A Story of Sophiatown*, Zed Books, London, 1987.
Meredith, M., *The State of Africa – A history of Fifty years of Independence*, free Press, London, 2005.
New African Yearbook 1981-2, IC Magazines, 1982.
Kabukuru, W., *From 'terrorist' to national hero*, New African, March 2007.
Nkrumah, K., *Towards Colonial Freedom*, Panaf, London, 1973.

Sawyer, P. and M. Bright, *British cash behind bid to combat Mugabe*, Observer, May 21, 2000.

Thomson, D., *Europe Since Napoleon*, Pelican Books, 1966.

Ajayi, B., *Patrick Wilmot and related National Issues*, Nigeria World, 16 June, 2005.

Wilmot, P., *Reflections on Nigerian Leadership: Murtala Mohammed and Southern Africa*, Africa Update Newsletter, Vol. Xiii, Issue 4, Fall 2006.

Chapter Sixteen

Transitions in the Horn of Africa

The Rise and Fall of the Somali Democratic Republic

To consider the state of Somalia at the start of the 21st century, we go back to the late 1940s. The British introduced forces of instability that would later threaten to destroy Somalia, when they decided to give the Ogaden, a land inhabited by Somali pastoralists to Ethiopia.

During World War II Italy was the colonial administrator of Somalia, which it had acquired as part of an agreement with Ethiopia. However, the Italian dictator, Mussolini, had to look after things on the home front so that the British were able to stage an easy re-conquest of Somalia by 1941.The first significant political party in Somalia was the Somali Youth league (SYL).

In 1948 the British gave the Ogaden part of Somalia to Ethiopia. The British held the territory till 1949, when it was decided by the victorious allied forces to give trusteeship of the territory to Italy for 10 years. The SYL opposed the plan to give Italy trusteeship and called for immediate independence. But Italian trusteeship was granted and Somalia did not become independent until 1959.

Things seemed to begin well as the Somali populace were politically aware and involved. But two issues loomed in the background of Somali politics that would later threaten the stability of the newly independent nation: 1) the emerging north south divide, 2) The disputed territory of the Ogaden region, which had been given to Ethiopia by the British in 1948. Internal conflicts in Somalia spilled out into external aggression towards Kenya and Ethiopia on account respectively of the disputed Northern Kenya which some believed was part of a greater Somalia and the Ogaden region.

Super-power east-west politics had an early role in the dynamics of Somali politics, because of Somalia's geographically strategic position governing routes of navigation in the Atlantic and Indian Oceans. Somali political parties soon allied with the communist block countries (such as Soviet Union and China). Somali forces were trained by the Russians in the mid 1960s. But later, in the late 1970s, Somalia developed relations with the United States. As Ethiopia was Somalia's bitter rival, relations between Somalia and the US cooled when the US began giving military aid to Ethiopia.

As in so many cases after independence, the political life of Somalia was blighted by the presence of corruption and inefficiency in government. The slide towards a military take over began when in 1969 a body guard assassinated President Abdirashid Ali Sharmarke whilst the prime minister was out of the country. A group of army officers monitored the crisis situation as the prime minister returned only to appoint a successor along ethnic lines. This made the likelihood of political crisis real for the observing military and they were given the excuse to step in with a peaceful overthrow of the civilian administration. The military junta were headed by a supreme military council that appointed Mohammed Siad Barre as the president and they pledged to rid the country of "tribalism, nepotism, corruption and misrule." The country was renamed the Somali Democratic Republic and the incoming regime pledged to live peacefully with its neighbours Kenya and Ethiopia without giving up the nation's claim to the disputed territories of Ogaden and northern Kenya.

Barre's regime remained in power for over twenty years with his overthrow coming in 1991. Barre proclaimed Somali Democratic Republic to be a socialist state in his first year in power. Initially the country's supreme military council gave priority to a serious programme aimed at economic and social development. Somali was made the official written language and attempts were made to increase the literacy of the Somali populace. A concerted effort was made to "de-tribalise" Somalis as this was seen as the great stumbling block to progress in nation building.

The turning point for the Barre regime was perhaps the 1977-1978 war with Ethiopia over the Ogaden region. The loss of the war produced a low national morale and greater opposition to Barre's rule began to emerge. This led to intensified political repression.

Barre had a close relationship with the US who replaced Soviet Union as main user of naval facilities at Berbera. As a result of this relationship Barre received some military aid from the US. By 1982 Barre was under international criticism for the detention of his political opponents. Political stability was weakened by raids of Somali dissidents into Somalia with the help of the Ethiopian military. Barre's positioned was also weakened by his often brutal and genocidal persecution of certain powerful clan-families: the Majerteen, the Isaaq and the Hawiye who occupied the strategic centre of the country. The latter led to Barre's downfall. In short, Barre created enemies who were becoming united and determined to see his overthrow. His brutal methods or those of his forces included the destruction of water supplies condemning people to death by thirst, rape and the destruction of grazing grounds and livestock.

The crunch came in 1990 when Barre sentenced to death 46 members of Manifesto Group who demanded human rights and called for elections. Public pressure forced Barre to drop the penalties. Barre retreated to his

147

bunker near the airport to save his skin. In May 1991 the northern part of the country declared itself independent as Somaliland but had not been recognised by the UN.

UN forces were sent in to alleviate famine conditions in the south of the country. Unusually this was led by US troops. Critics pointed out that before the crisis the Barre regime had granted nearly two thirds of the country's territory as oil concessions to American oil companies, Conoco, Amoco, Chevron, and Phillips.

Many Somalis opposed the foreign presence especially the presence of US troops and 24 UN peacekeepers and 19 US soldiers were killed in gun battles with local gunmen in Mogadishu. The UN withdrew in 1995.

The secession of the North was followed by the secessions of Puntland and the Rahanweyn resistance army, which were temporary with the proviso that they would re-join any Somali reconciliation to form a unified Somali central government. At the turn of the century, the country was in a situation of anarchy, with no functioning government, but with commerce thriving, particularly in the area of telecommunications.

Twentieth Century Ethiopia and Eritrea

The Abyssinians, as the descendents of the Axumites were known, created a civilization that had writing and was founded on a unique African form of Christianity. The line of the Emperor of the kingdom reputedly dates back to the love affair between King Solomon and the Queen of Sheba. The son born of their union was named Menelik. As heir to his mother's throne, he was to be the first emperor of the so called Solomonid bloodline.

At some point in the history of Ethiopia, the Solomonid line of descent was broken. However, much later, Emperor Tewodoros was to claim descent from the Solomonid line and re-introduce it in Ethiopian royal history. In 1896, the Ethiopian Emperor, Menelik II signed a treaty with the Italians giving them the regions covering modern Eritrea and Tigray. The Italians proclaimed to the European powers that the treaty had given them control over all of Ethiopia. The Ethiopians' protest that this was not the treaty they signed was ignored. The matter was settled on the battlefield when the Italians were defeated at the battle of Adowa in 1896. The independence of Ethiopia was then acknowledged.

When Menelik died his grandson Lij Iyassu succeeded to the throne of the emperor. Iyassu had come to admire the religion of Islam. But his ties to the Islamic faith displeased the Christian nobility, who, in 1916, were powerful enough to have him deposed. Menelik's daughter, Zaudita was then made the empress. On her death, her cousin Ras Tafari Makonnen, was made successor to the throne. He took the throne name of Haile Selassie on being crowned Emperor of Ethiopia. In 1935 the Italians invaded Ethiopia and Selassie was forced into exile in Britain. His pleas for the League of Nations to intervene had not been heeded, but five years later the Italians were defeated again by the Ethiopian forces, and Selassie was returned to his throne.

The crowning of Haile Selassie of Ethiopia had uncanny timing and was accompanied by an exceptional set of circumstances with biblical echoes. Dr Saba Saakana recalls the passages in the book of revelation which were interpreted as confirming Haile Selassie's divinity and ordained place on the throne of Ethiopia: "Revelation 19:19: And I saw the beast and the kings of the earth and their armies, gathered together to make war against him that sat on the horse, and against his army." Saakana notes that: "These signs were seen literally...to invest the power of divinity in Selassie I."

Indeed, the Rastafarian belief in the divinity of Haile Selassie I is a modern instance of the age old African tradition of divine kingship. It is also an instance of what Boahen and others acknowledge as "ethiopianism" where religious belief is used to articulate African people's aspirations for liberation from colonial shackles. For the Rastafarians, Selassie was indeed seen as a liberator. Saakana, however, paints a pragmatic view of the modern attitudes of young Rastafarians, who "...accept the cultural projection of Rastafarians", but "...refuse to acknowledge that Selassie is God".

Initially, Selassie promoted modernizaton of Ethiopia, establishing a University in Addis Ababa in 1950. Selassie worked with other African leaders of the time to build the Organisation of African Unity (OAU). But his rule stagnated and civil unrest set in.

A point of contention for Selassie was what to do about the region of Eritrea. Ethiopia was keen to lay claim to Eritrea because it gave access to the sea via the port of Massawa; otherwise Ethiopia would be a land-locked country. Selassie laid claim to Eritrea on the grounds that parts of it had been part of the old Ethiopian empire. The Eritreans, numbering about 3 million, were themselves divided over whether their province should become an independent state or remain a province of Ethiopia. The division of opinion was largely along religious lines; with Eritreans being split virtually 50/50 between its Muslim and Christian populations. Whereas the supporters of a continued union with Ethiopia were primarily Christians, the supporters of independence were primarily Muslims. The compromise of the UN was for Eritrea to become a federation of Ethiopia, with Ethiopia remaining in control of its defence, foreign affairs, finance, commerce and its ports. Eritrea retained freedom of religious worship, its own languages (Tigrinya and Arabic) and flag.

However, from the outset Selassie saw the federation of Eritrea as no more than a step towards total unification with Ethiopia. Any autonomy the Eritreans initially had was steadily eroded with its free press, trade unions and political rights dismantled. Then in 1958 its flag was abolished. In 1959 the laws of Ethiopia were extended to Eritrea and its languages, Tigrinya and Arabic were replaced by Amharic, the Ethiopian state language. In 1962, through Ethiopian influence on Christian Eritrean politicians in favour of union, the Eritrean assembly voted in favour of Eritrea's dissolution. Thereafter Eritrea became merely another part of the Ethiopian empire. The previously observed principle of even handed treatment of Eritrea's half Christian and half Muslim population was abandoned. Eventually, even Eritrea's Christian population became opposed to rule by Ethiopia and by the 1970s a movement had been established for the secession of Eritrea from Ethiopia. In December 1970, Selassie declared a state of emergency throughout the Eritrean province. The Eritrean movement for secession was led by the EPLF (Eritrean People's Liberation Front) and the ELF (Eritrean Liberation Front) which was supported by the Arab states, Saudi Arabia and Yemen and also Sudan.

In 1974 Selassie was deposed and killed in a military coup in which Lt. Col. Mengistu Haile Mariam became the new head of state. Mengistu's rule was managed through a military committee known as the "Derg". The Derg were ruthless and responsible for many deaths of the regime's opponents.

In 1977 Somali forces who had for ages considered the Ogaden to be part of Somalia, attacked Ethiopia, sensing that the country was weak and in disarray. A one year war between the two states broke out and Somalia was defeated, so that the Ogaden remained firmly in the control of the Ethiopians.

Mengistu eventually traded his military khaki for the suit and became civilian president of the country in 1987. However, drought and famine were to make the regime's position weak and insurrections in the northern regions of Tigray and Eritrea served to weaken the regime still further. The Mengistu revolution of 1974 had been an opportunity for Eritrea to gain independence; but retention of the port of Massawa was still seen as strategically important for Ethiopia in avoiding its land-locked status, and Mengistu's army, the Derg, instead intensified the Ethiopian war against Eritrea. In the meantime, in the contest between the rival ELF and EPLF movements, EPLF gained ascendancy.

Mengistu's decision to continue the war against Eritrea turned out to be a fatal mistake. The continued major assault on the Eritrean people including the bombing of civilians by air strikes only galvanised support for the secessionist movement. The Derg's prevention of access to food and medical aid from the Red Cross and other agencies hardened the people's resolve still further. The war waged by Ethiopia became unwinnable. By 1988 following a series of devastating losses, the Ethiopian army was demoralised. By 1989 the Tigray Peoples liberation army (TPLF) joined with other groups including EPLF in opposing the Mengistu regime to form EPRDF (Ethiopian People's Revolutionary Democratic Front). In 1991 the EPRDF forces succeeded in ousting Mengistu who went into exile in Zimbabwe. In 1991, the EPRDF and other groups made up a transitional government that oversaw a transition to civilian rule. Meles Zenawi was elected Prime minister and Negasso Gidada was elected President. Eritrea, meanwhile, gained its independence in 1993 ending 30 years of its struggle for independence.

Africans versus "Arabs": North-South Tensions in the Sudan

At a certain point in the history of modern Sudan, it was oil that fuelled the conflict between the Arab north and the African south. Since independence the largely Muslim and Arab north and the largely Christian (and traditional) and African south were divided by ethnic and religious tensions.

It could be said that all Sudanese are in fact Africans, only that some northerners claimed to have Arab genes that could be traced back to several generations, which some patently assumed made them superior to their southern Sudanese countrymen. There was a deadly absurdity about the "Arab" versus African violence. Says Professor Ali Mazrui: " There is first the very phenomenon of racial mixture and inter-marriage in the northern parts of the Sudan, coupled with the fact that a large proportion of Arab Sudanese are in fact Arabized negroes, rather than ethnically semitic. For many of them the Arabness is a cultural acquisition, rather than a racial heredity".

The fault lines for the north-south divide had been created before the time of independence when the senior posts in government were dominated by northerners. The army took control in 1958 and General Ibrahim Abboud moved to promote Islam and the use of Arabic language and built Muslim schools and mosques in the south, which followed mainly Christianity and traditional African religion. This led the African population of the south into organised resistance, represented by various groups but most popularly by the SPLA (Sudan People's Liberation Army) led by John Garang. General Abboud stepped down in 1964 and the northern politicians succeeding him continued the same Islamist policies towards the south.

Then in 1969 there was some relief for the south when the government was overthrown in a military coup staged by Gaafar Nimeiri supported by a committee named the National Revolutionary Council. His reason for overthrow of the government was chiefly its inability to tackle the southern problem and Nimeiri's approach to the problem was held up by both southerners and northerners as his government's most important achievement. Nimeiri agreed to allow the south a measure of local autonomy and a new constitution in 1973 established Sudan as a secular state, allowing southerners freedom from the yoke of previous government's attempts to impose Islam on the Christian and traditional African southerners.

However, Nimeiri was to be the architect of his own downfall. In order to increase his support base and appeal in the north of the country Nimeiri backtracked on his former commitment to a secular Sudanese state. To increase his support in certain quarters, Nimeiri recruited the Islamists Sadik Al-Mahdi and Hassan Al-Turabi, who strongly influenced the further Islamisation of Nimeiri's programme and political outlook. In 1983 Nimeiri declared an Islamic revolution in Sudan. The country then became governed by Sharia (Islamic law). This was imposed on all Sudanese, including Muslim, Christian and traditional African practitioners. Nimeiri's abandonment of his initial principles was a sign of his gradual loss of control of the country to Islamist politicians. His demise was completed when he also lost control of the economy, which was crippled by striking workers including doctors, nurses and civil servants. He was overthrown in 1985.

Sadiq Al-Mahdi became the prime minister, but he was soon deposed after victories by the southern rebels forced him into talks with the SPLA leader John Garang. Those Islamic radical politicians, who were opposed to a secular state, would not tolerate an agreement with the SPLA.

This was not before the SPLA attacks provoked the Khartoum government of Al-Mahdi to take revenge. Al-Mahdi encouraged armed Baggara Arab militias to plunder and attack the Nuer and Dinka villages, killing men, women and children or abducting them and taking them to the north to be traded or kept as slaves. In retaliation for an SPLA attack on a Rizayqat militia group, the survivors attacked 1000 Dinka men women and children sheltering in six railway carriages. The carriages were set alight and the men, women and children burnt to death. Those that tried to escape were stabbed or shot.

The coup of 1989 put Sudan under a new fundamentalist Islamist regime. The coup leader, general Omar Al-Bashir declared that Sudan would never again be a secular state.

Apparently, the racial superiority complex of the northern Sudanese had resulted in a programme of genocide by the Sudanese government-supported Janjiweed militia against the southern ethnic groups. But the root of this conflict was not merely a naïve race hate, but also due to the fact that the oil producing wealth of the nation lay in the southern part of Sudan.

Oil was discovered in the south of Sudan in 1978 and the American company Chevron began its oil exploration only to suspend operations in 1984 due to attacks by southern rebels. In 1992 the northern "Arab" dominated government persuaded Chevron to sell its 42 million acre concession. The area was then subdivided into smaller blocks and sold to other countries including those from China and the Far East. Oil became more crucial than ever to the Islamic government of Omâr Al-Bashir and unluckily for southern groups the oil lay in their territory, occupied mainly by Nuer and Dinka ethnic groups. The government undertook a campaign of ethnic cleansing, pushing the southern ethnic groups out to prevent rebel attacks from disrupting oil production.

Thus oil lay at the heart of much of the genocide by the "Arab" militia, spurred on by the warping of Islamic teachings in the interest of the Islamist government's agenda, proclaiming that Islam granted the "freedom of killing" and portraying the whole conflict between Arab north and African south as an Islamic Jihad. The government bombed villages and relief centres in air raids, whilst their militias massacred innocent civilians and abducted women and children into slavery. Much of the population were uprooted from their homes and faced with mass starvation, having to rely on relief supplies; although these were often cut off by the militias. Their refugee camps, including those of Darfur in later years, were under the watch of the government supported militias intent on further genocide, but held off only by very few African Union peacekeeping troops.

In the mid-1990s the threat of Sudan spreading its jihad through the region had alarmed neighbouring African countries. Events led Uganda to support the SPLA rebels against the Khartoum government. The Khartoum government in response supported the brutal messianic led Lords Resistance Army, whose leader Joseph Kony claimed to have a divine mission to create God's kingdom on earth, based on the Ten Commandments. But instead Kony's 'divine kingdom' proved to be a hell on earth with children and women mercilessly murdered and mutilated, raped and abducted into becoming child soldiers and slaves. Ironically, Kony's forces shared a similar religious fervour with the jihadist Janjiweed.

At one point Uganda's Museveni, a pan-Africanist, who had hosted the 7th pan- African congress in Kampala in 1994, declared that the conflict was colonial and that on this basis other member states of the African Union should intervene.

In 2007, the African Sudanese population in Darfur (predominantly Muslims) remained under grave threat of genocide from the Janjiweed, with many fleeing into neighbouring Chad, pursued by Janjiweed militia even into Chadian territory and spreading the conflict regionally, as neighbouring governments such as Museveni's had feared years earlier. By this date over 200,000 had been killed in the conflict which began in 2003 and over 2.5 million had been displaced from their homes.

Although lacking in resources, the Darfur region could not be considered as affected by troubles unrelated to earlier conflict involving the Janjiweed in the oil-rich southern territories. Darfur, had its own local history of tensions between the Baggara (who claim Arab descent) who are predominantly cattle herders and the surrounding African populations such as the Fur, Massalit, Zaghawa, Daju and Berti who are farmers, with scarcity of useable land and water being objects of contention for the "Arab" and African groups. The conflict ensued in 2003 when African groups rose up to resist their economic marginalisation in the region. The Baggara and Rizayqat militia groups, who were already carrying out atrocities against the Dinka and Nuer in the South of Sudan then turned on their rebelling northern neighbours in Darfur.

Despite the jihadist religious ideology of the Arab militias, the conflict is essentially ethnic, with the Africans of the Darfur region being predominantly Muslims.

The African Union forces which numbered only 7,000 and were poorly equipped were largely ineffective in protecting the Darfur civilians. In December 2006, African Union forces killed 3 civilians who were protesting at the AU troops' failure to protect them when 30 of their relatives were murdered by Janjiweed militia.

Bibliography
Chapter Sixteen - Transitions in the Horn of Africa
AL-JAZEERA, *AU troops kill 3 in Darfur*, Al-Jajeera.net, 11 Dec. 2006.
Arnold, G., *Africa – A modern History*, Atlantic Books, London, 2005.
Collins, R.O., *Disaster in Darfur: Historical Overview*, in S. Totten & E. Markusen (ed.), Genocide in Darfur – Investigating the Atrocities in the Sudan, Taylor & Francis, New York, 2006.
Clarke, S. (Saba Saakana), *Jah Music: Evolution of the popular Jamiacan Song*, Heinemann, London, 1980.
Cliffe, L. and B. Davidson (ed.), *The long Struggle of Eritrea for Independence and Constructive Peace*, Spokesman, Nottingham, 1988.
Mazrui, A., *the Multiple Marginality of the Sudan* in Sudan in Africa, editor Yusuf Fadl Hasan, Khartoum University Press, 1985.
Meredith, M., *The State of Africa – A history of Fifty years of Independence*, free Press, London, 2005.
New African Yearbook 1981-2, IC Magazines, 1982.
Post, K., *Ethiopianism in Jamaica: 1930-38* in Allen, C and R.W. Johnson (ed.) African Perspectives, University Press, Cambridge, 1970.

Chapter Seventeen

The Lords of War

Kabila and the Rwanda Connection

In the aftermath of the 1994 Rwanda genocide that claimed the lives of near to a million Rwandans, many Hutu fled to neighbouring Zaire, still under the control of the ailing President Mobutu. The Hutu refugee camps quickly became a meeting point for Hutu militia who had been involved in the massacres. By 1996, the Hutu militia together with Mobutu's Zairean forces were reported to be persecuting Zaire's Tutsi population, known as the *Banyamulenge*. In a convenient collaboration, the forces of Laurent Kabila, that had been fighting for the overthrow of Mobutu since the early 1960s, joined with the rebels of the *Banyamulenge* to form the "Alliance of Democratic Forces for the Liberation of Congo-Zaire". Kabila's forces were also supported by the newly installed, mainly Tutsi, government of Rwanda, led by the Rwanda Patriotic Front (RPF) under the leadership of Paul Kagame. The main interest for the RPF in supporting Kabila was not only the support of Zaire's ethnic Tutsis, but also it availed them of an opportunity to enter Zaire to flush out those escaping Hutu militia responsible for the 1994 genocide.

Kabila's forces launched an assault on Mobutu's Zaire government and within 7 months took control of over half the country. Kabila's forces pushed all the way to the capital, Kinshasha, ousting Mobutu's regime and installing Kabila as president of a renamed Democratic Republic of Congo in 1997. This name distinguished it from Congo, its northern neighbour, which is much smaller in size and was formerly a French colonial territory.

Later a rift emerged between Kabila and his former allies of the Rwandan Patriotic Front, when Rwandan forces were ordered to leave Democratic Republic of Congo (DRC). The Rwandans remained fearful of the Hutu militia who fled and were still resident in DRC and large areas of the DRC remained in the grip of a civil war, into the 21st century.

At the source of the continued instability in the Congo was the ongoing plunder of the country's valuable raw materials which had fuelled the actions of rebel groups. The collapse of the Congo state precipitated a "free for all" with an unprecedented case of even neighbouring African states joining in the scramble and, in cases, looting of the Congo's national resources in diamonds, gold and other precious metals including Coltan, used in mobile phones. According to Renton and co-authors, Angola, Zimbabwe and Namibia supplied troops to protect Kabila's government; but all protection came with the hope of repayment in diamonds. "By 2000 the Zimbabweans had secured the right to exploit two of the country's principle diamond areas …as exclusive owners for 25 years. Namibia and Angola also insisted that its interventions be rewarded with vital diamond concessions". In the case of Rwanda and Uganda we see a period of naked theft in the Congo. In 1997 gold was Uganda's largest export earner, which as Renton and co-authors note is extraordinary for a country that does not have gold reserves. In the instance of Rwanda, Renton and co note that "In regions occupied by the Rwandan army, local communities were also forced into mining. …Walikale people … were required to mine coltan".

There became an increased interest in the mineral coltan by the late 1990s. Indeed, it was celebrated as a wonder metal and US multinationals were among the most interested parties. The often quoted position that the US has no more strategic interest in Africa became totally false; if by strategic interest we do not exclude economic ones. We may bear witness to large quantities of cobalt and coltan from the Congo, required for the construction, for example, of the International Space Station. Renton and co-authors remind us that the coltan and diamond trades have played a large role in funding war in the region. "By the end of the 1990s, the DRC was the fourth largest producer of diamonds in the world…, diamonds were flowing through neighbouring countries at an astonishing rate."

The Rwanda Genocide of 1994

The recent wars in the Congo and the genocide in which close to a million Rwandans died in 1994, share a common backdrop of increasing instability in central Africa, where arms are proliferating to create a mushrooming of many militias that are bringing a deadly new chaos and brutality to the region. In Uganda, for instance, the Lords Resistance Army was abducting children into its armed forces and many militias were using the rape of civilians as a weapon in their wars. Even in the DRC, despite the end of two wars, the chaos and the conflict continued as many of the militia - for instance, the militias in the Congolese Katanga region – refused to be disarmed.

The Rwanda crisis was the end of the line of a long history of conflict between Hutu and Tutsi in Rwanda and in neighbouring African countries. Colonialism had served only to worsen the bitter rivalries as both the Germans (1890-1916) and the Belgians (1916-1962) created a monopoly on education and high profile government jobs for the Tutsis. This helped to keep the Hutu in a subservient position.

The resentment that had been growing over a long while led to revenge attacks on Tutsis in 1959, when there were riots and over 20,000 Tutsis were killed. This led to an exodus of Tutsis to neighbouring Burundi (which had its own history of Tutsi-Hutu conflict), Tanzania and Uganda. The lead up to the Hutu uprising began when in July 1959 the death of the traditional ruler, the Mwami of Matara II led to the seizure of power by a Tutsi clan that plotted to eliminate the Hutu leaders. The new Mwami fled the country.

The Belgian colonial government introduced political concessions, bringing forward the independence of the colony. In 1960, the election results brought in a provisional government with Joseph Habyarimana as President, whilst Gregoire Kayibanda was Prime Minister. In 1961 a UN supervised referendum brought the Hutu majority party, the Parmehutu into power. Kayibanda became the country's first President in 1962 and remained until his overthrow in 1973. In the interim, the Tutsi formed guerrillas who staged military raids, provoking reprisals and leading to the massacre of many more Tutsis, driving more into exile into neighbouring countries.

Kayibanda was ousted in a military coup led by Hutu General, Juvenal Habyarimana, in July 1973. This ended a period of instability in which disturbances occurred in various parts of the country. The Parmehutu was replaced by the Revolutionary Movement for National Development (MRND), which was controlled by the military. The new arrangement was made legal by elections held in 1978.

Deterioration of the Rwandan economy led to the loss of popularity of Juvenal Habyarimana's government. Meanwhile, Tutsi refugees in neighbouring Rwanda supported by moderate Hutus formed the Rwanda Patriotic Front (RPF) with the aim of overthrowing Habyarimana, to enable their return to their homeland. Under pressure Habyarimana exploited the ethnic tensions created by the conflict in order to bring the moderate Hutus back to his support. Tutsis inside Rwanda were accused of assisting the RPF rebels.

Then in April 1994, President Habyarimana's plane mysteriously crashed killing Habyarimana and the President of Burundi who was also on board. The mainly Tutsi RPF were accused of shooting down the plane and a campaign of blame and vengeance was immediately set into motion by President Habyarimana's guards. Leaders of the political opposition, including Tutsis and moderate Hutus, were hunted down and murdered. The slaughter spread as Hutu military officials, politicians and businessmen organised militias, which recruited ordinary Hutu civilians, sometimes forcing them to murder their Tutsi neighbours and also enticing them with money and the promise that they would gain the land of Tutsis they killed. The enticements to violence spread more quickly, thanks to radio propaganda. Within 100 days over 800,000 Rwandans were massacred. It was indeed a genocide, although the United States of America and western governments refused to term it as such as this would then have required them to take action. On the death of ten of its personnel, the UN withdrew and the world watched passively as the genocide unfolded.

After the death of Habyarimana, the RPF continued its war against Habyarimana's government forces. In July 1994, the rebel RPF captured the capital, Kigali, and declared an end to the war. The victory of the RPF prompted the exodus of Hutu refugees into neighbouring Zaire (now Democratic republic of Congo - DRC). Many of these refugees have since been implicated in the massacres of Tutsis after the death of Habyarimana.

UN troops and aid workers thereafter arrived in Rwanda to restore order and meet basic needs. In a gesture of reconciliation, the RPF installed a Hutu President, Pasteur Bizimungu, and the majority of cabinet posts went to RPF members.

In the search for justice in the aftermath of the genocide, 500 people have been sentenced to death for taking part in the genocide, while 100,000 have been jailed. Despite this, many of the ringleaders of the killings remain at large, escaping to neighbouring countries and even to Europe were some alleged ringleaders are known to have claimed asylum. The effort to bring those responsible to justice continues.

Charles Taylor and the Diamond Sponsored Conflicts of the Sierra Leone-Liberia Region

In Sierra Leone a generation of childhood has been lost to the bloody greed of warlords and international companies for its diamond wealth. In 1991 Charles Taylor started a war when he caused fighting through his attempts to control the diamond field of south Sierra Leone, near the Liberian border. Over a period of 11 years 50,000 people died and 20,000 were left mutilated. Three quarters of the population had been displaced.

Charles Taylor, who has brought a new type of gangsterism to Africa's politics, did well out of the war in Sierra Leone. The country's diamonds during the war years were smuggled out through Liberia and handled by traders acting on Charles Taylor's behalf. Monrovia acted as a major centre for laundering diamonds from Angola. Liberian exports during the 1990s ranged from 300 million dollars a year to 450 million dollars a year. Taylor represents a new and worrying trend in African conflicts and regime over-throw which Arnold aptly describes. For Arnold these conflicts "had more to do with power hungry warlords seeking control than any more ideological question of a ruling philosophy on behalf of the people as a whole".

Taylor supported Guinea rebels to overthrow President Lansana Conte by providing bases in Liberia. But Conte retaliated by providing bases for LURD (Liberians United for Reconciliation and Democracy).

Taylor was singled out by western governments for an arms embargo. This was not explicable in comparison to the actions of the western governments in Rwanda, and other examples where a government clearly implicated in crimes against humanity were nevertheless not subject to any arms embargo. A UN tribunal indicted Taylor for war crimes in Sierra Leone. The Taylor affair has illustrated the power that western governments do have, when they choose to prevent massive loss of African life due to conflict in Africa. Western governments imposed an arms embargo and trade sanctions on Charles Taylor's Liberian government and a travel ban on its officials. An article in the New African attempts to explain the western double standard in regard to Taylor. Says Baffour Ankomah in the May 2006 issue of New African: *"In 2002, Taylor...committed political suicide by refusing to allow the Americans to exploit Liberia's offshore oil on terms very disadvantageous to Liberia. Instead he wanted the Chinese who have excellent offshore technology to do the job on better terms for Liberia. ...if he had allowed the Americans to exploit the oil, he would still be in power today, and the current circus about war crimes would not have arisen in the first place."*

As Ankomah notes further on in his article: if the west had the power to act so decisively to stop Taylor in Sierra Leone then why not in other parts of Africa? In Sierra Leone the embargo on the diamond trade that was funding Taylor's government was effective in cutting off the finances of the RUF rebels who were supported by Taylor's government and the cause of the maiming and butchery of helpless civilians and recruitment of child soldiers. At least that was the effect until, according to Guy Arnold, a British airline transported the lethal goods of a Gibraltar based arms dealer to the RUF rebels in 2000.

After attacks by CIA trained guerrillas based in neighbouring Guinea (after refusal of Taylor to allow America to exploit its offshore oil), Taylor agreed to stand down in a deal that granted him immunity from prosecution for war crimes. This was after some 200,000 Liberians had died in the civil war of the past decade.

It is clear that Charles Taylor's diamond-sponsored gangsterism helped precipitate the collapse of Sierra Leone. After Taylor's NPFL (National Patriotic Front of Liberia) caused fighting in their bid to take control of southern Sierra Leone diamonds in 1991, the state of Sierra Leone was destabilised by his support of the Sierra Leone rebel RUF (Revolutionary

United Front). A coup in Sierra Leone on 20 April 1992 removed President Joseph Momoh and brought Captain Valentine Strasser to power. Strasser's new regime did not prevent the slide of the country towards civil conflict. Strasser was ousted in another coup in 1996, then elections were held in which Ahmed Tejan Kabbah of the Sierra Leone People's Party was elected President, and following negotiations with RUF leader Foday Sankoh, achieved a temporary peace. A third coup in the 1990s decade was mounted by Johnny Paul Koroma. ECOMOG (Economic Community of West African States Monitoring Group) then sent a peacekeeping mission, led by Nigerian troops to restore order. In February 1998, ECOMOG forces, principally Nigerian, fought their way to the centre of the capital, Freetown, to dislodge the illegal military regime of Koroma, and Kabbah was restored to power. Rebels of the government fled to neighbouring Liberia, where a strife torn Sierra Leone was seen as an opportunity for continued Liberian exploitation of the southern Sierra Leone diamonds. These rebels joined the ranks of the Liberian-supported RUF, which became reorganised and strengthened by hundreds of mercenaries from the Ukraine, who were attracted by the lure of Sierra Leone's diamond riches. The mercenaries were not alone in their greed. It is well known that even the Nigerian peacekeeping forces under ECOMOG (despite the good will of many and their overall positive effect in restoring Kabbah's elected government) were not all necessarily attracted by the need for restoration of justice as much as the promised diamond wealth of southern Sierra Leone. A huge assault on Freetown was undertaken by RUF rebels. They were pushed back by ECOMOG forces, but the attack resulted in the loss of 3000 civilian lives as well as the massive destruction of the capital. In the desperate situation, Kabbah was persuaded by both the Nigerian and British governments to restart negotiations with the rebel RUF forces, whose brutal campaign of mutilation of helpless civilians had received worldwide attention. A peace accord between Kabbah's government and the rebels collapsed when the RUF kidnapped 500 UN troops stationed as peacekeepers. Full scale fighting between the rebels and the Sierra Leone army resumed. The peace accord had provided for the freedom of the rebel leader Foday Sankoh and his installation as vice-President. Then, an extraordinary thing happened. Upon all the horrendous suffering of African people under the yoke of bad leadership, there occurred one of the rare and notable instances of real people power exercised in Africa. On 8 May 2000, 10,000 ordinary Sierra Leoneans took to the streets of Freetown and marched towards the house of Foday Sankoh, who was seen as responsible for the continued atrocities of RUF members against the civilian populace. The police fired on the crowd and Sankoh escaped. The inability of the UN troops to control the situation led to the deployment of

1000 British troops. Sankoh was captured on May 17th after a series of defeats for the rebels. Kabbah then removed Sankoh's immunity from prosecution in order for him to stand trial. The rebel RUF still retained control of the southern diamond producing zone and thus the financial means to continue their war. Then by 18 May 2001 the RUF and pro-government militias signed an agreement to end hostilities. By September 2001, Kofi Annan announced that 16,000 fighters had been disarmed; whilst 9,000 remained to be disarmed. In January 2002 the civil war was declared to be over by President Kabbah. A war crimes court was established in Sierra Leone in May 2002, and Kabbah was easily re-elected, beating Ernest Koroma of the All People's Congress.

In July 2002 a Truth and Reconciliation Committee (TRC) modelled on the South African TRC was established.

The end of the war in Sierra Leone left questions about the integrity of African leadership in the region. It plummeted to a new low with two West African heads of state colluding to illegally acquire the resources of another country at the cost of fomenting civil war in that country . We are not only talking of Charles Taylor at the centre of this West African crisis. It is clear that Charles Taylor in Liberia wanted a share of Sierra Leone's diamonds and was prepared to cause conflict leading to the loss of thousands of lives to get them; whilst France's ally in the region Blaise Campaore of Burkina Faso was trading arms to the RUF rebels in exchange for diamonds, further fuelling the conflict and the atrocities. What Thomas Sankara (the assassinated military president of Burkina Faso) once said about military leaders is equally applicable to both Campaore and Taylor, despite one being a soldier and another being a civilian: *"A soldier without ideology and political education is a criminal in power"*.

It was a situation that was dangerous for other West African states because such conflict could spread through the region. This is what determined Nigerian involvement in the conflict. It was not an involvement popular with the Nigerian public, especially when it emerged that the intervention cost Nigeria hundreds of lives and 25 billion US dollars. Nigerians were infuriated by the cold-blooded execution of 2 of its journalists, reportedly at the command of Charles Taylor. Yet as part of the deal, to get him to resign from office and leave the region in peace from his brand of state gangsterism, Taylor was to go into exile, free from prosecution, with Nigerian protection.

Museveni and the Gangsters of God

Uganda is yet another region that became embroiled in the conflagration of civil conflicts that bedevilled African states in the last years of the 20th

161

century. President Yoweri Museveni battled one of the most bizarre and sinister threats to African peace at the turn of the century. Joseph Kony's Lord's Resistance Army was the most prominent of threats to the stability of Uganda; charging itself with the mission of establishing God's kingdom on earth. It all appeared to begin with an uprising in the north of Uganda where 6000 followers of a spiritual medium and prophetess known as Alice Lakwena (Joseph Kony's aunt) attacked Museveni's government, apparently to counter the continued marginalisation of the Acholi people. The followers of Lakwena were eventually defeated by Museveni's National Resistance Army in 1987; but there was great loss of life. At this point, Museveni's army that had had high moral standards and shown remarkable restraint for a force that had engaged in years of civil war, lost its moral high ground with brutal retaliation against its opponents. To an extent this was a measure of the extent to which Museveni had lost control of his once disciplined army.

Museveni had been the chief opponent of Uganda's first Prime Minister, Milton Obote, in Uganda's 1980 elections. Obote had become Uganda's first prime minister at its independence in 1962 and was then ousted in a coup led by General Idi Amin, who infamously proceeded to expel the Asian population of the country in 1972. Many of the Asian families (who were given 90 days to leave the country) subsequently settled in Britain. Amin, a leader responsible for the massacre of many of his own people, including Acholi and Lari troops, was eventually overthrown by the forces of Julius Nyerere of Tanzania in 1979. Amin had attacked Tanzania in 1978, which responded by invading Uganda and joining with rebel Ugandan forces, the Uganda National Liberation Army formed by Yoweri Museveni and Lt. Col. David Oyite-Ojok, to drive Amin out. Elections in 1980 were won by Obote and his Uganda People's Congress Party which defeated Museveni's Uganda Patriotic Movement. The situation leading to Museveni's take over of power emerged with the increasing violence from Obote's army against the civilian population in the north of Uganda. The violence increased dramatically during 1983 and large numbers of refugees were created. These people, already vulnerable, became a further target for the army which attacked them in retaliation for guerrilla attacks which were now taking place. By 1985, the country was out of Obote's control. That year the NRA went on the offensive and in July the army mounted a coup as Obote fled into exile to Zambia. The country was led by General Tito Okello. But he eventually stood down after a peace pact with the NRA in December 1985. NRA gained control of the country's capital, Kampala and Museveni was sworn in as President in June 1986.

Before Museveni's encounter with the Lord's Resistance Army in 1987 he had gained much respect and support from the people for the discipline of his army. However, the brutal methods of the Lords Resistance Army which included rape, child abduction, slavery and maiming served to infect the NRA with the same vengeance, brutality and inhumanity. Needless to say, the Lords Resistance Army established fear rather than a kingdom in accordance with the Ten Commandments as they claimed they desired. Despite Museveni's offers of amnesty to the LRA their resistance to Museveni's government forces continued into the 21st century with periodic resurgences in violence.

Bibliography

Chapter Seventeen – Lords of War

Ankomah, B., *A pound of flesh, but in whose interests?*, New African, May 2006.
Arnold, G., *Africa – A modern History,* Atlantic Books, London, 2005.
BBC News, Africa, *Kabila: The Rwanda connection*, (http://news.bbc.co.uk/1/hi/world/africa/144517.stm)
Hatzfeld, J., *A Time for Machetes: The Rwandan Genocide: The killers speak*, Farrar Straus and Giroux, New York, 2005.
Meredith, M., *The State of Africa – A history of Fifty years of Independence*, free Press, London, 2005.
New African Yearbook 1981-2, IC Magazines, 1982.
Renton, D., Seddon, D. and L. Zeilig, *The Congo: Plunder & Resistance*, Zed Books, London & NY, 2007

Chapter Eighteen

HIV/AIDS and Medical Intervention in Africa

In the late 1980s, in a crowded lecture hall of a British university an audience of young men and women were chattering away. Silence swept across the hall as the lecturer who was to deliver a talk about the origin of AIDS appeared. The silence was broken by a wave of laughter when the lecturer opened with the message that: Yet again, something new and exotic had come out of Africa. He was, of course referring to the still relatively recent emergence of a new disease called AIDS (Acquired human Immuno-deficiency Syndrome).

Apparently, most of the African and African-Caribbean students in the hall were not so amused. Rather, it was another mark of embarrassment associated with negative perceptions of their mother continent. Yet the lecturer was merely expressing a view that was rapidly gaining ground in the mainstream of academic circles. Previously it had been an American disease: first discovered in 1981 among the gay communities of Los Angeles and New York.

Soon the "Out of Africa" proponents of AIDS origins had their theory: the so called "cut-hunter" theory. This supposed that the disease simply jumped species from monkeys to humans when a hunter who had slain an African chimpanzee for bush meat, had either been scratched by the animal or cut himself whilst butchering it and contaminated his blood with a chimpanzee form of the AIDS virus. It was believed that SIV (Simian Immuno-deficiency Virus) in African primates was the ancestor of HIV, the virus causing AIDS. In 2006, a team of American scientists led by Beatrice Hahn, concluded that the disease originated from a certain chimpanzee eaten as bush meat by hunters from Southern Cameroon.

Predictably, many of the local Cameroonians were not convinced. Hahn's team obviously did not see it as relevant to confirm her theoretical conclusions with evidence from any local oral history of an AIDS-like disease occurring among hunter communities. One suspects any such corroboration by local oral history accounts would have been hard for Hahn's team to come by. The life of the peoples of the Cameroon rain forest, the Baka, is well documented. The Baka hunt monkeys for food, and in regard to their living in balance with their environment they are a meticulous people, even scientific, with their own methods of environmental conservation, medicine, hunting and fishing. Yet they leave us no reports in their documentary biography of their people dying from AIDS-like illnesses. Indeed, it should be a miracle that forest peoples like the Baka, who have been hunting and eating monkeys for possibly thousands of years, have not become extinct from AIDS.

This particular weakness of Hahn's theory, the failure of the epidemic to emerge locally in bygone times, will not easily go away. In fact, it is surprising (on this basis alone) that respectable scientists still adhere to the theory, given the existence of more plausible theories. Early studies (e.g. Brun-Vizinet and Jaeger et al.) found that monkey-eating hunter gatherer forest communities across West and Central Africa showed no evidence of HIV or SIV infection before the late 1980s. Where the very few instances of recent infections have been present, they have been found to originate from contact with the urban African (Bantu) population rather than from monkeys. Furthermore, in an article in the Village Voice, of November 1999, which is completely supportive of Hahn's theory, Mark Schoofs reports on one concern that the AIDS researcher, Preston Marx, still has about the theory of African AIDS origins: "...if such a vast ocean of immunodeficiency viruses has long existed, why did an epidemic happen only now? Why not during the slave trade, when millions of Africans were taken from the areas where both HIV-1 and HIV-2 originated? Here was a massive mixing of peoples, and the slaves were often raped, giving the virus ample opportunity to spread. And yet, no epidemic flared up....This is what obsesses Marx: 'Something that has to do with the 20th century has changed the ecology between SIV and HIV and has allowed these epidemics to occur. And we don't understand what that is' ".

The danger is, of course, that Marx and fellow researchers may well be pondering that question forever. The 'cut-hunter' theory, proposed as early as 1985, was already accepted and little criticism or challenge of the theory had gained public attention until the 1999 publication of the *River* by Edward Hooper, who was avidly championed by the late Professor William Hamilton, a renowned evolutionary biologist from the University of Oxford. The two had combined their efforts to try and prove an alternative theory of AIDS origin before Hamilton died in 2000. For a long time one of the pieces of evidence used to support the African origins of AIDS and thus the cut hunter theory, was the apparent "discovery" that a Manchester seaman who had died from a disease contracted whilst out in Africa died from AIDS. Hooper's work proved that the samples from the remains of the sailor concerned were false positives for HIV. Had Hooper not rigorously tested this finding, the world would not have known any better.

Hooper's OPV (oral polio vaccine) theory proposed that AIDS was introduced into the African population inadvertently by (World Health Organisation) WHO scientists in the late 1950s in the course of oral polio vaccine trials. In the trials carried out between 1957 and 1960 over a million Africans in the former Belgian colonies of central Africa, from babies to adults, were given a live oral polio vaccine that had never been tested on humans. The theory proposed that the vaccines, which were prepared in laboratories in America and Belgium, were prepared in chimpanzee kidneys that were infected with SIV. These kidneys were from chimpanzees sampled from research stations in the former Belgian colonial territories.

The theory aroused a great deal of hostility from some influential scientists and debate was stifled by the refusal of mainstream journals such as Nature and Science to publish Hooper's work after Beatrice Hahn and fellow scientists published a rebuttal of the theory. Also refused publication was Hooper's letter of reply to the rebuttal. Nevertheless, the OPV theory explained some things better than the cut-hunter (CH) theory and fitted with some impressive correlations.

- The cut-hunter theory cannot explain why there are three types of HIV as it proposes one source of AIDS from an infected chimp killed for bush meat in the Cameroons. But the OPV theory holds that the three types of HIV correspond to the three areas in Africa were the oral polio vaccine trials took place in the late 1950s.

- If the cut-hunter theory is true and AIDS jumped the species barrier after being in the African population since time immemorial, why now? Cut-hunter theorists claim the disease had always been present in Africa but only became an epidemic when roads and urbanisation opened up central Africa. But as already noted by Marx, we still have no explanation for why the AIDS epidemic did not then break out during the slavery era. The OPV theory holds that the epidemic was caused during the mass vaccination of over 1 million Africans, at the dawn of the independence era, 1957-60.

- The cut-hunter theory required that the infected hunter did not infect anyone in West Africa, but travelled 600 miles down the Congo river to infect the local central African population there. OPV theory does not have this weakness.

- Hooper notes the explosion of HIV infection in rural western Burundi long before it appeared elsewhere in the continent happened in the very villages where a large trial of a polio vaccine was made in 1958

- In a continent as vast as Africa, 64 percent of all AIDS cases seen up to and including 1980 come from the same towns and villages (all in the former Belgian colonies of Congo, Rwanda and Burundi) where the OPV was fed to Africans in the 1950s.

- Again, given the vast size of the African continent, some 11.6 million square miles (or over 20 percent of the earth's total land area), it is surprising that everyone of the 46 earliest HIV-positive blood samples from Africa comes from within a mere 140-mile radius of one of the various vaccination sites.

The key point however is that right or wrong; Hooper's work raises crucial questions about the conduct of European and American medical scientists on African populations. Effectively, the million or so Africans involved in the trials, were used as guinea pigs for the safe medical treatment of western citizens. The massive vaccine trials were of little or no benefit to Africans at the time, when, according to Hooper, 19 out of every 20 Africans had a natural immunity to polio.

In the last 40 years of the 20th century, after these oral polio vaccine trials, the conduct of western medical science in Africa did not improve. Very often unsuspecting African populations became the guinea pigs of drug trials in the traumatic circumstances of medical emergency. The primary offenders were large American pharmaceutical companies.

The case of clinical trials in Kano, Nigeria, in 1996 run by Pfizer exposed the danger of this type of intervention. At the time of a meningitis epidemic in this part of Nigeria, Kano had the only infectious diseases hospital in the area. Conditions were dirty and overcrowded with drugs and equipment scarce. Doctors from Médécins San Frontieres came with anti-biotics and set up emergency clinics to treat up to 120 patients arriving at the clinic per day, at the height of the epidemic. 200 children who arrived at the hospital with their anxious parents were recruited into the trial instead of being given the routine treatment. The drug, Trovan, used in this instance had only been tested on one child previously in the US and that child was an emergency case where no other options were available. According to Pfizer, just under 6 percent of the children in the trial died. But according to other reports, up to 50% of the children in the trial later died or suffered from serious side-effects. We may never know to what extent the trial saved lives or lost them; but Pfizer claimed to have saved 189 lives. However, parents of the children suing Pfizer, have claimed the control drug Pfizer used in the trials, which was a routine anti-meningitis treatment was responsible for the successes rather than Trovan, which left some children both deaf and dumb. Questions were raised about the lack of evidence for consent from the trial recruits and a letter from the Kano Hospital Ethics committee giving approval for the trials was produced one year after the trials were ended. This letter was backdated to March 1996 and presented to the US government. But hospital director Dr Sadiq Wali confirmed that the hospital had no ethics committee until October 1998, making the letter fraudulent. The incident points not only to the unethical behaviour of American pharmaceuticals but also the lack of integrity of some individuals in authority in African countries who give big companies access to recruit the African public into trials without proper understanding and consent. In some cases, corruption among state and local officials plays a role. The question is to be asked why the Nigerian authorities allowed Pfizer scientists into the area to in the first instance.

One would think that African parents like any other parents given the informed choice would not subject their sick children to an experiment when routine treatments are available, as they were in the case of the Kano epidemic.

One objection to this type of trial generally was that in some trials patients' treatment was maintained in order to observe the outcome despite their condition not improving on the treatment. In some cases (called the "control group" cases) a placebo (that is, no treatment at all) would be given to make a comparison with patients that had been given the real drug. This happened in cases in the late 1990s involving the trial of AIDS drugs on 12000 HIV-positive pregnant women in Ivory coast, Uganda, Tanzania, Zimbabwe and other African countries, sponsored by the US Centre for disease Control In this vein American companies were violating the 1995 Helsinki Declaration of the World Medical Association that the best available therapy must be given to human subjects, including those in control groups. US companies were even violating the Nuremberg Code of Research Conduct adopted after World War II in response to the practices of Nazi doctors. The Centre for Disease Control defended its use of placebos saying that in the absence of research none of the target group would benefit. Yet the studies violated ethical standards that were strictly enforced to protect US citizens, but not enforced to protect Africans. In some cases the powerful AIDS drug AZT, which would never be tested on children in America was given to African and Asian children as young as 3 months old.

In actual fact, the target African populations were always too poor to ever afford the drugs that were tested on them; so that the trials could not be defended on the grounds that they were of benefit to African populations.

The future did not promise improved African protection from drug trials, as an increasing number of American companies were searching for clinical evidence to license potentially very profitable drugs on the drugs market. US giant pharmaceuticals were putting their weight behind a new move to relax the Helsinki Declaration to allow the use of placebos and hence remove a vital legislative protection barrier from the African public.

The threat and menace presented by US companies landing on African soil would be countered if only African countries had in place the much needed, responsible, accountable government bodies staffed by people of sufficient integrity not to be bought by the inducements of the big US and other companies. It was within the power of these officials to give undue access for the recruitment of the African public into drug trials, without their full understanding or consent and with substandard levels of protection.

On the warfront against AIDS, things looked decidedly more positive for Africa in 2005 with the discovery by South African and French AIDS researchers that the simple practice of circumcision was a far more effective protection against AIDS than even an AIDS vaccine. Initial results showed that circumcision reduced the risk of contracting AIDS by 70 percent.

Statistics from the World health Organisation in 2005 showed that the tide of the AIDS epidemic was slowly turning in Africa's favour, with the rate of infections falling in 6 out of 11 countries monitored. The continent, however, may not yet have seen the worst of the effects of the HIV/AIDS epidemic. The report noted that "Countries like Burkina Faso, Burundi, Kenya and Zimbabwe have joined the ranks of Uganda, where HIV prevalence declined in the early to mid-1990s". Success in Uganda was thanks to Yoweri Museveni the Ugandan leader's robust approach to tackling HIV/AIDS, which provided an example of good practice for other African leaders who were, less forthright in tackling the problem. Southern Africa remained the most affected sub-region with HIV prevalence stabilising around still unacceptably high levels. Some countries in southern Africa had HIV prevalence levels in excess of 25 percent. In east Africa the prevalence remained high at 7 percent whilst most West African countries have stabilised below 5 percent. These infection rates may be compared, for reference, with the rate in Britain, for instance, which was measured at just under 0.1 percent in 2004, with an estimated 50,000 people being HIV positive.

Bibliography

Chapter Eighteen - HIV/AIDS and Medical Intervention in Africa

Bosely, S., Ailing Ethics, the Guardian, 20 January 2001.

Brun-Vizinet, F., Jaeger, G., et al., Lack of evidence of human or Simian T-lymphotropic viruses type IIIinfection in Pygmies, Lancet, 1986 Apr 12;1(8485):854.

Hooper, E., The River: A Journey back to the Source of HIV and AIDS, Allen lane, London, 1999.

Hopkin, M., HIV-like Virus Found in Wild Chimps, Nature, 22 May 2006

Keele, B.F., Hahn, B.F., et al., "Chimpanzee Reservoirs of Pandemic and Nonpandemic HIV-1", [Science Express: 10.1126/science.1126531]; P. M. Sharp, "Where AIDS Came From" [Webcast]; 13th Conference on Retroviruses and Opportunistic Infections; Denver, CO, USA; February 5-8th, 2006.

Kuttners, R., U.S. Science's Cruelty Overseas, Boston Globe, 27 April, 1997.

Ndembi, N., Habakuk, Y., Takehisa, J., Takemura, T., Kobayashi, E., Ngansop, C., Songok, E., Miura, T., Hayami, M., Kaptue, L., Ichimura, H., HIV 1 type infection in Pygmy hunter gatherers is from contact with Bantu rather than nonhuman primates, AIDS Research and human retroviruses, 2003 May; 19(5):435-9

SAN FRANCISCO CHRONICLE 2005. Circumcision May Offer Africa AIDS Hope. Procedure linked to much lower rates of new HIV infections, San Francisco Chronicle, 6 July 2005.

Schoofs, M., AIDS: The Agony of Africa, Village Voice, Nov. 24-30, 1999.

WORLD HEALTH ORGANISATION, 2005. HIV /AIDS Epidemiological Report for the WHO African Region, 2005 UPDATE, Harare, Zimbabwe, December, 2005.

Yasuoka, H., The sustaining of Duiker hunting for baka hunter gatherers in South East Cameroon, African Study Monographs, Suppl. 33: 95-120. May 2006.

Chapter Nineteen

A Tale of Two Revolutions

Revolutionary Leadership

What kind of leadership in Africa has been revolutionary? We must take care to be correct when talking about revolution. One can in a general sense talk about an African revolution that had brought about the so called "winds of change" consisting of the various events like the 1945 Pan African Congress that raised awareness and created a movement that drove African states towards independence and, in many more protracted and violent cases, towards armed struggle and liberation from the former colonial power. But on the internal level of the individual state there are few examples we can readily point to of real revolutions in Africa. Two examples resonate as instances of revolutionary leadership that existed in the context of independent or liberated African states. There are many examples of leadership that were revolutionary at the phase of struggle; but their revolutionary nature died soon after liberation or independence was achieved or aborted due to the assassination of the leaders. The two examples of revolutionary leadership before us are Julius Nyerere's "African socialism" pursued in Tanzania in the period 1967-75 and Thomas Sankara's "democratic and popular revolution" of 1983-87.

Before presenting these two examples it is timely to say what we mean by revolutionary leadership. By revolution we do not mean revolutionary slogans or rhetoric. We mean creative programmes which in some way strive to break the chains of Africa's dependence on the neo-colonial structures handed over to states at independence. The former colonial countries did their best to ensure that these structures were maintained so they could have continued access to Africa's raw material resources beyond independence.

We see that a key ingredient of revolution is creativity – a power to create a change that will in the long term lead to real African self determination rather than dependence on the West for perpetual investments and handouts. This is what both Julius Nyerere and Thomas Sankara set themselves to achieve. This creativity was employed to create concrete programmes of action that we can point to years after the endeavour as true examples of revolutionary leadership and revolutionary action which the people are by and large supportive of. We can not say that in both cases we had unquestioned success in these areas; but in each case we are witness to the presence of a firm political will in this direction.

One might wonder if any African leader of integrity has managed to survive and implement a progressive programme of governance for his country with outside support rather than sabotage. In this vein the late President Julius Nyerere of Tanzania stands out as a dignified exception. But most likely, the lack of interference had everything to do with the fact that Tanzania had no oil, precious metals or other valuable raw materials than any genuine desire to give good African leadership a free reign. Had Tanzania been blessed (or should one say cursed) with precious raw materials, there is little doubt that there would have been western pressure for Nyerere to follow free market (capitalist) policies to facilitate western access to cheaply obtainable precious raw materials rather than indulge in a socialist experiment.

The ideology of Nyerere's system of government was called African Socialism and Tanzania became a one-party state on 5th July 1964. Tanzania was formed through the amalgamation of the states of Tanganyika and Zanzibar earlier that year, having gained its independence in December 1961. Julius Nyerere, the leader of the Tanganyika African National Union (TANU) became its first prime minister; but resigned almost immediately in January 1962. He chose to concentrate on building up the party from its grassroots; involving the people of Tanzania at every level. Perhaps the most important political event in the life of the country was the Arusha Declaration of 1967, which proclaimed the country's policy of socialism and self reliance. By many accounts Nyerere's African socialism was credible because of his own personal example of simple tastes, egalitarianism, compassion and dislike of elitism. Nyerere's socialism emphasized slower, more organic growth of the country's wealth through self reliance and the development of the peasant agricultural economy. Foreign investment was to be used only as a supplement to indigenous development efforts.

In 1967 Nyerere began his Ujamaa programme whereby he hoped to establish self sufficient agricultural cooperative villages called Ujamaa villages. Nyerere hoped that this would raise agricultural productivity of the nation. The mistake perhaps that Nyerere made was to initially make the programme of Ujamaa on a voluntary basis, hoping that sufficient numbers of the population would take it up of their own accord. This led to the take up being too low. Eventually villagers were coerced into leaving their villages for an Ujamaa village. Still the measures did not yield more food crops as hoped. Worse was to come when in 1974-75 there was a shortage in the production of cereals. By 1975, with an accompanying drought to make things worse the country had to be rescued through IMF assistance for food aid. More pressure was put on the Tanzanian economy by the rising cost of fuel, which by 1980 was costing the Tanzanians 60 percent of their total annual budget. After Julius Nyerere was re-elected for the fifth time in 1980, he announced that he would be standing down at the next election in 1985. The Tanzanian economy weakened during the decade and it became clear that Nyerere's grand project of African socialism had failed, at least economically. But in other ways it had succeeded. Despite the economic failure of Ujamaa, he had created a benevolent moral and social climate not to be matched in any other African state. By 1985 his government had given the country 23 years of stability and had survived a coup attempt in 1983. He remained popular through out with the majority of the people still loyally in his support. Nyerere was succeeded by Ali Hassan Mwinyi who was elected president in October 1985.

The Revolution of Thomas Sankara in Burkina Faso

Thomas Isidore Noel Sankara was one of Africa's truest of revolutionary reformers for progress and social justice. He was, without doubt, a compassionate leader and above all, in his brief years at the helm, he showed himself to be incorruptible, as the name of the nation *Burkina Faso* implies. Sankara's revolution (1983-87) may be regarded as one of the most radical and creative on the African continent since the independence of the 1960s. But Sankara's radicalism had a growing influence on Francophone Africa which was not appreciated either by France or by Houphouet Boigny of neighbouring Ivory Coast, who saw the growing popularity of his leadership as a direct threat to their own moribund regimes. Sankara established close working relations with Jerry Rawlings of Ghana, and the two discussed the possible union of their countries.

Upper Volta (as Burkina Faso was formerly called), gained its independence on 5 May 1960. Maurice Yameogo was the first president of the Republic of Upper Volta, who was elected in that same year and then re-elected in 1965 with 99 percent of the votes. However, on the 3 January 1966 a popular uprising resulted in the fall of Yameogo's government, and Lt. Col. Sangoule Lamizana became the head of government. Yameogo was arrested for embezzling £1.2 million, but given an amnesty in 1970 and refuge in Ivory Coast.

Lamizana was later replaced in another coup following continued wrangles over disputed election results in 1978. Lamizana's government was toppled in a coup on 25 November 1980 and Col. Saye Zerbo became the new head of state. Zerbo's rule was characterised by conflict between the trade unions and the government. On 7 November 1982 yet

Figure 17 Sankara addresses the United Nations (UN photo)

another coup briefly brought in major Jean-Baptiste Ouedrago. Then on 4 August 1983 a further coup brought Sankara to power. He appointed Blaise Campaore as his deputy in the position of Minister of state to the Presidency. Sankara named his revolution "the democratic and popular revolution". The ideology of the revolution was defined by Sankara as anti-imperialist.

The achievements of Sankara's dynamic revolution were a model for African renaissance and revolution into the 21st century and included

- Abolition of unjust tributes received by chiefs.
- Employment of women in government.
- Banning of female circumcision.
- Promotion of contraception and a robust approach to tackling HIV/AIDS.
- Raising of the literacy rate from 12 percent to 22 percent.
- Sale of the government fleet of Mercedes Benz cars and the adoption of a more environmentally friendly and fuel efficient vehicle as the official car of ministers.
- Conversion of the army provisions store in the capital Ouagadougou into a state owned supermarket.
- The nationalisation of all land and mineral wealth in the country.
- 2.5 million children were vaccinated against meningitis, yellow fever and measles with Cuban medical assistance reducing infant mortality in Burkina Faso from 280 deaths per 1000 to 145 deaths per 1000 within two years.

- The taxing of civil servants and military salaries to fund education and health projects in 1984.
- The launch of a campaign on 1 January 1985 to plant 1 million trees to halt the advance of the Sahara desert [*the policy of tree planting in the West African region, promoted by Sankara's revolution, reaped benefits later in 2006 when scientists observed that trees planted in neighbouring Niger were halting the advance of the desert, and hence alleviating the conditions of drought and famine in the region which had reached crisis point in 2005]*
- The undertaking of a UN assisted programme in 1986 to combat river blindness.

Sankara's revolution was not dogmatic, and aimed to do away with those aspects of traditional culture that resulted in the unjust treatment of peasants on the land. The payment of taxes to chiefs for no other reason but tradition was unjust and had to be abolished. The role of women was integral to Sankara's revolution: Women were to be involved, bearing equal responsibility at all levels including decision making.

The elements of Sankara's revolution were laid out fully in his speeches to the people. One of his goals for Burkina Faso was self sufficiency in food production. Thus agriculture was to be the 'lever' for industrial development. Around this the revolution consisted of reforms that would transform an African society:

i)   Agricultural or agrarian, reforms that make agricultural production the 'lever' for industrial development
ii)   administrative reforms that make the administration inherited from colonialism operational purging it of the evils that characterise it, including unwieldy bureaucracy and all its consequences (including increased opportunities for corruption),
iii)   Educational reforms that promote a new orientation for education and culture and end illiteracy
iv)   Reform of the structures of production and distribution (the storage and distribution of food and fair distribution of national resources being, of course, key problems to address in Africa in the 21st century).

It seems that Sankara was well aware of the example that his revolution might set for other revolutions in Africa and beyond. Although he knew of the special nature of Burkina Faso's revolution he had seen the revolution as a small part of a whole. For Sankara all revolutions are connected despite time and distance meaning that his struggle was part of a universal struggle encompassing the Black World from Ouagadougou to Harlem and also the struggles of the past, as if all humanity had a common revolutionary path: "Our revolution in Burkina Faso embraces misfortunes of all people. It draws on the totality of man's experiences since the first breath of humanity. We wish to be the heirs of all the revolutions of the world and all the liberation struggles of the people of the Third World".

Nevertheless, it seems that Sankara was too honest and compassionate a political leader to live. On the 15th October 1987, Sankara and 12 other officers were killed in a coup organised by his former colleague, Blaise Campaoré. Campaore's coup was welcomed by Ivory Coast, Togo and France who feared Sankara's influence in the region. Campaore reversed the tide of Sankara's revolution: civil servants and military pay was restored, ceasing the previous education and health projects; Sankara's supporters were detained without trial and one of them, the lecturer Guillame Sessouma died during torture.

Although the World Bank report of 1988 praised the high standard of financial management during the Sankara revolution, whilst noting the increasing incidence of corruption since the Campaore takeover; the IMF in 1993 still loaned Campaore's Burkina government 67 million dollars on the condition that it implemented free market policies. In June 1993, an official visit of Blaise Campaore to France, established him as France's favourite ally.

Bibliography

Chapter Nineteen – A Tale of Two Revolutions

Arnold, G., *Africa – A modern History*, Atlantic Books, London, 2005.
Davidson, B., *Modern Africa – A Social and political History* (2nd ed.), Longman, New York, 1983.
Freund, Bill, The *making of Contemporary Africa: The Development of African Society since 1800*, Macmillan, London, 1984.
Gailey, H., *History of Africa – from 1800 to present, Vol.II*, Krieger Publishing Co., New York, 1971.
Meredith, M., *The State of Africa – A history of Fifty years of Independence*, Free Press, London, 2005.
New African Yearbook 1981-2, IC Magazines, 1982.
Nyerere, J., *Ujamaa: Essays on Socialism*, Oxford University Press, 1968.
Polgreen, L., *In Niger, Trees and Crops Turn Back the Desert*, New York Times, 11 February, 2007.
Thomas Sankara Speaks: The Burkina Faso Revolution 1983-87, translated by Samantha Anderson, Pathfinder Press, New York/London/Montreal/Sidney, 1988.

Chapter Twenty

The State of Africa: A Question of leadership?

Examples of bad leaders in Africa supported by the West illustrate the double standards of some western commentators who have readily cited the question of poor leadership as the "first and foremost reason" for the continent's lack of progress; but ignored the fact that western states have been propping up many of Africa's most serious leadership failures both militarily and financially since the independence era of the 1960s.

It is alarming that all of the examples cited ahead involve France. Perhaps this should not be surprising, as it indicates the nature of France's role in Africa, and the frequency of French state intervention in African affairs. This negative intervention contrasted with French non-governmental organisations that have done invaluable work.

Mobutu Sese Seko proved to be a valuable asset to the French and Americans. In August 1970 the American President, Richard Nixon, described him as a leader of "stability and vision", citing his handling of the Zaire economy as an example to other African nations. This was despite Mobutu's well known massive level of theft from his country's riches, often with the collusion of some of the Congo's increasing number of western investors in copper, cobalt, industrial diamonds and other minerals. Mobutu's level of theft was legendary. By the 1980s Mobutu had a fortune of an estimated 5 billion U.S. dollars. Although a guarantee of western interests made Mobutu valuable to the west, he was useless to his people. His government was corrupt, inept and allowed the country to degenerate whilst his personal wealth expanded. Hospitals closed for lack of medicines. Staff were never paid and therefore deserted their posts. Massive imports were needed to feed the nation. Yet all along, Mobutu was supported by the French and the Americans who continued to arm him and bail him out financially.

Emperor Bokassa, the dictator of the Central African Republic came to power in 1965 in a violent coup. His brutal regime remained in power for 14 years. He was throughout supported by France, which continued to bail out Bokassa's regime despite human rights violations and rampant corruption. France was willing to front the embarrassment of supporting such a despot in order to get its hands on Central African Republic's uranium for its nuclear programme. Even when Bokassa made his coronation as emperor, France footed the bill. Not until Bokassa murdered 100 school children and this made the world news did the French cut support for Bokassa. The French then removed Bokassa in 1979 and installed David Dacko as president.

In Rwanda the French supported the government of Juvenal Habyarimana and continued to arm his government even after it became clear that his government was involved in the genocide against Rwanda's Tutsi population. This was clear to the French by April 1994; yet a shipment of arms from France was sent to Habyarimana's government in June 1994. A report into human rights abuses in Rwanda published in March 1993 by a set of human rights experts held President Habyarimana and his "immediate entourage" responsible for human rights abuses against Tutsis living in Rwanda.

In Togo, General Gnassingbe Eyadema who ruled for 38 years had broken the African record for longest reigning head of state at the time of his death. He died whilst still in power in 2005. Eyadema had led the assassination of Togo's first president, Silvanus Olympio, back in 1963 and assumed power in 1967. In 1991, after 24 years in power (supported by France despite his poor record on democracy and human rights), Eyadema bowed to public pressure for opposition parties to operate and for a national conference. The national conference was used to protest against the brutality of Eyadema's regime, and evinced years of abuse of Togolese human rights. The conference boldly led to the draft of a new constitution, the scheduling of elections and the choice of Kokou Koffigoh as prime minister. But Koffigoh was rendered ineffective, being forced to defer to Eyadema. In 1993 the presidential elections resulted in Eyadema winning 98 percent of the vote. He was the only candidate, as the electoral commission disqualified the only other candidate, Gilchrist Olympio (a son of the late first president). Eyadema was succeeded by his son Faure, appointed by the army in February 2005, despite the objection of the African Union that this was unconstitutional.

The final example goes back to 1992 in Congo-Brazzaville. Pascal Lissouba had won the presidential elections there, defeating the country's former military dictator, Denis Sassou-Nguesso, who had been in power since 1979. Although as military dictator Sassou-Nguesso had presided over a one-party Marxist state, he had been befriended and supported by France for one simple reason: oil. Sassou-Nguesso, whilst in power, had allowed the French oil companies, Elf Aquitaine and others to take up to 85 percent of Congo-Brazzaville's oil revenues back to France, leaving the Congolese with a paltry 15 percent. So naturally, on assuming power President Lissouba moved to improve his country's revenue from its own oil to 33 percent, which was better, but still paltry. This ensured the demise of Lissouba's short-lived government. Elf Aquitane set out to destroy the new arrangement, calling on Sassou-Nguesso's support. The situation was not in Lissouba's favour. Having lost the presidential election, Sassou-Nguesso, who had only introduced elections under public pressure to hand over to a civilian democracy, was still hungry to regain control of the country. Lissouba's position was not secure due to the fact that the Congo-Brazzaville army was dominated by loyal Mbochi - Sassou-Nguesso's ethnic group. Lissouba established his own militia to protect his presidency. Civil war ensued and France flew in its troops ready to evacuate its nationals from Zaire whose government under Mobutu was on the verge of collapse (or more likely to intervene against Lissouba if this was needed to protect French interests). The conflict enabled Sassou-Nguesso to call for a transitional government to reorganise the conflict ridden country and "organise credible elections". Omar Bongo of Gabon was called in as a mediator (with blatant vested interests as he was France's ally and the father in law of Sassou-Nguesso). Meanwhile Sassou-Nguesso's Cobra militia easily took key points in the city of Brazzaville and he was restored to power. The French foreign ministry spokesman announced that "It is a good thing". It was a good thing for the French economy, as Sassou-Nguesso immediately reduced the 33 percent share of oil revenues won by the ousted President Lissouba down to 20 percent to secure French support for his return to power.

These shameful examples of African leadership above, supported by the west, are among the worst examples of an African elite class that had tightly held onto power since the independence era of the 1960s. The inevitable and most radical solution for Africa is to do away with this class, if this is at all possible. Various authors have recognised this and advocated accordingly. When Chinweizu is asked the question: 'What is the problem with African leadership?' he says: "In one word, it is **compradorism**. In brief, Imperialism and Arabism are only able to dominate, exploit and confuse us through their local agents, their fifth column in our midst, the caste of Black Compradors. This pseudo-bourgeois class-stratum that led the decolonisation movements in Africa was a caste of comprador-African agents of white supremacy. If we don't grasp that point, we will understand nothing and everything else we know will only confuse us!"

Chinweizu, and many other writers, singularly blame Africa's situation on the debilitating effects of the African elite class, often schooled in the west and serving the interests of the neo-colonial countries. Uchendu Egbezor reaches that same conclusion about the elite in Nigeria, blaming the country's elite for maintaining unchanged the colonial structures that condemn the country to be trapped by bad leadership, as the elite refuse to relinquish their tight reign on power. Chinua Achebe, who has long advocated that Africa's problems lie principally in the poor quality of leadership, cites the same singular ingredient of African failure. He also infers the neo-colonial credentials of the elite and the source of their outside support when he says: "We have not been lucky with the leadership we have had since independence. Part of it is deliberate. Part of the hoax called independence, is to give us leaders who do not understand what happened to us. As long as they are running things, they run Africa to the ground."

The neo-colonial elite classes, represented in the extreme by Mobutu, Bokassa and their ilk, have, as so many writers have noted, driven Africa into the ground. Frantz Fanon, as Chinweizu recalls, lamented on the uselessness of this elite class. In addition to being corrupt, this class created no iota of progress in Africa since independence. In fact, this ruling class has sent Africa backwards. Fanon is telling a deep truth when he says: *"the bourgeois phase in the history of under-developed countries is a completely useless phase. When this caste has vanished, . . . it will be seen that nothing new has happened since independence was proclaimed, . . . [that] that caste has done nothing more than take over unchanged the legacy of the economy, the thought and the institutions left by the colonialists. . . . and that everything must be started again from scratch. . ."*

How often has one heard it said that at least the Western elites, although like-wise tainted by corruption, have at least ensured maintenance of the national infrastructure of roads, health services, water and electricity supplies, etc. in their own countries.. The extremities of wealth and poverty in Africa have created extremities of greed. In Africa and other Third World regions, within the elite classes, we witness that even the minimum of obligations to public service are jettisoned. Politicians see themselves, not as servants of the public. Rather, the public are obligated to the wealthy elite and their families.

But to leave the question of leadership at this point and say only that it is a question of the neo-colonial elite is surely not enough. Can it be guaranteed that after the removal of this class, Africa will still not be haunted by the same problems? We witnessed the bloody nature of Rawlings' revolution, which eliminated virtually the entire clique of post-independence Ghanaian leadership. Yet this did not, in the long term, eliminate corruption.

Otonti Nduka would probably argue that an elimination of the elite today would make no permanent difference. Because, tomorrow there will be others to fill their shoes, and they in turn would become the new elite. For Nduka, the key lies in the weak value base of modern African leadership. In Nigeria at the turn of the century, for instance, corruption was endemic and the values that promoted such a state of affairs ran through the society from top to bottom, affecting both leaders and subordinates.

Nduka's concern is underdevelopment rather than merely leadership and (with the support of other authors) he identifies many of the day to day symptoms, causes and elements of African underdevelopment: -

- Inadequate supply of skilled labour.
- Low productivity and low per capita income.
- Poor attitude to work.
- Systematic corruption.
- Lack of theoretical scientific knowledge (although it could be countered that Africa's problem is not producing scientists and mathematicians; but rather gainfully employing them. Many of Africa's Universities – supposedly, the key to African development – have ceased to function due to the usual evils cited by Nduka: "tribalism, nepotism, bribery and corruption").
- Failure to operate a democratic nation state; in particular, the peaceful transition of power that follows an election outcome, through the agreed democratic processes. Again, Nduka notes that this failure is traceable to the operation of the usual negative forces: *"tribalism, nepotism, bribery and corruption on the part of the electorate and the elected representatives, the rigging of elections and above all, the attempt to run a democratic polity without genuine commitment to the principles of honesty and fair play."*

Virtually all of the elements of underdevelopment Nduka cites as responsible for Africa's state appear to be value based. For Nduka the role of warped values is more fundamental than bad leadership in explaining Africa's predicament: *"the weakest link in the chain of development efforts remains the weak value base which adversely effects both individual and collective attempts at development, including those of the leaders who are either born or selected or rigged into positions of leadership or assume the leadership of the country through the barrel of the gun."*

Ultimately, Nduka advocates an ethical revolution and the creation of an African foundation for the promotion of right values.

At the Dawn of the 21st century it can be said that in Africa there are the best of leaders and there are the worst of leaders.

On the one hand, one could contend that there were very few world leaders outside Africa in the last 40 years of the 20th century that matched the moral integrity and stature of a Mandela, a Nyerere, a Sankara or a Desmond Tutu. Leaders like Mandela, Sisulu and others in South Africa had to find particular strength to survive incarceration. They retained their humanity in the face of inhumanity, compassion and absence of bitterness in the face of hatred. Sankara, Nyerere and others exemplified **incorruptibility** and the courage and creativity to put into action strategies for Africa's independent existence outside the eternal cycle of international aid and debt payments.

Then on the other hand there were those leaders of the likes of the Mobutu's and the Bokassa's. These leaders were propped up by western governments over almost the complete 40-year period from independence to the turn of the 20th century, always bailed out of trouble economically and militarily. They were supported to remain in power by the same nations that championed democracy when it suited them (U.S.A and France) even against the desperate wishes of their people to be rid of them. In the same camp were also ruthless and corrupt leaders like Abacha of Nigeria whose stolen billions sat in European and American bank vaults whilst their countries continued to wallow in growing poverty and debt.

So we observe that in Africa two extremes of leadership are seen. This phenomenon has not gone unnoticed. Says Robert Rotberg of Harvard University: "Leadership in Africa is typified more by disfiguring examples ...than by positive role models. Other clusters of developing nations exhibit wide variations in leadership quality, but none is so extreme in its range."

Not acknowledging that colonialism or neo-colonialism might have played any role in creating Africa's leadership deficit, Rotberg argues that the reason for this deficit was that African countries, in contrast to the Asian and Caribbean countries had relatively shorter periods of colonialism and hence less time for democratic leadership to be nurtured. He says: "Compared to the Asian or Caribbean experience, colonial rule in Africa was brief, with settled foreign-run governments in much of Africa for only about 50 years. There was little time, especially in the least devolutionary cases like Congo, to nurture democracy or responsible leadership." Rotberg's audacity here is left to speak for itself.

It is the common view that the problem of Africa is the preponderance of poor leadership. The start of the 21st century saw the emergence of a growing number of initiatives on leadership; all purporting to address the problem of Africa's "leadership deficit". One example of these initiatives – the African leadership Council – boasts the involvement of African ex-heads-of-state (General Yakubu Gowon of Nigeria and Ketumile Masire of Botswana).

The Council (whose guiding light is none other than Robert Rotberg of the Harvard Kennedy School of Government) is one example of the kind of leadership programme that might raise concern over the level of true independence in the development of Africa's future leaders. Although we would all recognise and appreciate the values put forward in the

Council's manifesto; there is genuine concern that Rotberg openly advocates *ideological* choices of leadership model for Africa. For instance, it is not the advocation of a Seretse Khama as a leadership model that is worrying, so much as the clear dissuasion from following African socialist models like Nyerere, Sankara and even the anti-colonialist spirit of Nkrumah.

It would seem that for Rotberg, Africa's success must lie in retaining colonialism's legacy: *"Seretse could have done otherwise...The rest of Africa largely followed president Nkrumah...in renouncing colonial traditions.."* Rotberg is clearly telling African leadership to steer clear of revolutionary models (Nyerere, Sankara and Nkrumah) and in so doing, Rotberg's intervention through the African leadership council will be seen by many as purely and simply an ideological dictate on the direction of future African leadership. For what strategic purpose? Safe guarding long term western business interests, most likely.

Africa, like any region, has had its share of poor leaders. But Africans have had great and inspiring leaders. We have recognised them when they have come along. We have too often mourned them when they have passed on, all too soon. Sankara and Nyerere were great leaders. Sankara stands out for giving the continent one of the best blue prints for revolutionary reform. Nyerere and Sankara too, with some prudent adjustments perhaps, have pointed the way for agricultural reform and self-sufficiency in food production.

Murtala Mohammed's words at the OAU summit in Addis Abbaba, Ethiopia on 11th January 1976 warn us that Africans need not be too hasty to let outside experts guide us along the leadership path. For we are bound to ask, in whose interest are our future leaders being guided? Murtala speaks at a time when his role in galvanising African nations in support of Angola against U.S. and apartheid South African sponsored aggression, marked a key point in modern Africa's history. This time African nations were not going to be bystanders whilst a sister African state was bullied and violated through the use of western sponsored mercenaries as happened in the case of Lumumba's Congo. But a familiar pattern was yet again repeated when Murtala was assassinated barely a month after he uttered these words at the same OAU summit:

Africa has come of age. It is no longer under the orbit of any extra continental power. It should no longer take orders from any country, however powerful. The fortunes of Africa are in our hands to make or to mar. For too long have we been kicked around: for too long have we been treated like adolescents who cannot discern their interests and act accordingly. For too long has it been presumed that the African needs outside 'experts' to tell him who are his friends and who are his enemies.

183

The time has come when we should make it clear that we can decide for ourselves; that we know our own interests and how to protect those interests; that we are capable of resolving African problems without presumptuous lessons in ideological dangers which, more often than not, have no relevance for us, nor for the problem at hand. [Murtala Mohammed. November 1938 - February 1976]

Murtala's words described the Angolan problem from an African perspective very precisely, in so far as the Angolan war was a struggle by Africans for decolonisation and freedom from Portuguese and western colonial rule, in which Angolans freely chose to accept the assistance of Cuban forces against the American-hired mercenaries and forces of racist South Africa. It was not, as popular history books like Meredith's *State of Africa* would confuse us to believe, a conflict between East and West in which the Angolans were merely the helpless pawns of communist regimes. This simplistic "East versus West" analysis of the situation denigrates and belittles the aspirations of Africans for colonial freedom to nothing worth any consideration in historical terms. This patronising stance of Europeans on the Angola question at that time, which has its extension in the telling of the history of Africa today, is precisely what Murtala condemned when he noted that Africans are not children to be told who to befriend and who to consider as enemies. The "East versus West" style of analysis, disguised the bare facts: that the West wanted to get its hands on Africa's precious materials, and needed to use the pretext of fighting communism as a front for its military involvement to crush the African liberation movement of that region, and safeguard its economic interests. Murtala's government saw this clearly and were in the position to alert other African nations to the fact that that they had the power to act in the Angolan people's favour.

The question of African leadership cannot be taken out of the context whereby the neo-colonial environment stifles the emergence and survival of good African leadership. In spite of the conditions, Africa has produced outstanding leaders, as well as the usual preponderance of bad examples found on every continent. It should not be pretended that it has been in the economic interests of Africa's former colonial powers to have good African leaders, stridently protective of African interests. This is why we have witnessed in the past, and sadly may continue to witness in the future, the assassinations of the Lumumbas, the Cabrals, the Murtala Mohammeds and the Thomas Sankaras of Africa.

Bibliography

Chapter Twenty - The State of Africa: A Question of leadership?

Arnold, G., *Africa – A Modern History*, Atlantic Books, London, 2005.

Chinweizu, *Talk to Black Heritage Summit, Plenary Session*, Nigerian Institute of International Affairs, Lagos, 4 December, 2006.

Davidson, B., *Modern Africa – A Social and political History* (2nd ed.), Longman, New York, 1983.

Egbezor, U., *Nigeria: Breaking the Stranglehold of the Neocolonial Elites*, Iroko Press, Leeds (UK), 1996.

Fanon, F., The *Wretched of the Earth*, Penguin Books, Middlesex, 1983

Meredith, M., *The State of Africa – A history of Fifty years of Independence*, Free Press, London, 2005.

Nduka, O., *The Roots of African Underdevelopment and other Essays*, Spectrum Books Ltd, Ibadan, 2006.

Rotberg, R., *The Roots of Africa's Leadership Deficit*, Compass I, 2003.

Thomas Sankara Speaks: The Burkina Faso Revolution 1983-87, translated by Samantha Anderson, Pathfinder Press, New York/London/Montreal/Sidney, 1988.

VANGUARD (Lagos), *The Problem with Africa Remains Leadership – Achebe*, Vanguard, 8 January, 2007.

INDEX

A

Abacha, Sani, 110, 182
ABAKO, 113
Abeokuta, 67
Abreha and Asbeha, 42
Abu Simbel, 16, 19, 29, 33
Abyssinia (Ethiopia), 93, 98, 99
Acheampong, Ignatius, 107
Achebe, Chinua, 179, 185
African land use, 143
African population (decimation by slavery), 60, 67, 91
African Socialism, 171. 172
African Union (AU), 106 153, 154, 178
Afrikaners, 100, 140
Afrikaner Broederbond, 140
Agricultural reform, 183
Ahmose I, 16, 27, 28, 32,
Akhenaton (Amenophis IV), 27, 30, 31, 32
Akuffo, Frederick, 107
Al-Bakri, 46
Al-Bashir, Omar, 152, 153
Alexander of Macedonia, 41
Alexandria, 43, 76
Algebra, 77
Al-Khwarizmi, 77, 79
Al-Mahdi, Sadiq, 152
Alodia (Alwa), 43
Amazulu, 64, 69-70
Amenemhet, Nymare, 25
Amenemhet, Nukaure, 25
Amenirdis I, 37, 40
Amenose, 28
Amharic, 150
Amin, Idi, 162
Amina, 70, 92
Amistad, 60
Amun (Ancient Egyptian divinity), 16, 32, 36, 37, 40, 83

Anaximander, 82
Anaximenes, 82
ANC (African national Congress – South Africa), 140
ANC (African National Congress – Zimbabwe), 186
Angola, 61, 64-65, 93, 95, 109, 128-131
Animism, 77-80, 136, 158, 183, 184
Annan, Kofi, 161
Anu, 20
Apophis, Aawserre, 16, 17
Aristotle, 76, 80, 81, 82
Asclepius, 22, 78, 79
Ashurbanipal, 37, 40
Aspelta, 40
Assab, 93
Assyrians, 37
Astronomy, 3, 12
Aten (Egyptian sun god), 31, 32
Averroes, 77
Awolowo, Obafemi, 107
Axum, 3, 39-44, 98, 148
Azikiwe, Dr Nnamdi, 107

B

Badouin, King of Belgium, 114
Bala Usman, Yusuf, 109
Balewa, Tafawa, 107, 108
Bambata, 100
Bantu, 50, 69, 141, 165
Banyamulenge, 155
Barclay, David & Alexander, 55
Barre, Siad, 147
Bassa script, 98
Bechuanaland(Botswana), 93, 100
Benin, 70-71
Benin Bronzes, 61
Berbers, 46, 49, 73, 75, 147

186

Bernal, Martin, 78, 80, 81
Biafra, 108
Biko, Steve, 141
Black Consciousness Movement, 141
Black majority rule, 136, 141
Boahen, A. A., 91, 92, 149
Boigny, Houphouet, 173
Bokassa, Jean Bedel, 177, 180, 182
Botswana, 93, 100, 137, 182
British East African company, 93
British South Africa company, 94
Bull Horns Formation, 69
Burkina Faso, 161, 169, 173-176
Burton, Richard, 99
Burundi, 68, 96, 157
Busia, Kofi, 106

C

Cabral, Amilcar, 129, 132, 133
Caesar, Augustus, 41
Calendar (Lunar), 3, 12
Cambyses, 41
Cameroon, 93, 164, 166, 170
Campaore, Blaise, 161, 174, 176
Capitalism, 88, 91, 99
Catholicism, 113
Chandler, Wayne B., 19 21, 24, 33, 73, 75
Chimurenga (Zimbabwe war of liberation), 94, 136-139
Chinweizu, 179, 180
Christianity,
    - general, 76, 95, 106, 113
    - Ethiopian, 42, 43, 44, 148
CIA (Central Intelligence Agency), 104, 105, 122, 129, 131, 133, 159
Colonial land policy (British), 142-144
Coltan, 155, 156

Columbus, Christopher, 48, 54, 55
Congo (Brazzaville), 178-179
Congo (former Zaire), 12, 75, 92, 94-95, 101-102, 104, 105, 112-127
Constantinople, 43, 72
Coptic Church, 43-44
Corpus Hermeticum, 78, 79
Cotton production, 54, 57, 89, 90
Criminal Laws Amendment Act (S.Africa), 140
Crown Lands Ordinance (Kenya), 143
Cuba, 109, 126, 129, 130, 131, 135, 136, 142, 174, 184

D

Dahomey, 60, 64, 67-68, 93, 96
Dan Fodio, Usman, 96
Darfur, 138, 154
Davies, H.O., 107
De Clerk, F.W., 141
De Medici, Cosimo, 78, 79, 80
De Witte, Ludo, 117, 120, 125
Deism, 77
Demi-urge, 79
Democratic Republic of Congo (DRC), *see Congo*
Diamonds trade, 100, 128, 155, 156, 158-161, 177
Dinka (Sudan), 152, 153, 154
Diodorus, 26
Diop, Cheikh Anta, 8, 10, 20, 33, 50, 51, 61, 73, 74, 81, 98
Djoser, 14, 21
Dogon (Mali), 62, 63, 82, 83, 85
Dongola, 17, 36, 43, 44
Douglas, Frederick, 91
Drug trials, 164-169
Dubois, W.E.B., 75, 106, 133
Dutch East India Company, 99

Hieroglyphs, 41
Hilliard III, Asa, 30
HIV/AIDS - Cut hunter theory of origins, 164-169
HIV/AIDS – Oral Polio Vaccine Theory(OPV), 165-167
Hochschild, A., 101-102
Horn of Africa, 146-154
Hutu (central Africa), 68, 69, 155, 156, 157, 158
Hyksos, 15, 16, 17, 26

I

Ibadan (Nigeria), 67
Ibn Battuta, 46
Ibn Khaldun, 46, 48
Ice Age, 8, 9
Igbo (E. Nigeria), 20, 57, 82
Imhotep, 14, 21, 24, 25
IMF (International Monetary Fund), 107, 173, 176
Indian Removal Act (American colonies), 54
Industrial revolution (financed by slavery), 87
Intermediate period (ancient Egyptian/Kemetic), 15, 16, 23
Isandlwana (defeat of the British at), 69, 100
Ishango bone, 3, 12, 13
Isis, 29, 40
Islam, 42, 43, 44, 48, 49, 66, 72, 74, 98, 99, 109, 110, 151, 152
Ivory Coast, 93, 98, 103, 173
Islam, 42, 43, 44, 48, 49, 66, 72, 73, 74, 75, 98, 99, 109, 110, 148, 151, 152, 153
Ivory Coast, 93, 168, 173, 176

J

Jameson, Leander Starr, 100

Janssens (Belgian General), 117

K

Kabbah, Ahmed Tejan, 160, 161
Kabila, Laurent Desire, 125, 155-156
Kalahari desert, 12, 135
Kalenjin (Kenya), 143
Kama, Seretse, 137
Kamose, 14, 15, 16, 17, 26, 27
Kasa Vubu, Joseph, 124, 126
Kashta, 36, 40
Katanga (Democratic Republic of Congo), 95, 102, 114, 117, 118, 119, 120, 121, 125, 156
Kathrada, Ahmed, 141
Kaunda, Kenneth, 137
Kenya, 106, 142, 143, 144, 146, 147, 169
Kenya African Union (KAU), 143, 144
Kenyatta, Jomo, 106, 142, 143, 144
Keynes, John Maynard, 80
Khafre, 14, 22, 23, 27
Khoisan (Southern Africa), 12, 49
Khufu, 22, 23
Kimathi, Dedan, 142, 143, 144
Kony, Joseph, 153, 162
Koroma, Ernest, 161
Koroma, Johnny Paul, 161
Kush, 15, 16, 17, 27, 30, 36, 37, 38, 39-44
Kuti, Fela Anikulapo, 110

L

Lake Chad, 41
Lake Victoria, 41
Lamizana, Sangoule, 173
Leadership, 171-184

League of Nations, 135, 149
Leibnitz, Wilhelm, 77, 80
Leopold II, King of Belgium, 92,
93, 101, 102, 114, 117, 120
Lesotho, 69
Liberia, 158-161
Lion of Judah, 39
Lissouba, Pascal, 178, 179
Liverpool & Manchester
Railway, 87
Lord Lugard, 97
Lord's Resistance Army, 162,
163
Lumumba, Patrice, 112, 126
LURD (Liberians united for
reconciliation & democracy),
159

M

M'siri, 94, 95
Machel, Samora, 133, 134
Madagascar, 93
Makuria, 43
Malcolm X, 125
Mali Empire, 47, 48, 49, 63
Malcolm X,
Mande people, 47, 48
Mande script, 98
Mandela, Nelson, 140, 141, 142,
144, 181
Mansa Musa, 48, 49, 56, 61
Mansa Uli, 48, 49
Marxist-Leninism, 130, 133
Mass production, 61, 88, 91
Massawa, 93, 149, 150
Master and Servants Laws, 100
Mathematics, 3, 12, 82
Mecca, 48, 49, 57
Memphis, 37
Menelik, 39, 98, 148
Menes, 19, 21, 73
Menkaure, 22, 23

Mercenaries, 15, 117, 118, 126,
129, 131, 160, 183, 184
Meroe, 3, 36, 40, 41, 42,
Meroitic script, 14
Metallurgy, 3, 12
Missionaries, 59, 95, 106, 113
MNC (Congolese National
Movement), 113, 114
Mobutu, Desire, 121, 123, 124,
125, 126, 129, 155, 177, 179,
180, 182
Mohammed, General Murtala
Ramat, 108, 109, 131, 183, 184
Momoh, Joseph, 160
Mondlane, Eduardo, 133
Monotheism, 31
Moors, 72-77
Morocco, 48, 72, 73, 74, 75, 93
Mozambique, 61, 96, 128, 129,
132, 133, 136, 139
MPLA, 82, 97, 98, 99
Mugabe, Robert, 134, 136, 138,
139, 145
Muom script, 98
Musa, Kankan, 62
Museveni, Yoweri, 153, 162-163,
169
Mutnofret, 28
Mwenemutapa, 49-50
Mwinyi, Ali Hassan, 173

N

Nama (Namibia), 135
Namibia, 96, 129, 130, 134, 135,
136, 139, 156
Napata, 36, 38, 39, 40, 41
Nastasen, 41
Natal (South Africa), 69, 100,
141
National Union of south Africa
Students (NUSAS), 141

CPSIA information can be obtained
at www.ICGtesting.com
Printed in the USA
LVHW092120210223
740061LV00004B/642

9 780955 713101